IMAGES
of America

WENTZVILLE

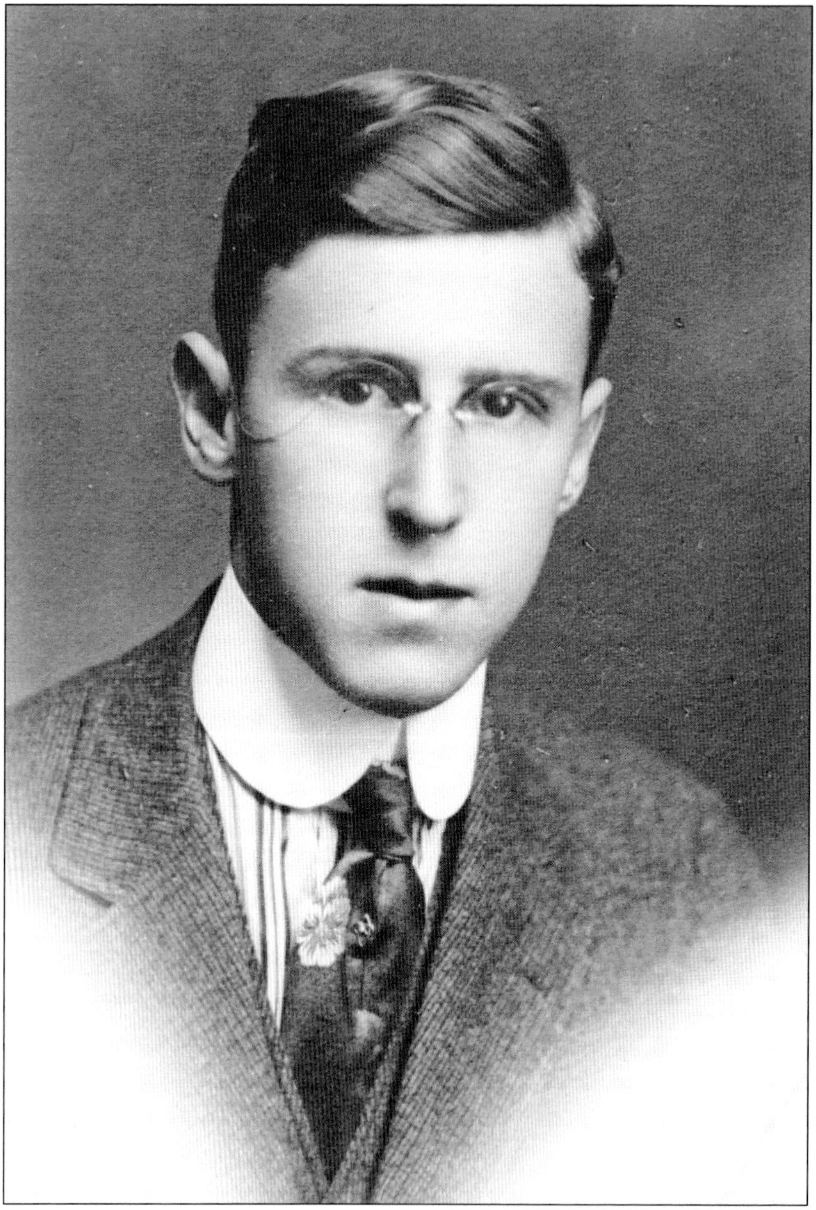

This 1898 photograph shows 18-year-old Charles Richards. "Charlie" became known as "Mr. Wentzville" because of his tireless volunteer work with local and county organizations. He was president of the Lions Club and the first president of the Community Club. In addition, he was chairman of the St. Charles County US Savings Bond program for 20 years and was in charge of the bloodmobile program for many years. (Wentzville Community Historical Society.)

On the Cover: West North Main Street (now West Allen Street) between Blumhoff and North Linn Avenues is shown around 1915. From left to right are the Blumhof Cash Clothing Store, Freese Ford Dealership, Wentzville Ice Cream Parlor, Schulte Brothers Meat Market, and the Heady (Wentzville House) Hotel. This was the first block in town to have electric lights in 1916. George Freese bought the Blumhof store and expanded his automobile dealership to include Fordson tractors. (Wentzville Community Historical Society.)

IMAGES
of America

WENTZVILLE

Deborah Bowman and Larry Marshall

ARCADIA
PUBLISHING

ISBN 978-1-4671-2823-0

Published by Arcadia Publishing
Charleston, South Carolina

Printed in the United States of America

Library of Congress Control Number: 2017959246

For all general information, please contact Arcadia Publishing:
Telephone 843-853-2070
Fax 843-853-0044
E-mail sales@arcadiapublishing.com
For customer service and orders:
Toll-Free 1-888-313-2665

Visit us on the Internet at www.arcadiapublishing.com

Dedicated to the enduring memory of Betty and Conrad Shutske.
Your love will warm our hearts forever.

Contents

Acknowledgments

This book is not intended to be a comprehensive history of Wentzville, but it contains the highlights gleaned from information available to us. The authors profoundly thank the board and membership of the Wentzville Community Historical Society for allowing them unlimited access to their archives and use of their historical photographs; specifically, thanks to board members Rick Anselm, Anne Boedeker, Gloria Ehll, Gary Mittelbuescher, Matt Swanson, Tony Thieman, and William Vehige. All photographs, unless noted in the caption as being from the O'Fallon or St. Charles County Historical Societies, are courtesy of the Wentzville Community Historical Society.

In addition, the authors are indebted to the O'Fallon Historical Society (Lewis Swinger) and the St. Charles County Historical Society for assistance with information and photographs used in this book. Thanks also go to the National Archives, *Actual Detective Stories* magazine, and the *Wentzville Union* and *St. Louis Post-Dispatch* newspapers.

We owe thanks as well to all the people working diligently to preserve and restore historic Wentzville, especially the Wentzville Main Street Association and president Chris Gard, the American Legion, and the Downtown Business Association. Particular thanks go to the City of Wentzville, especially Dan Lang and Doug Forbeck, for providing us with information regarding the planning and development of Wentzville.

Finally, we sincerely thank the early historians of Wentzville, whose written notes helped us immeasurably: Barbara Mittelbuscher, Gerry Matlock, and Dorris and John Denny. Their past dedication to recording Wentzville's history showed a deep respect and love for the town. We hope that this volume will do the same for future generations.

INTRODUCTION

Wentzville, Missouri, is in western St. Charles County, about 40 miles west of St. Louis. The town earned the nickname "Crossroads of the Nation" by being positioned where Highway 40/61 and Interstate 70 meet. In recent years, it has been the fastest-growing city in Missouri. Its early years showed less impressive growth, but the early citizens were determined, hard-working folks.

In 1828, Rev. Joseph Smith Allen, along with his wife, Rachel, and their three sons, Smith, William, and Robert, came to Missouri from Heady County, Virginia. Reverend Allen became a successful farmer as well as a minister. One of his sons, William, was a voracious reader and became well educated. Like his father, William became a farmer, but he also grew active in St. Charles County politics. In 1845, at the age of 33, William was elected to the Missouri State House of Representatives, where he served two terms as a member of the minority Whig party. Four years later, he was elected to the Missouri State Senate. One of his greatest achievements was being instrumental in getting the North Missouri Railroad to come through St. Charles County. William M. Allen wanted to create a new village along the railroad, so he offered to donate a tract of his land for the easement. He convinced other local farmers to give property as well and offered to donate land for a station.

The plan worked; the railroad accepted the offer and agreed to build a station. Allen laid out and platted the town in 1855 and then had to come up with a name. Allentown? Williamsburg? But naming the town after himself was not William Allen's priority. Instead, he decided to name it after his good friend and chief engineer of the North Missouri Railroad, Erasmus Livingston Wentz, who helped him lay out the village.

The original 1855 town plat shows that Wentzville stretched from Church Street to Lewis Street, seven blocks east along Main Street. William Allen became the first station agent for the railroad. He built a large house at the east end of town for his big family in 1856. He said he built it as a showplace and hoped the home would someday have historical significance in this community, perhaps becoming a museum. The house was torn down in 1962.

Tobacco was the major crop in Wentzville between 1850 and 1880. The region extending for miles in all directions from Wentzville was tobacco country; nearly every farmer had a tobacco barn. Area names associated with the tobacco business included Paul Brown, George S. Myers, John Thompson, Charles and John E. Richards, Robert and Caleb Dula, John and James T. Drummond, Joel E. Carr, Hut and Jim Lacy, S.A. Grantham, James Tatum, John F. Bornhop, Wesley Sherman, W.H. Muzzy, J.W. Savage, Benjamine C. Pearce, and J.C. Goodrich. The Civil War had a profoundly negative effect on the tobacco industry in Wentzville. The Battle of Wentzville, fought alongside the railroad tracks just west of town, brought the war to Wentzville in a very real way.

Allen was not content to be a farmer and station agent; instead, in 1858, he and his friend W.A. Abbington started the first mercantile in Wentzville. The Wentzville Mercantile was a three-story frame building on the southeast corner of Church and Main Streets. Another early business was Compton's Saddle Shop, also on the corner of Church and Main Streets. Main Street was rutted and often muddy, and it was not uncommon to see masses of cattle, sheep, geese, and other animals being herded down the street to holding pens, where they waited to be loaded onto trains. Several of the streets in the older part of Wentzville are named after early citizens: Linn, Talley, Whitehead, and McRoberts.

Before long, businesses started to be built on the north side of the railroad tracks. In 1876, Fritz Schierbaum built a home on the corner of what is now Linn Avenue and East Allen Street, formerly North Main Street. This building was home to many businesses after the Schierbaum family moved out, including Citizens Bank and the post office. The building still stands.

Directly east of his home on Allen Street, Fritz Schierbaum built his first Wentzville business, the Schierbaum Blacksmith Shop. Later he made it a much larger building, known as Schierbaum Implement and Wagonmakers, which provided goods and services to farmers and townspeople. An old ad proclaimed, "Schierbaum has it, will get it, or will make it." The building also served as a meeting place for the town. The second floor was called the Opera House. Here the town held dances, meetings, and parties, and the Magic Lantern moving picture company came to town once a week to show Hollywood's latest silent films. The Opera House also served as Wentzville's first city hall.

On the east side of Schierbaum Implement and Wagonmakers sat a livery feed and sale stable, built in 1890. Charles E. Musick bought it in 1907. The Musick family built an elaborate home on South Main Street; it was called a "farm in town" and was actually a dairy farm. The Musick family hosted many major town picnics and celebrations at their home. The building was later used as apartments until it was torn down in the 1970s. Charles Musick was the alderman of Ward 1 from 1890 to 1904, when he was elected mayor for one term. He was later elected city marshal. On July 17, 1929, Musick was struck and run over by a westbound Wabash freight train. He was one of many Wentzville people to be killed by trains through the years, including one of the town's first doctors, Horace Talley, who was hit and killed while on his way to treat a patient.

Wentzville's first newspaper was called the *News at Wentzville*. It was started in 1867 and was published in Wentzville until 1870. In 1891, W.S. Dickey started the *Wentzville Union*, a weekly newspaper that lasted for over 80 years until the late 1970s. The first telephone came to Wentzville in 1908. The switchboard was located on the second floor of the Wentzville House Hotel and was run by Addie Lusby Anselm and her sisters Cordelia and Elsie. The Wentzville Farmers Telephone Company had a list of rules, which included no talking longer than five minutes, no profanity, and no listening to other people's conversations. Soon a bigger building was needed, so Cordelia and Elsie rebuilt their home to make room for the telephone company within. That building still stands at 205 Allen Street.

Businesses, buildings, and people have come and gone through the years, but Wentzville has continued to grow and thrive. History sometimes contradicts itself, depending upon which source is being used, but this book presents unique photographs and examines life through the early years of Wentzville, based on newspapers, historical society archives, personal writings of early citizens, and recorded interviews. Wentzville's history is rich and interesting, and the Crossroads of the Nation is proud to retain a small-town feeling, no matter how large it grows.

One

From Wentz We Came

The city of Wentzville is located in western St. Charles County, Missouri. Its location is 38°48'41" north, 90°51'26" west. According to the US Census Bureau, Wentzville has a total area of 19.98 square miles, of which 19.96 square miles is land and 0.02 square miles is water.

Established as a village in 1855, Wentzville was incorporated in 1872 and became a city of the fourth class in 1903. It has had a long and rich history despite being rocked by natural disasters, citywide fires, and the Great Depression. Early Wentzvillians banded together heroically in times of need to overcome the hardships of the past and ensure the future of their city.

From a small farming community to the rapidly growing city of today, Wentzville has endured and thrived. It enjoys a geographic advantage over other locations in St. Charles County. The transcontinental railroad started it all. The North Missouri Railroad was built through Wentzville in the 1850s, setting the town on a trajectory of growth that made it the Crossroads of the Nation at the intersection of US Highway 40/61 and Interstate 70 in the 20th century. The growth continues at a tremendous pace. Between 2000 and 2017, the population of Wentzville went from 6,800 to over 40,000 residents. This put the city in the top 10 fastest-growing cities in Missouri; forecasts state that Wentzville will keep up this pace for another decade.

One reason for Wentzville's growth came in 1983, when the General Motors Corporation decided to locate a new automobile manufacturing plant here, which was the spark needed to outpace other communities in the area. The decision to locate here was based on the centralized transportation infrastructure offered by both the railroad and highways.

City government records from 1872 to 1890 were lost in fires that plagued the town in its early years, but there are still names, personally written memories, and newspaper articles about the men and women who founded the town and their families and businesses. This truly is "from Wentz we came."

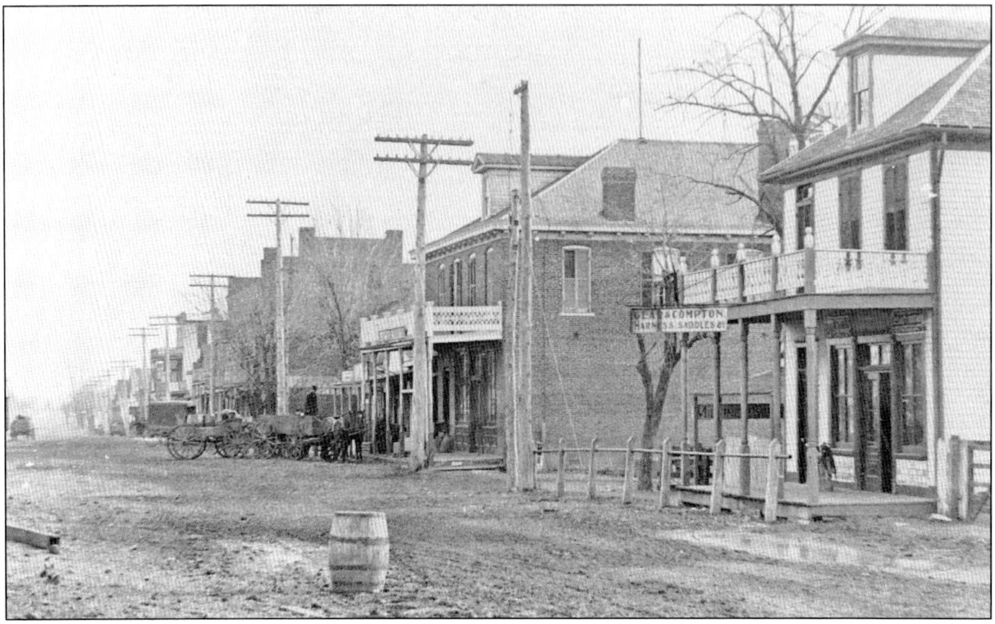

Welcome to South Main Street, looking east around 1870. Wentzville had been founded nearly 15 years ago when this photograph was taken. Almost all the buildings shown here have been lost; only the white three-story building in the distance remains. It used to serve as the Masonic lodge (third floor), a church (second floor), and a school (first floor). This photograph was obviously taken before Wentzville had a formal public works department.

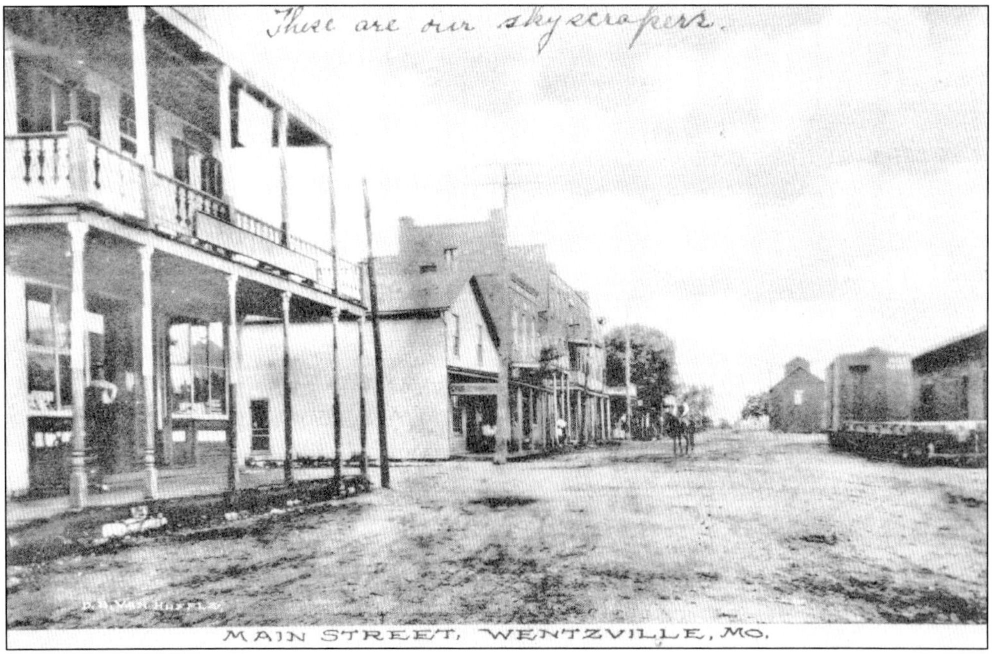

This is South Main Street, facing west, around 1890. Wentzville looked rustic as it headed into the 20th century. A horse and rider appear to be greeting shop owners from the middle of the street. On the near left, D.B. Van Huffle stands in the doorway of his drugstore. Some long-forgotten jokester wrote across the top, "These are our skyscrapers."

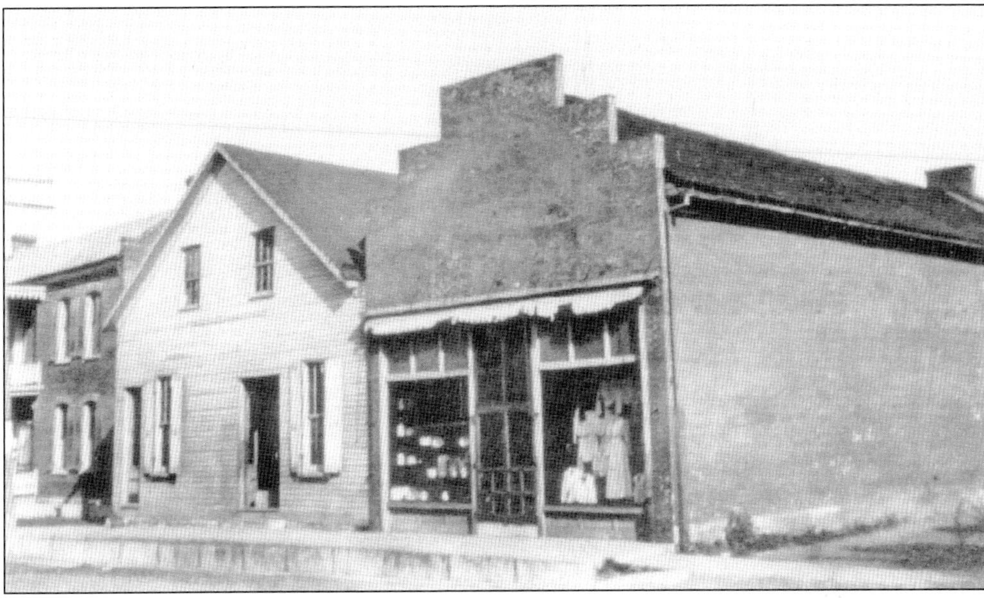

The Henry Michel Dry Goods store, shown here around 1870, was originally owned by Rudolph Peters, who sold it to Michel in the 1860s to avoid the destruction the Civil War brought to Wentzville. Michel partnered with his brother-in-law Ernest Dierker to form the Michel-Dierker General Merchandise store. Dierker later retired, and in 1872, Michel sold the store to Henry Koenig. Note the dresses, jackets, and assorted dry goods in the windows.

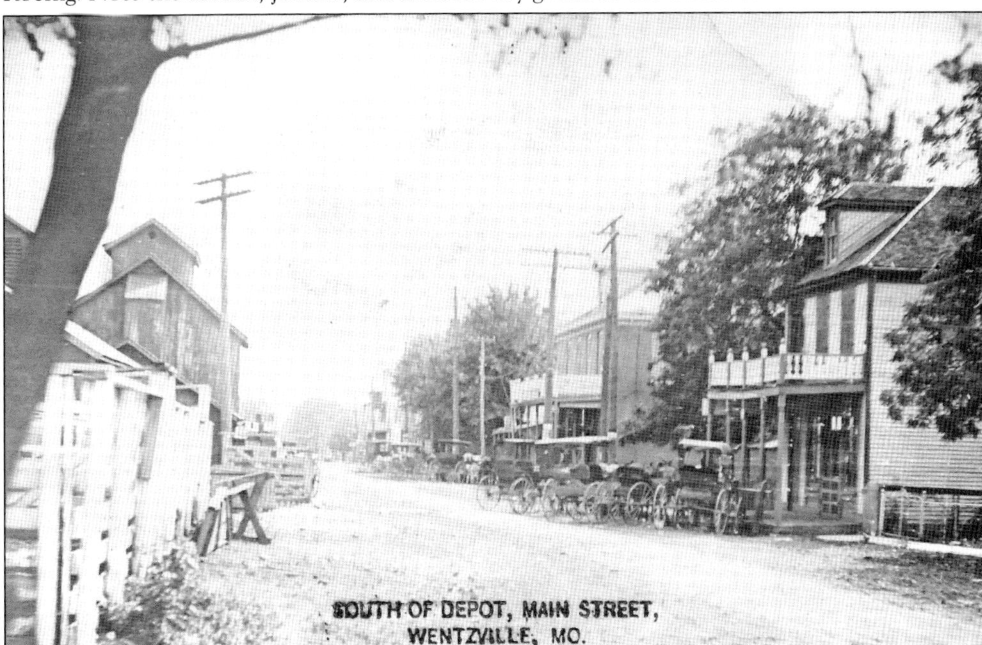

This postcard from 1880 shows South Main Street looking west. Townspeople often saw cattle, sheep, and geese being herded down the middle of the road into the railroad holding pens for delivery to the outside world. On the south side is Compton's Saddle Shop, and next door is the Wentzville Mercantile. The buggies show that this was the busiest street in Wentzville. (Roland Temme.)

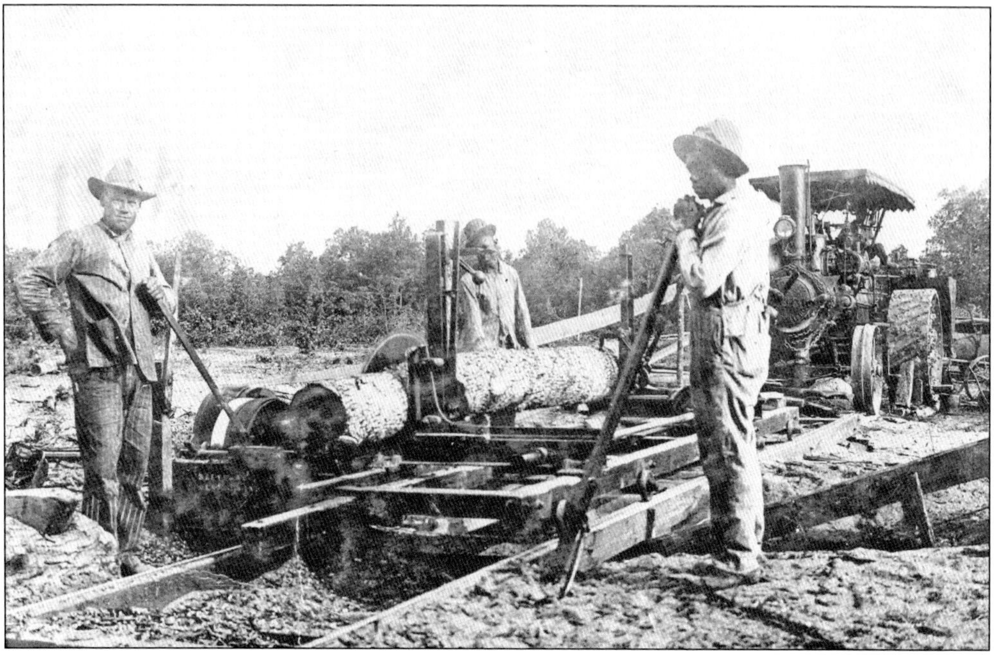

In the late 19th century, some industrious Wentzville farmers started a lumber business using steam tractors to drive the sawmills.

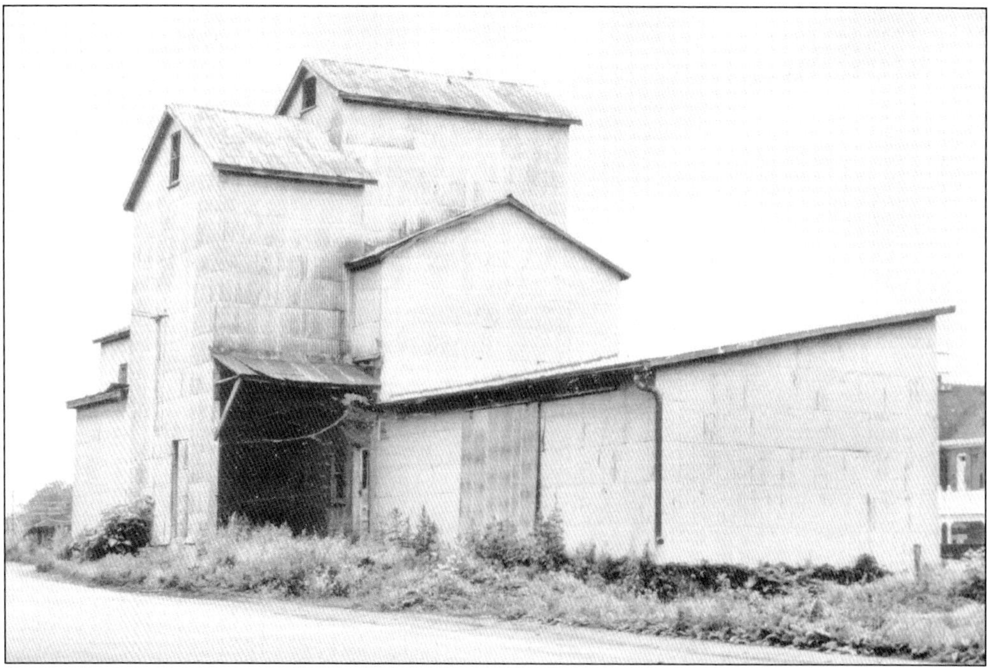

The Karrenbrock Flour Mill ceased operation in the early 1930s, but its grain elevator was left abandoned until it was razed by the city in 1963. Over the years, ownership was disputed, and as the building fell into disrepair, it was used by hobos for shelter. Children often played there until angry parents pressured the city to tear it down. (Wentzville Community Club.)

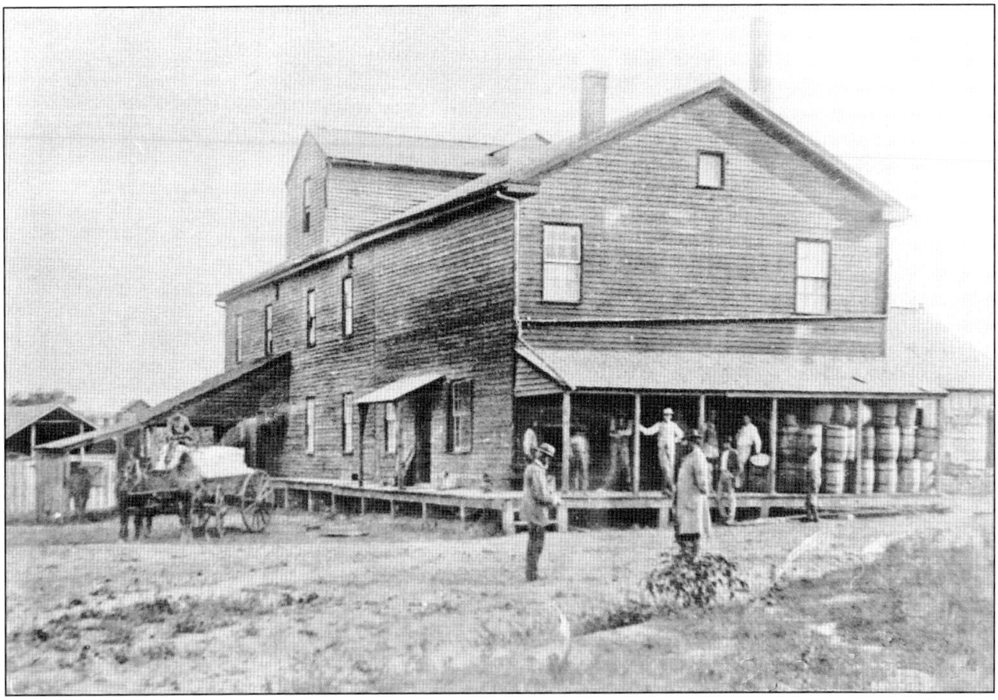

This building was constructed to house the Muzzy and May Tobacco Factory. When the factory closed in the mid-1880s, the Peerless Flour Mill moved in. Peerless stayed until the early part of the 20th century. Located on Mill Street (currently Wall Street), the old mill was later converted to a residence.

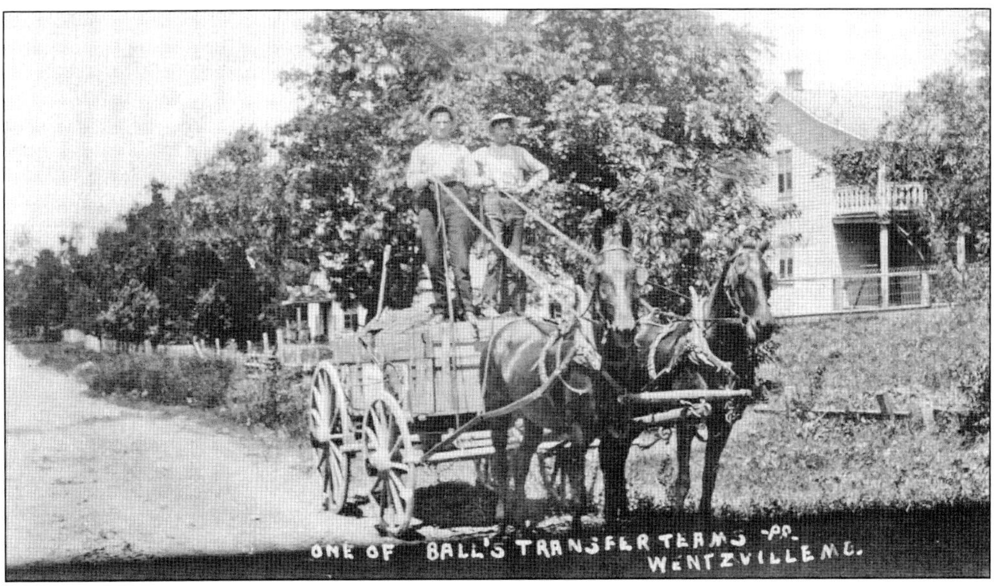

Ball's Transfer Teams, owned by Marshall Elliot Ball, carried freight throughout Wentzville. Ball also owned the Ball Livery and Feed Barn and served as Cuivre River constable and Wentzville city marshal from 1902 to 1904. He was married to Mayme Dierker, the daughter of hotel owner George Dierker. In 1895, Mayme was named by the *St. Louis Post Dispatch* as one of the "five most prominent belles of Wentzville."

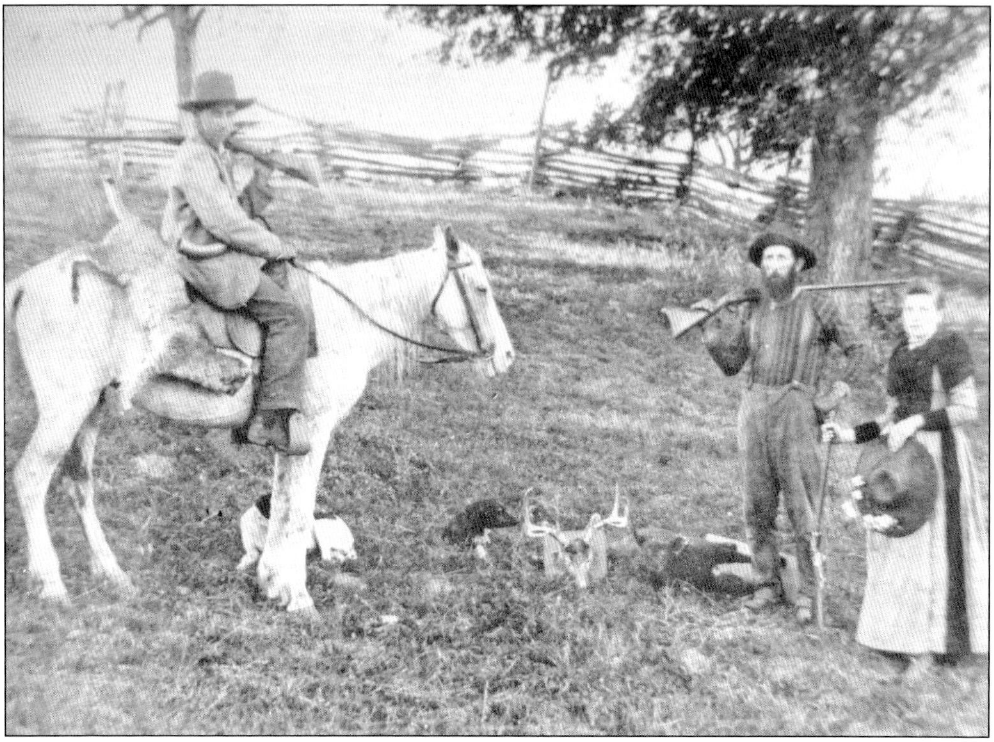

In the early days of settling St. Charles County, living off the land was important to survival. These pioneers appear to have been very successful at their craft. The origin and location of this image of pre-Wentzvillians is unknown.

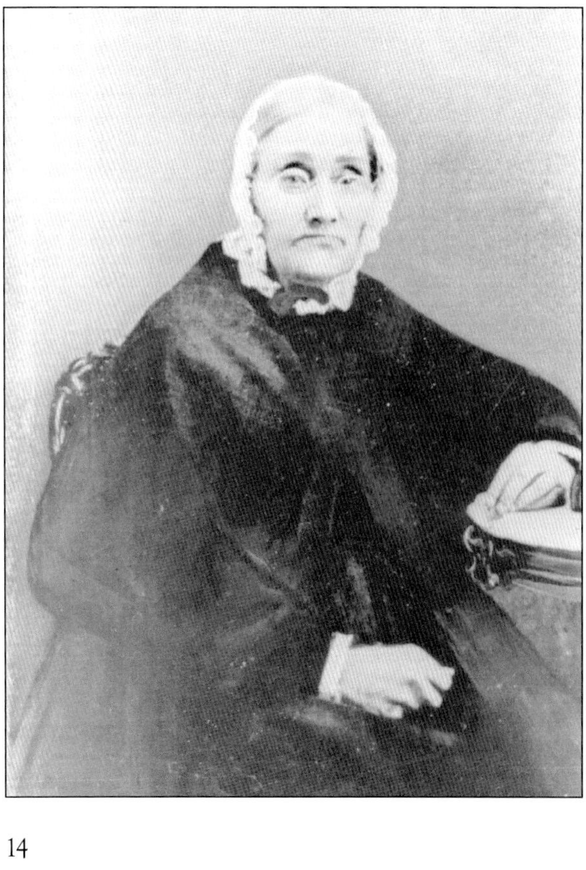

Missouri F. Long was born in 1814 in western St. Charles County, in the area of what is now Wentzville, and died on January 22, 1883, in Pollock, Sullivan County, Missouri. She was married to Frederick Yardley, who was born in Kentucky and died between 1849 and 1855. This is the oldest known photograph from the area that would become Wentzville.

Mayme Dierker Ball was born in 1875 in the Wentzville House Hotel, which her father, George Dierker, built in 1861. Mayme graduated in literature and music from Synodical College in Fulton, Missouri, and was said to be a fine singer. The *Post Dispatch* described this "belle of Wentzville" as "having wealthy family connections, dark hair and eyes, graceful, and a splendid entertainer."

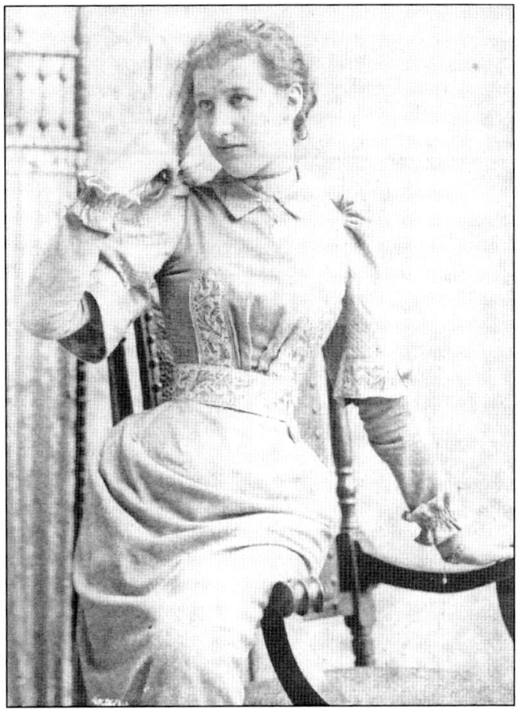

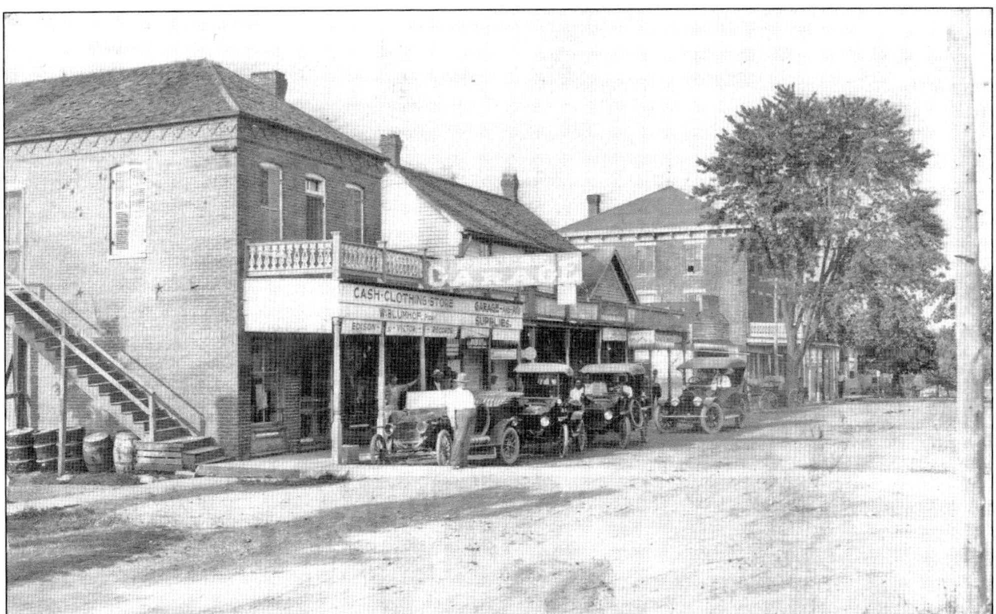

This view of West North Main Street (currently West Allen Street) was taken in 1915. William Blumhof ran his Cash Clothing Store until about 1917, when George Freese bought him out and opened Freese Ford, Wentzville's first automobile dealership. Freese, an industrious fellow, tired of waiting for the city to bring electricity to Wentzville, so he bought a generator, ran the wires, and installed lights in every building on this block.

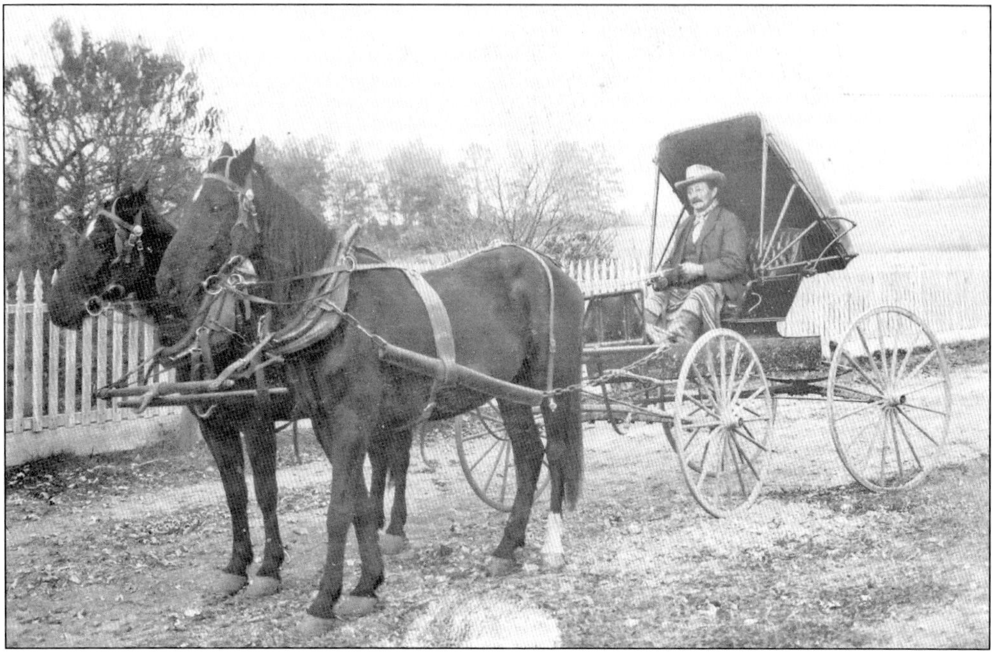

Charles Ruebling, alderman of Ward 1 in Wentzville, is driving in style in 1916 as he takes a buggy into town.

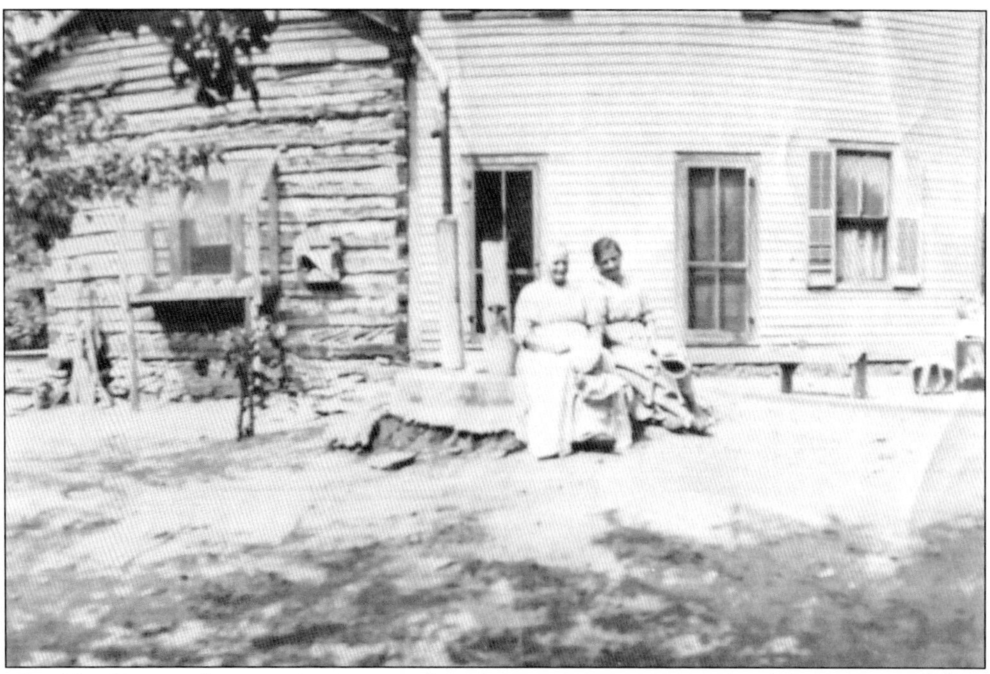

The Alex Hemmer home is shown around 1880. Hemmer's mother and wife have removed their bonnets to pose for a photograph. The home was originally built of logs (as can be seen on the left). Later, he added a more modern two-story addition.

On the left is the Schierbaum home; in the foreground is Wentzville's chemical fire department building. The octagonal building held the town's firefighting equipment: buckets, sand, and a wagon. It was built in the center of town so that volunteers from all over town could have quick and easy access. The upper level served as a bandstand where Craven's Band entertained at many celebrations. (Clara and George Schierbaum.)

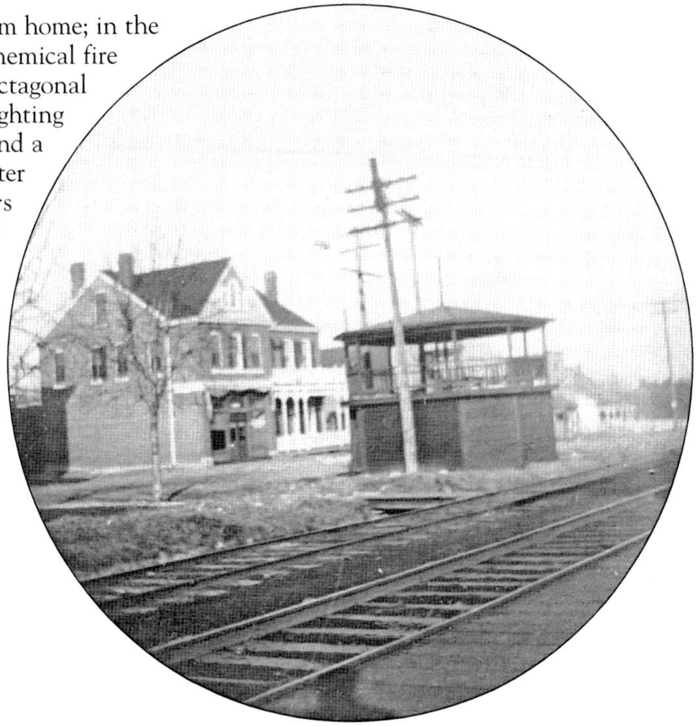

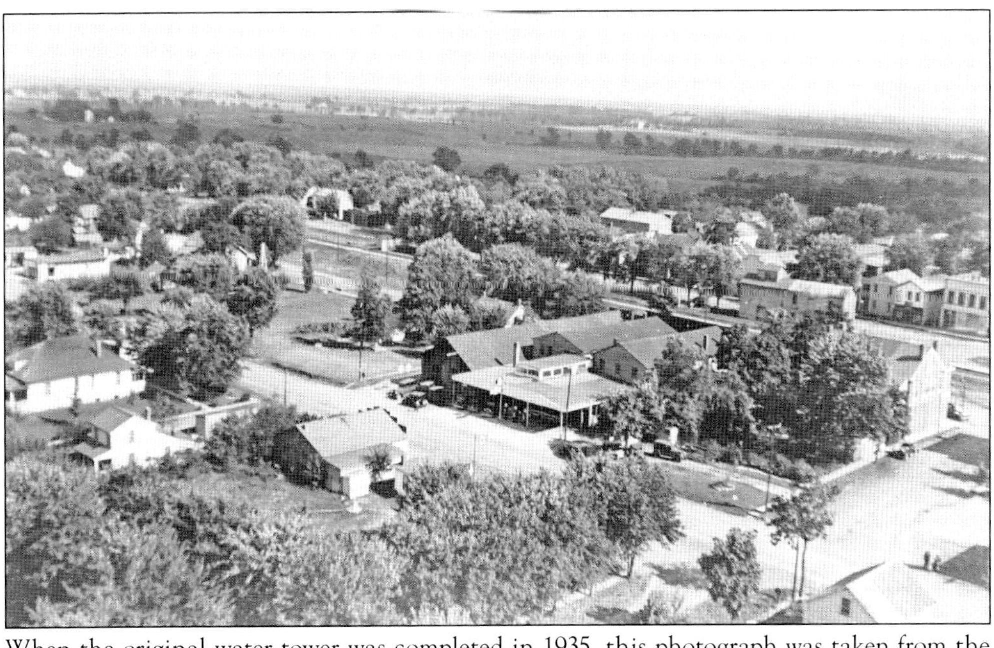

When the original water tower was completed in 1935, this photograph was taken from the top, looking southeast. On the lower right is the intersection of Old Highway 40 (now Pearce Boulevard) and North Linn Avenue. Schramm Chevrolet can be seen in the center; behind it on East North Main Street (now East Allen Street) is Reuters Blacksmith Shop. (Eugenia and Adolph Buescher.)

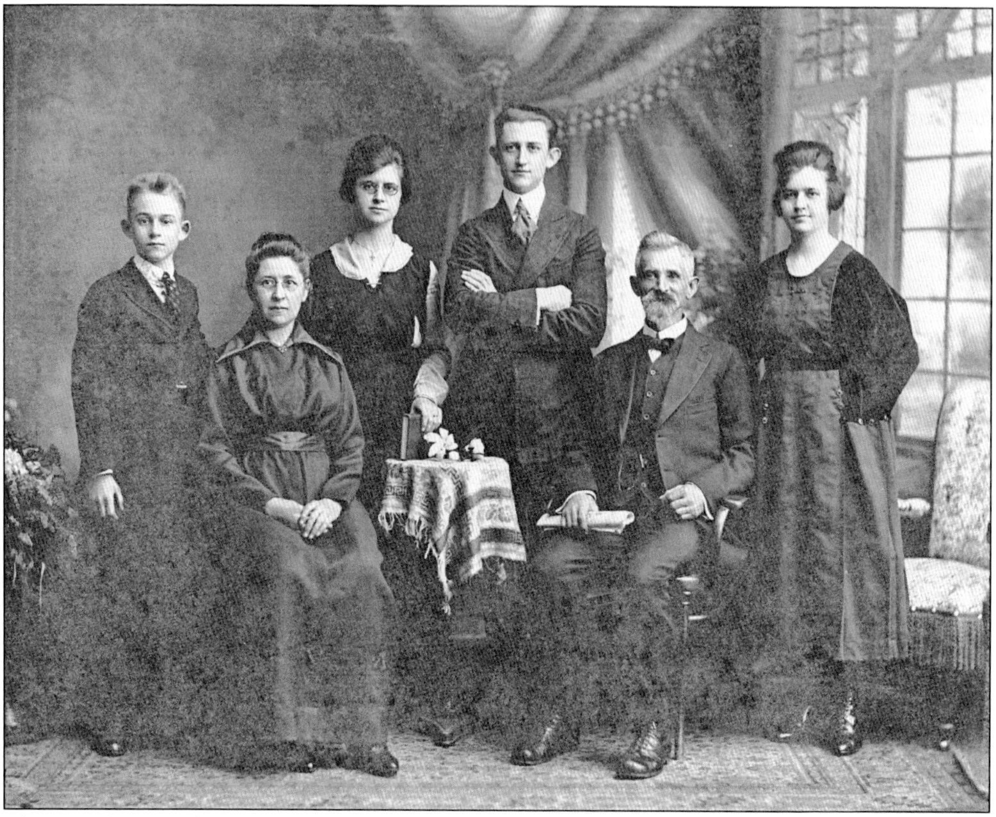

The Buescher family was prominent in business around Wentzville. Mr. and Mrs. Charles Buescher are seated. Their children, standing from left to right behind them, are Carol, Elsie, Adolph, and Olga. Charles partnered with John H. Koenig to open the Koenig-Buescher store, a mercantile that served Wentzville in the early 1900s.

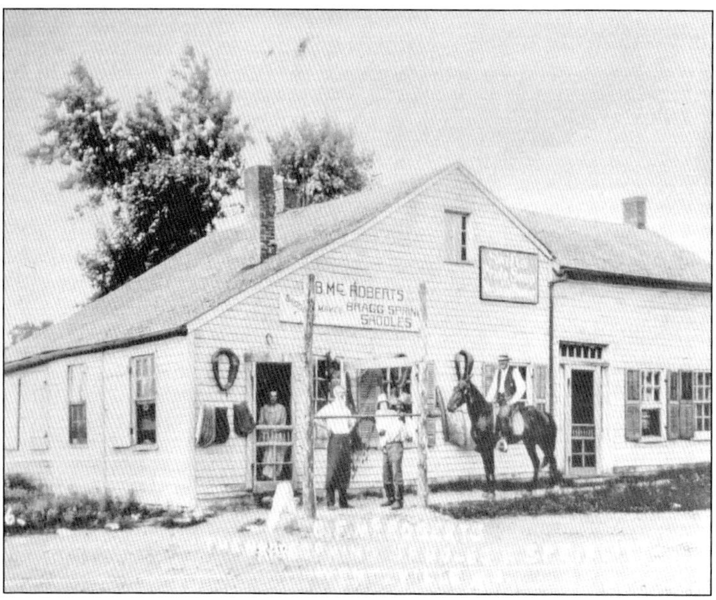

Fenton Blackburn McRoberts partnered with his brother-in-law, John R. Bragg, to create the famous Bragg Spring Saddle. Invented and patented in 1869 (patent No. 90,990), the award-winning saddle was a favorite of the US Cavalry and was a hit at the St. Louis Agricultural and Mechanical Fair in 1871. "Uncle Fent," at left in this photograph, was loved by the children of Wentzville. Bragg is on the horse.

These men were the movers and shakers in 1910 Wentzville and include mayors, businessmen, a newspaper owner, a banker, and a stable owner. From left to right are (first row) C.T. Richards and brother John E. Richards; (second row) C.E. Musick, George Lovell, William McCoy, Fred Chauncey, and Milton A. Gannaway; (third row) Fenton McRoberts, George Dyer, George Brown, and William Karrenbrock. These influential men gathered to celebrate the birthday of a good friend, John E. Richards.

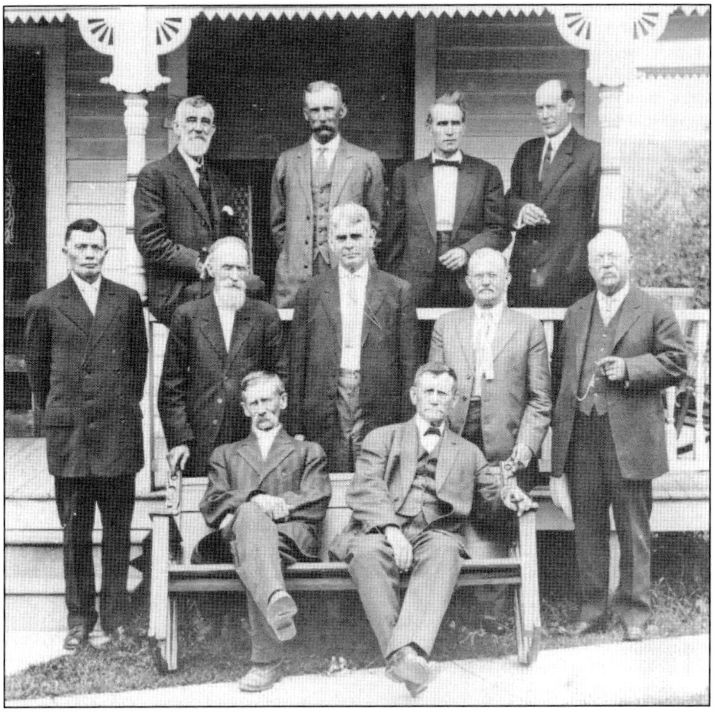

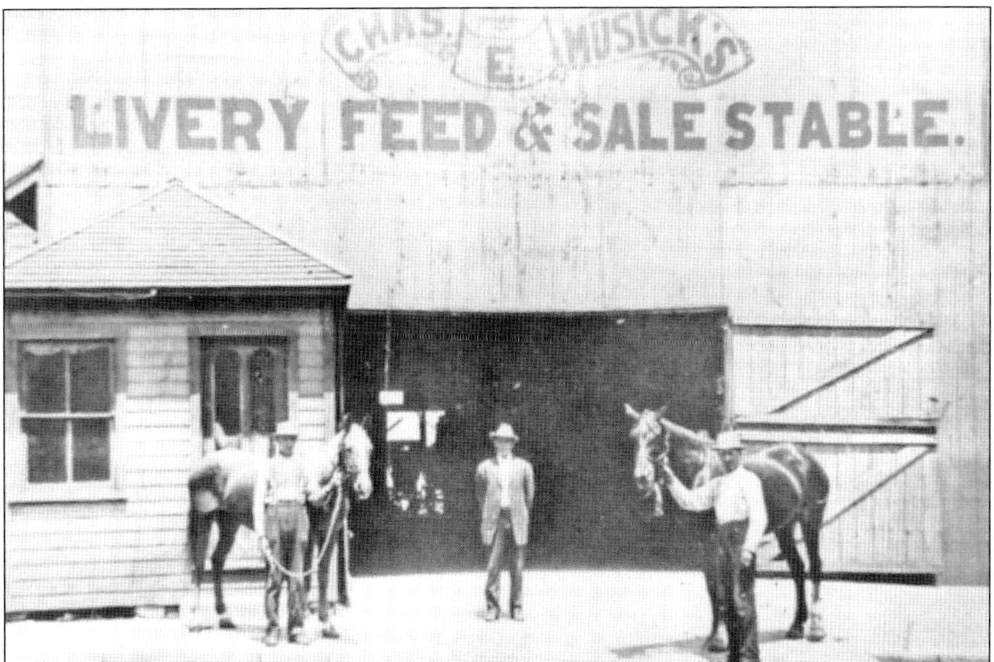

Charles Edward Musick, the owner of a stable, is shown here standing between his stable managers Sam (left) and Tom Sidebottoms. The stable was built in 1890; Musick bought it in 1907. Musick, mayor of Wentzville from 1904 to 1906 and city marshal from 1914 to 1918, met a tragic end when he was killed by a Wabash freight train in July 1929. Newspapers say he had gone deaf and did not hear the train approaching.

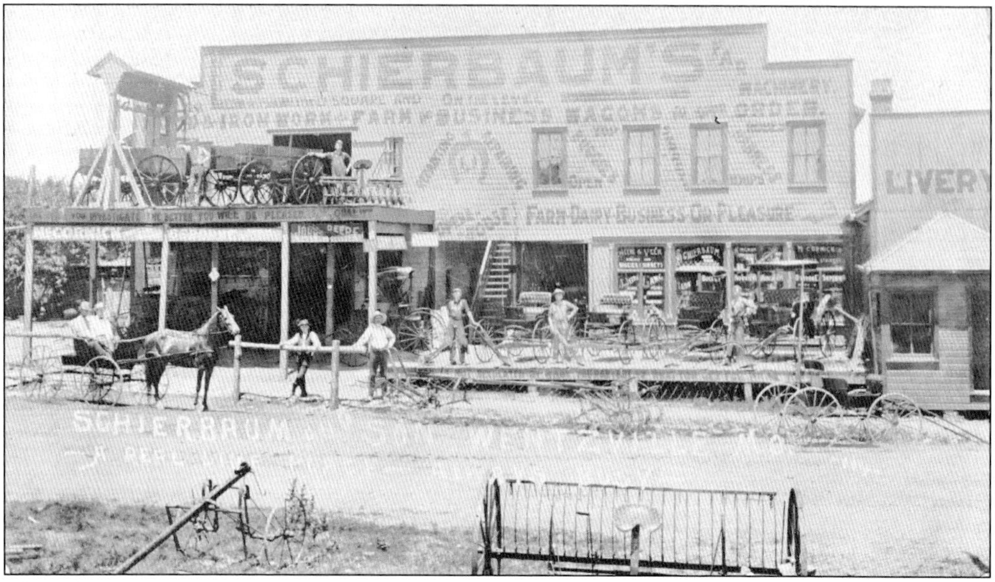

The Old West comes to life in this 1890s photograph of Schierbaum's Implement and Wagonmakers. Fritz Schierbaum built this interesting structure in the mid-1880s. The stairs in the center lead to the Opera House; on the left is a wagon lift to the second floor—Wentzville's first elevator. The space upstairs was the original city hall and was used for dances, meetings, and showings of silent films from Hollywood.

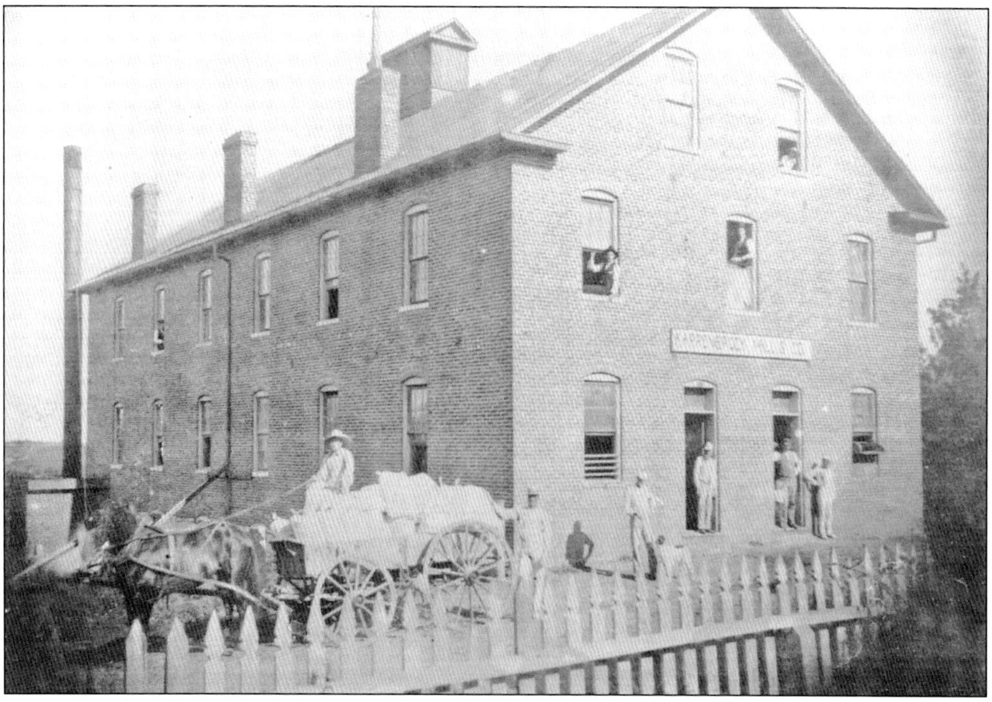

The Karrenbrock Flour Mill, shown around 1882, was erected in the early 1860s as the Dula and Carr Tobacco Company. It was located on the corner of Fourth and Elm Streets for over 140 years before it was razed in 2002 to expand a parking lot for the Wentzville Public Works Department. Today, a tombstone marks the spot where the building stood.

Two

Trains and Tobacco

When Wentzville citizens complain about the loud train whistles or grow impatient over being forced to wait at a crossing, they should realize that without the trains, the city would not exist. When Sen. William Allen, who was also a tobacco farmer, learned that the North Missouri Railroad planned to run a track across the country, he used his senatorial influence to convince Erasmus Livingston Wentz, principal engineer of the railroad, to run the track directly through his property, making it easy for him and his neighbors to ship crops to the market. Allen donated a strip of his property for the train as well as money for building Wentzville's first train station and fulfilled his promise to Wentz to name the resulting town after him.

William Allen founded Wentzville in 1855, and the first trains came into town in 1857, enabling nearby farmers to send crops and livestock to large cities. Tobacco was the main crop in this area from 1830 to about 1880. Tobacco companies began to spring up, including Myers and Pearce, Brown Tobacco, Carr and Dula, and Savage and May. At one point, Wentzville was home to about 17 tobacco companies. In the years after the Civil War, many of the smaller companies were sold to major companies or moved from Wentzville into St. Louis. The train, however, remained an important force for area farmers, many of whom continued to grow tobacco on a smaller scale. Tobacco barns on individual farms were a common sight.

In 1889, the North Missouri Railroad became the Wabash Railroad. The trains carried not only crops but also passengers, and Wentzville began to grow along with the railroad. Livery stables, blacksmith shops, restaurants and bars, clothing stores, banks, and even a hotel sprang up, largely to serve the railroad, but people and residential construction followed, making the town grow steadily.

The lesson to be learned is this: When Wentzvillians are late for a meeting because they had to wait for a train, they can tell their boss that they should be grateful. Without the trains, Wentzville businesses would probably not exist today.

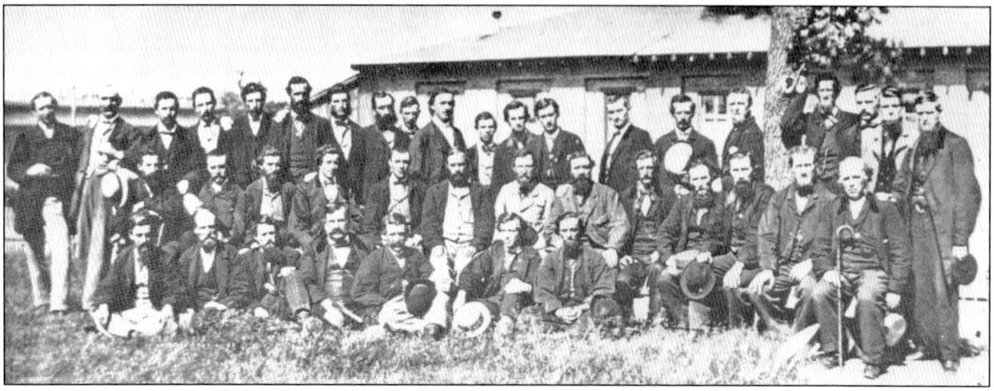

Until recently, photographs of the town's namesake, Erasmus Livingston Wentz, were elusive. Pictured here is a group of US Military Railroad superintendents; among them is Wentz, seated on the far right with his cane. During the Civil War, his arthritis was so severe that he needed the assistance of a cane. Wentz is the reason Wentzville exists today, a century and a half later. (National Archives.)

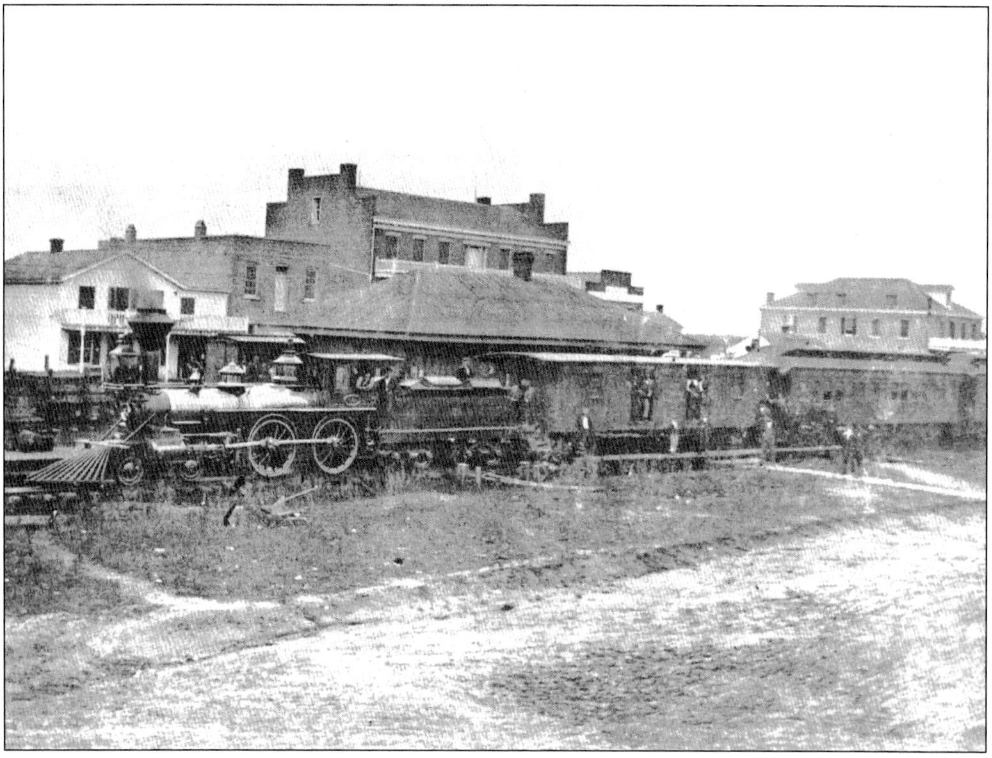

The railroad was key to Wentzville's growth; farmers were suddenly able to ship their livestock, tobacco, and other crops to large cities easily and quickly. The first locomotive rolled into Wentzville in 1857. This is the earliest known photograph of a train in Wentzville, taken in 1878. The large building behind the station is the Thompson Hotel. From its balcony, ladies often waved at travelers as they came into town.

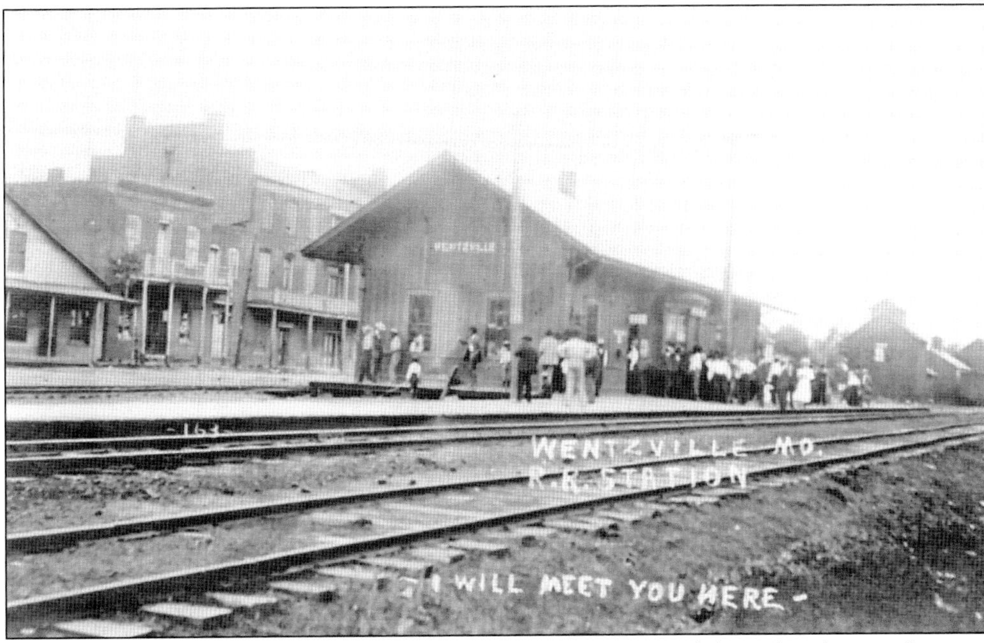

The train station was a busy place in Wentzville for 100 years, until the railroad stopped serving passengers. These two postcards each show a different era. Above, around 1880, the station is seen in connection with the buildings on West South Main Street. The large building in the background is the Thompson building; at the time, it was occupied by the post office and the Savage and May Tobacco Factory. That building burned down around 1883. In the bottom photograph, a freight car sits on the spur from the main track on the south side of the station, as passengers and greeters gather trackside. This photograph was taken around 1910, when the Wentzville Station was still a very popular place to gather. Both photographs were taken looking west.

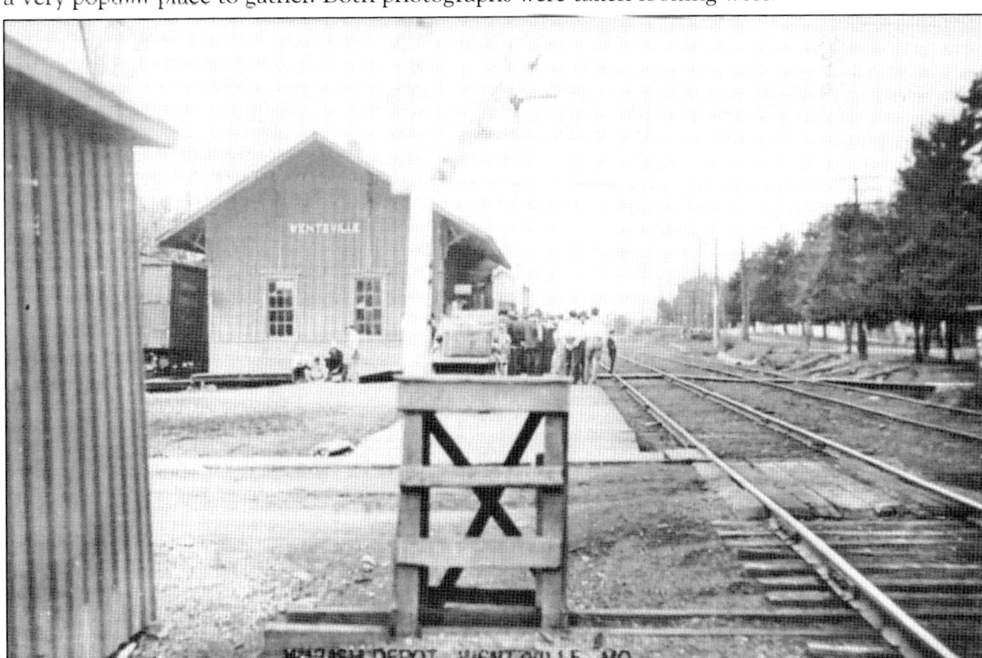

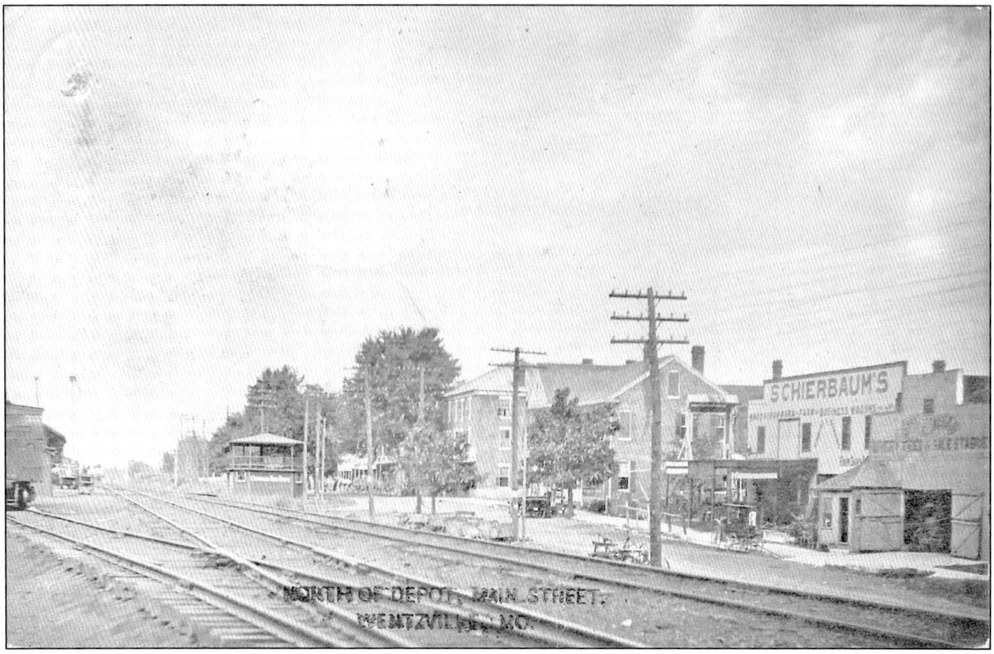

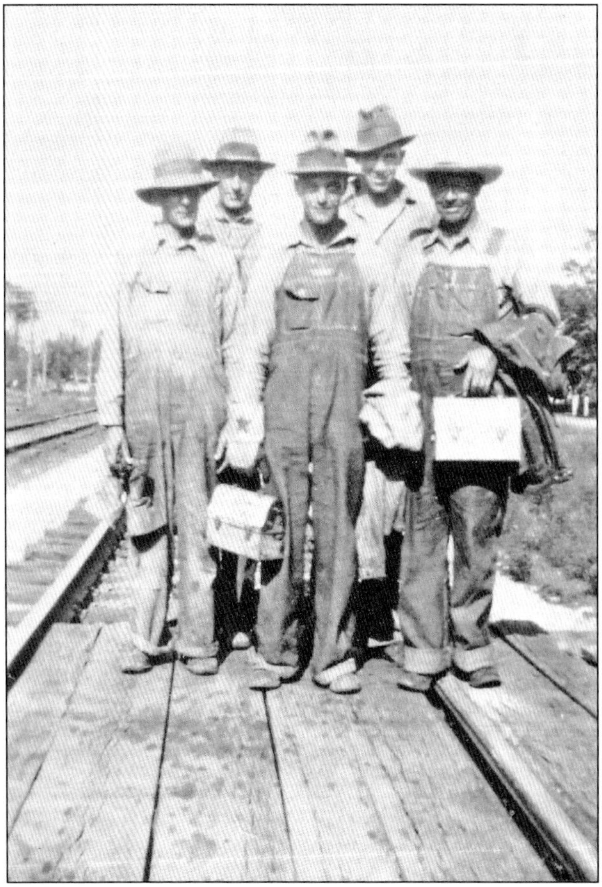

Taken from a postcard around 1910, this photograph has been a valuable tool for Wentzville historians; it has allowed them to find the relationship of the town's early buildings. Photographs like this one answer many questions, because street names change, structures are razed to make room for more modern buildings, and written descriptions leave room for interpretation. This is what Wentzville looked like around the beginning of the 20th century.

The Wentzville section of the Wabash Railroad maintenance crew is shown here, ready to eat their lunches, at the McRoberts Crossing around 1940. From left to right are (first row) Evo Schmucker, Clarence Mamle, and foreman George Jackson; (second row) unidentified and Gurden Simons. Jackson retired after 33 years with the railroad, 27 as foreman. He was the father of Omar Jackson, Arlene Kersting, and Ruth Temme. (Ruth Ann Temme.)

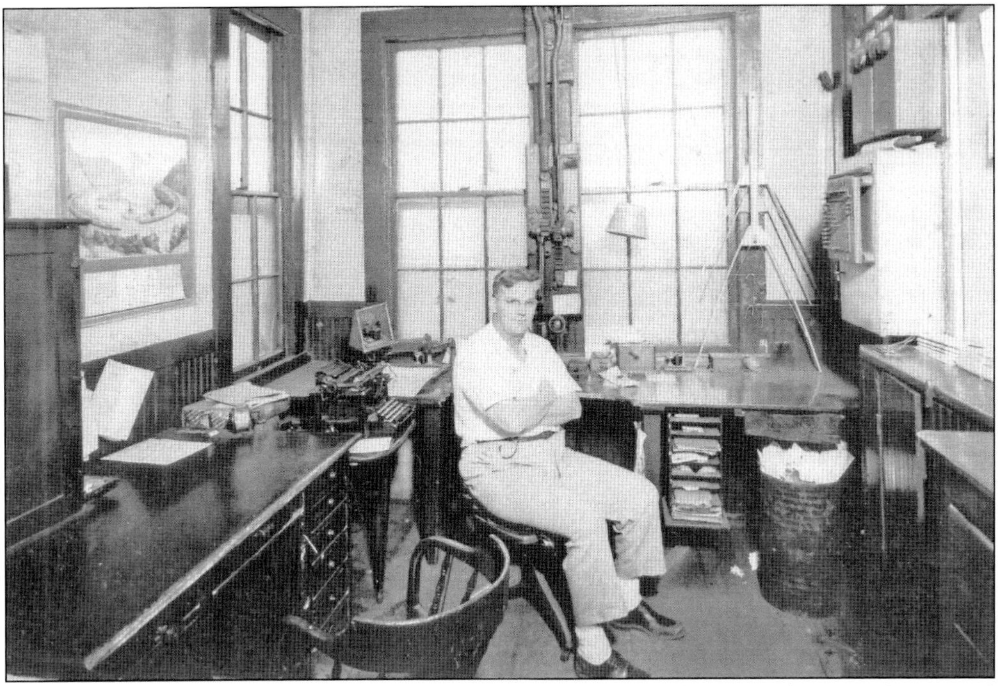

John M. Carter assumed the position of Wabash agent in Wentzville in April 1946 and remained until the station closed. He began his railroad career in Montgomery City, Missouri, where he pitched for the college baseball team. "Lefty," as he was nicknamed, hoped for a career in professional baseball, but blowing out his arm in the minors ended that dream. (Jane Carter-Bartig.)

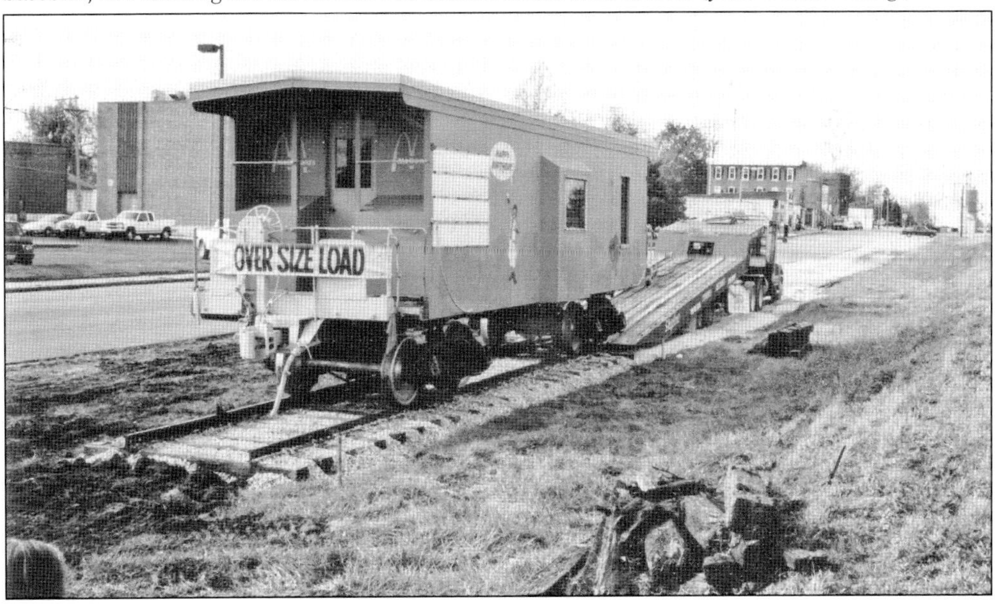

The historical society's caboose is shown being placed next to the tracks on South Main Street in November 2000. Acquired from McDonald's in St. Peters, Missouri, it had been used as a party house. It was rolled off a flatbed truck onto tracks, starting the city's downtown revitalization. Today it is a mini-museum with a bandstand deck and beautiful landscaping, including benches for sitting and dreaming of olden days.

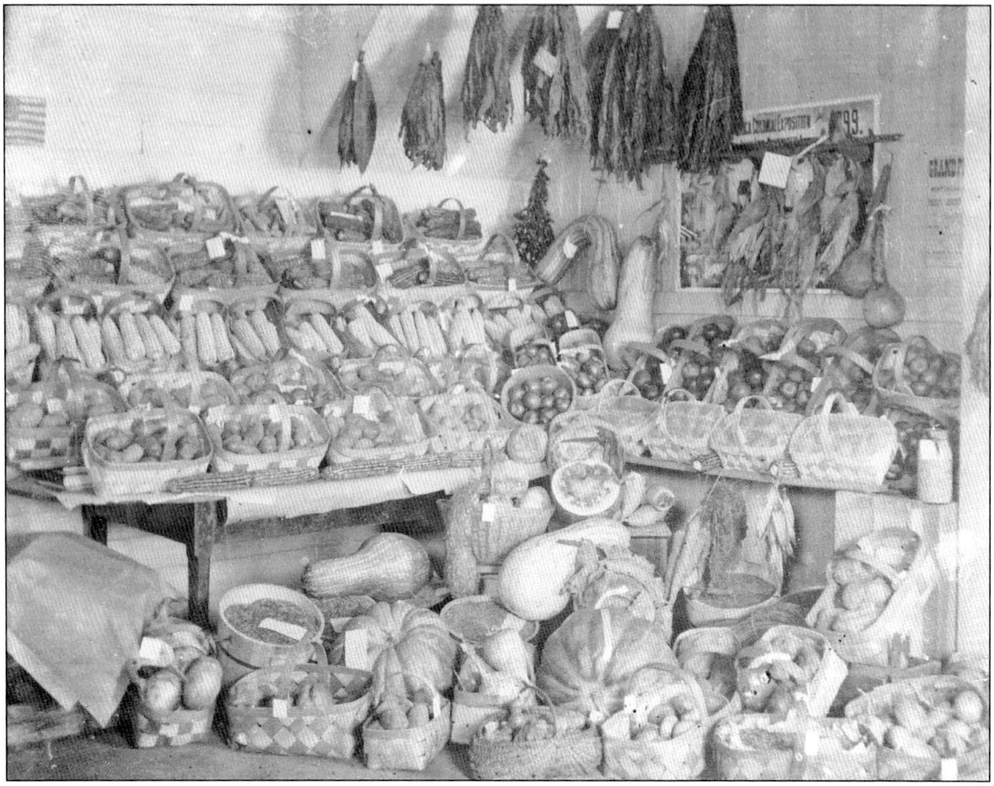

Crops grown in Wentzville farms and gardens are displayed at the 1934 St. Charles County Fair. Among the corn, melons, potatoes, grains, onions, and fruits, a variety of dried tobacco can be seen. Tobacco was the primary crop in and around Wentzville from 1830 to around 1885. By the time this photograph was taken, it was not uncommon to see small tobacco barns throughout the area. (Eugena Karrenbrock.)

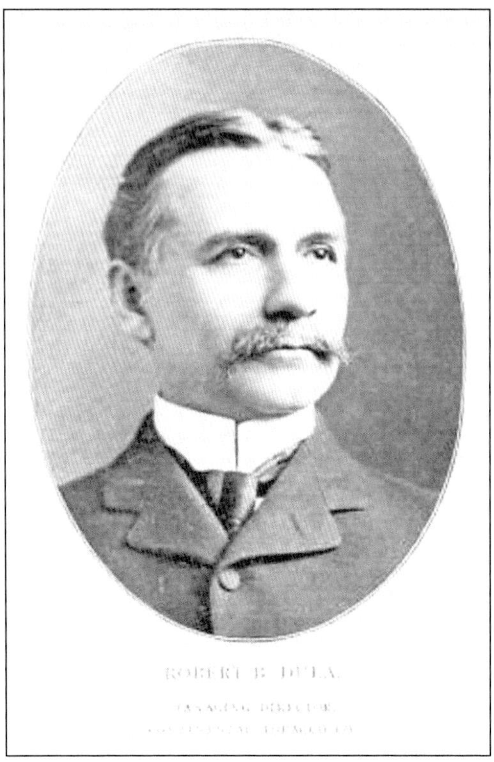

Robert Byron Dula, born in 1848, emigrated from North Carolina to Flint Hill, Missouri, where he taught in a country school. He moved to Wentzville and married Josephine Carr, sister of Joel Carr, then partnered with his brother-in-law to found the Dula and Carr Tobacco Company in 1863. They sold the business in 1885 to the St. Charles Tobacco Company. Dula died in 1926.

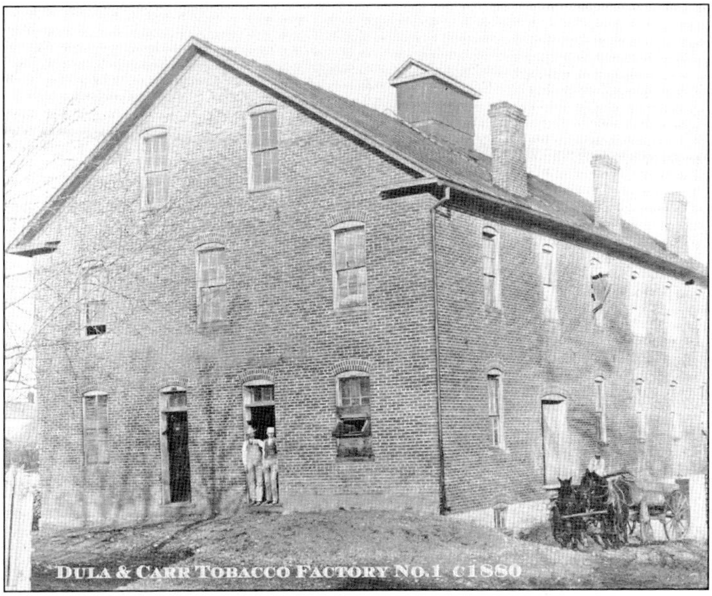

The Dula and Carr Tobacco Company Factory No. 1 operated in this structure between 1863 and 1885. In 1892, Henry William Karrenbrock used the building for a new roller-system flour mill, the Karrenbrock Milling Company. The mill ceased operation in the early part of the 20th century. In 1932, the Acme Garment Factory moved in, offering jobs to Wentzville citizens throughout the Great Depression. (Octavia Evans Sigman.)

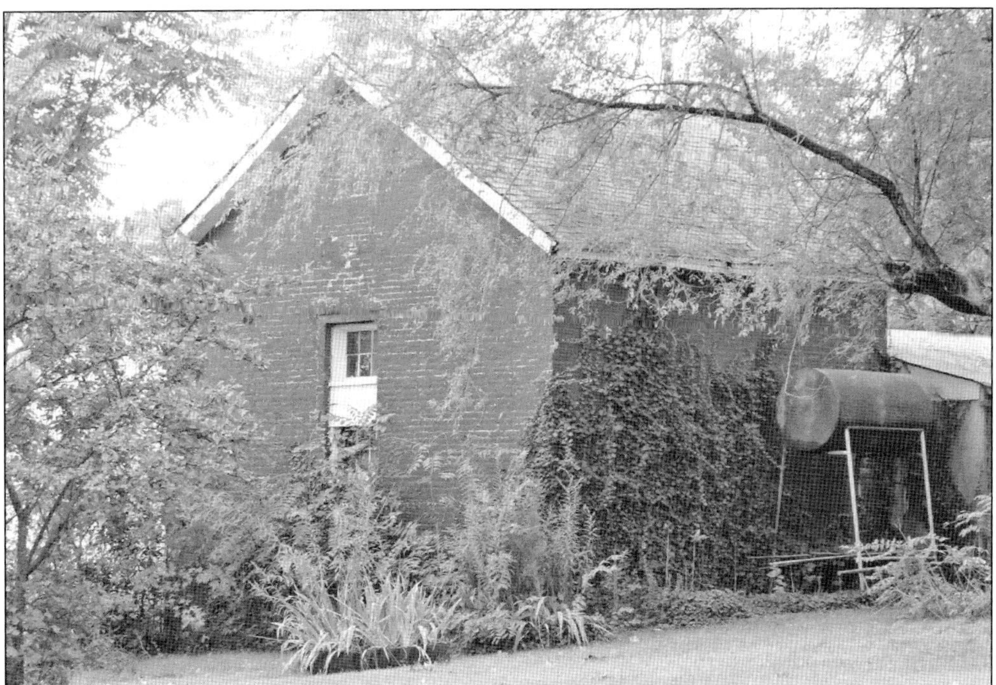

The Dula and Carr Tobacco Factory No. 2 is located directly behind Robert Dula's home at 408 East Main Street. Dula transported tobacco from the main factory to this location, nearer the railroad freight station, and prepared the crop to be sold to larger companies in St. Charles, where it was processed.

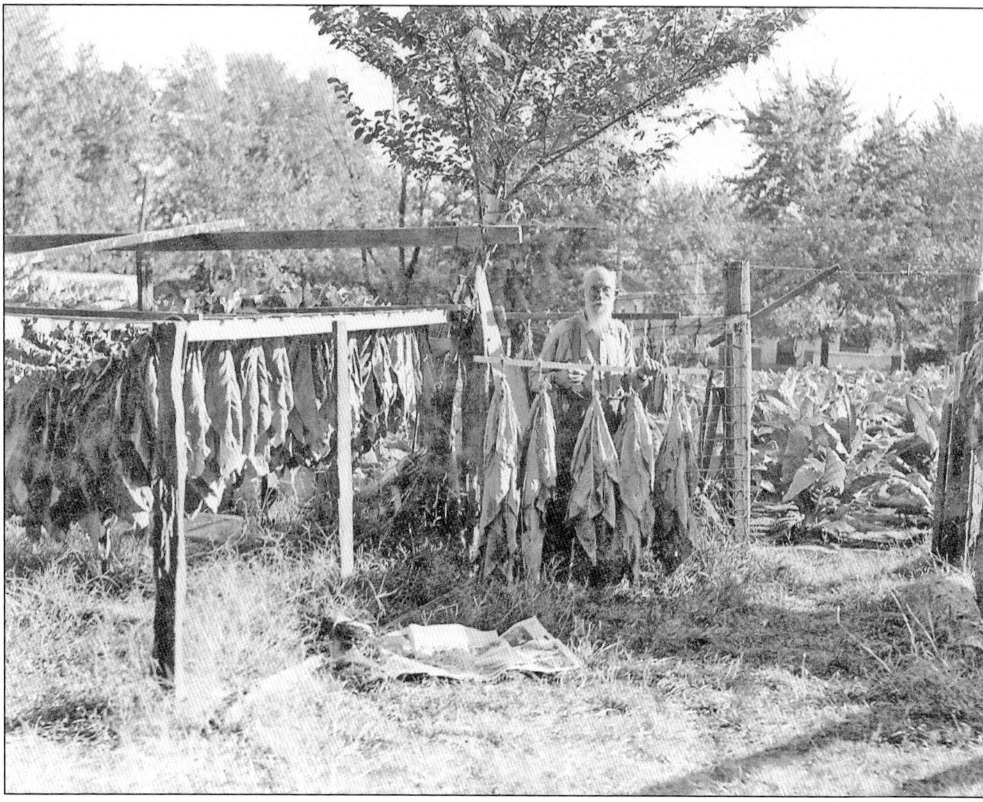

J.B. Muschany is seen in his tobacco field behind his home near Wentzville. Individual farmers grew and dried tobacco leaves long after the large tobacco companies left town. (Lewis Swinger, O'Fallon Historical Society.)

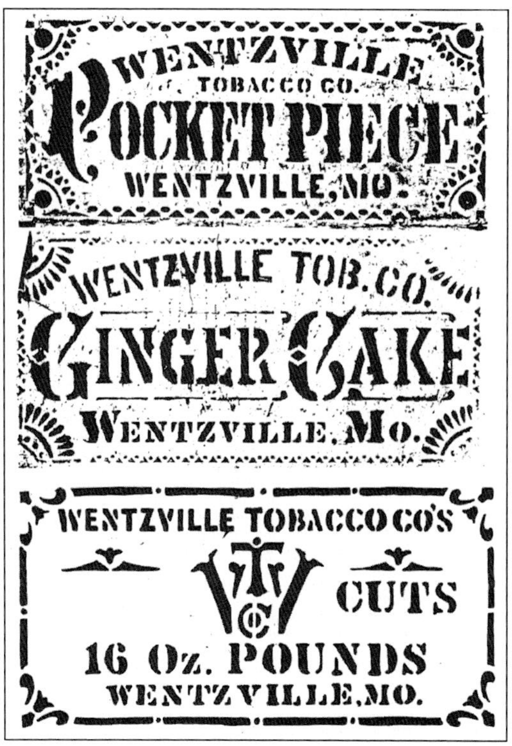

These are the Wentzville Tobacco Company's stencils used to identify some of the types of tobacco products it produced. Each of these stencils was 8 by 18 inches; they were for plug and cut chewing tobacco. (Penny Pitman.)

Three

The People Who Came Before

Studying Wentzville history will put readers in touch with people of the past, ghosts of citizens they will never get to meet, but the endeavor will also give readers a fondness for these people and this beautiful, friend-filled town. Walking through the older part of Wentzville, history lovers may be able to catch glimpses of people and buildings that many modern-day citizens cannot see. They might envision a thousand long-gone friends, and they will earn the gift of seeing how their lives and businesses still affect the city today. What would they say if they saw their homes destroyed, their businesses forgotten, or their civic centers moved from their beloved downtown to the newer part of the city?

Some of the homes in this chapter are still standing, but the overwhelming majority of the people are gone; only their images remain. Many of the older homes in the Village Center have been restored to their original beauty. Still others are being saved by citizens who care about Wentzville's heritage.

The future of Wentzville is bright, not only because the town is growing so rapidly, but because the city government realizes that history is important. Although Wentzville received its fourth-class charter in 1903, it held a rural status for many years. The residents had numerous setbacks. A tornado tore through town in 1915. A fire in 1931 destroyed most buildings in a three-block area, prompting citizens to erect a water tower in 1935 to put an end to the out-of-control fires. Business owners fought to get electricity. The population rose and fell, based on the town's circumstances, but by 1940, it had reached 752 people.

What would the founders and early citizens of Wentzville think if they could see the town today? They would be pleased that they are remembered. Maybe they do know—maybe the old-timers remain, standing in front of their homes and businesses, keeping an eye on their beloved town.

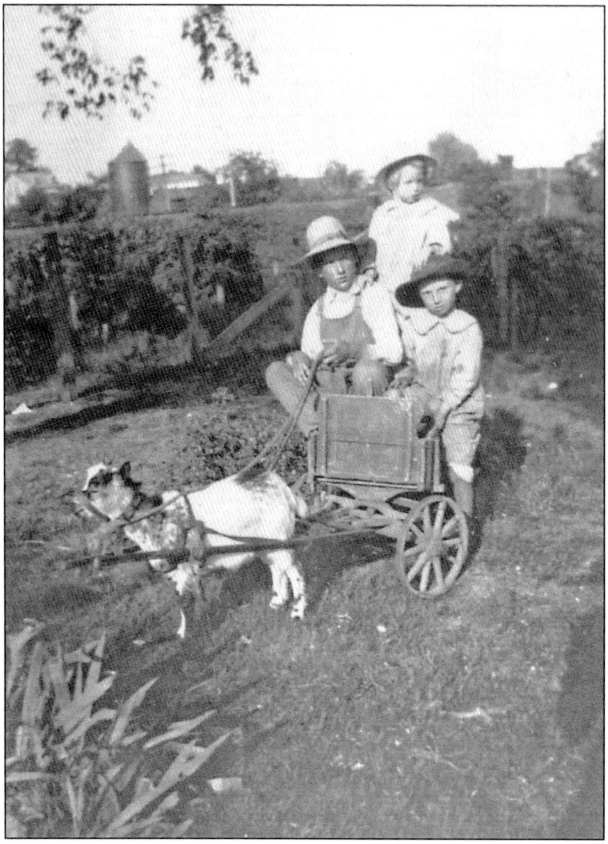

The Rottger children are pictured on their farm near Wentzville. From left to right are Rick, Hellen, and Lawrence. Clearly they needed a bigger goat.

This tobacco plantation mansion was built by the founder of Wentzville, William M. Allen, in 1856. In 1916, when this photograph was taken, it was the home of Milton Gannaway (seated at center) and family. To the far left is his brother-in-law Richard King. King owned the famous million-acre King Ranch in Texas. He came to Wentzville frequently to visit with his sister.

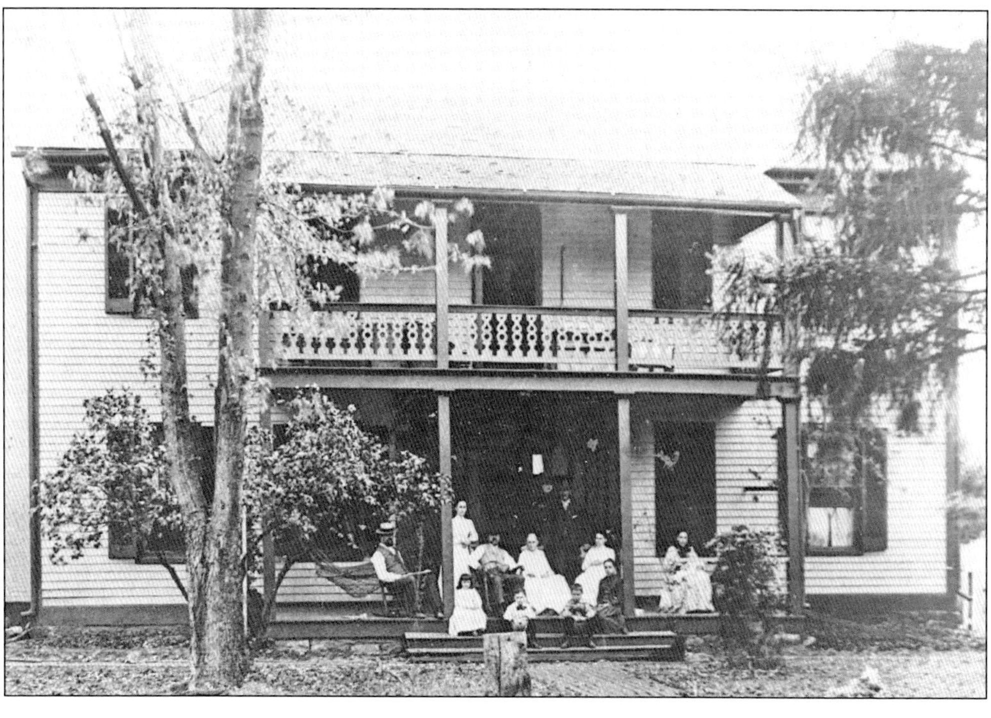

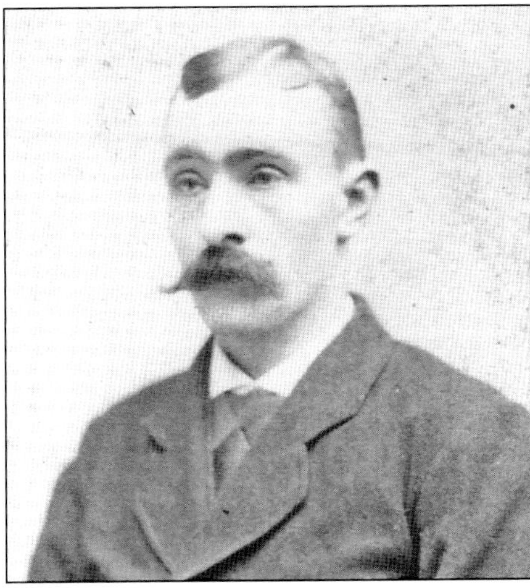

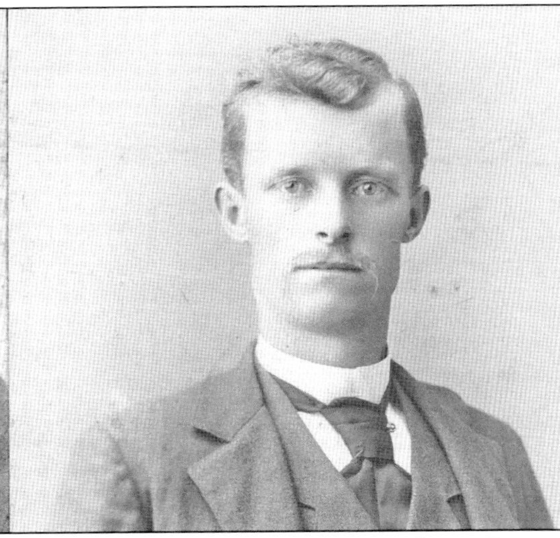

On the left is John F. Bornhop (1856–1933). He worked for the Savage and May Tobacco Factory, was justice of the peace, a Wentzville assessor and collector in 1892, postmaster from 1897 to 1914, and owned the *Wentzville Union* newspaper in 1917. On the right is Ed S. Walker, who lived from 1865 to 1937. Walker was a founding partner of the Wentzville State Bank.

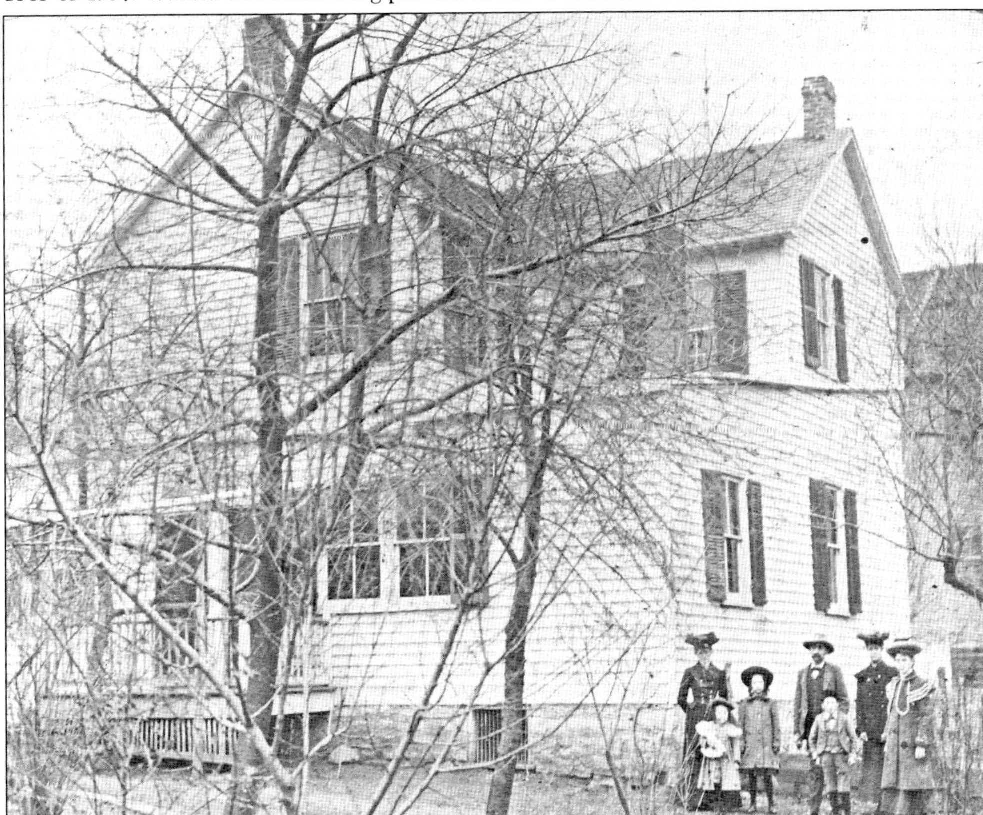

This majestic-looking home, pictured around 1890, is where the John F. Bornhop family lived. This influential man of Wentzville married Wilhelmina "Minnie" Catherine Clobes on June 23, 1886. John died on their 47th wedding anniversary in 1933. They are posed here with their children.

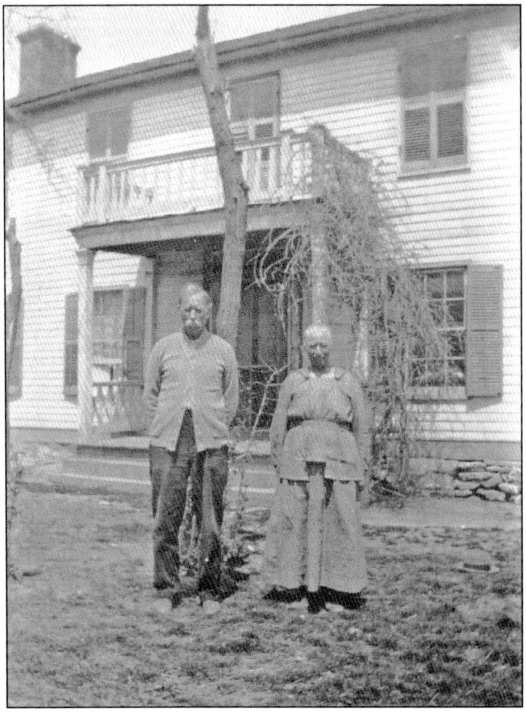

Phillip Post and his wife stand in front of their Wentzville home around 1900. (Bernice Post Strong.)

Oney Williams, his horse Charles, and his dog Tootle pose for a charming picture on East North Main Street (East Allen Street today) in 1915. This photograph was taken looking south across the railroad tracks. The large building in the background is the Koenig mansion, today the location of CenturyLink. The photographer was standing about where the post office is today.

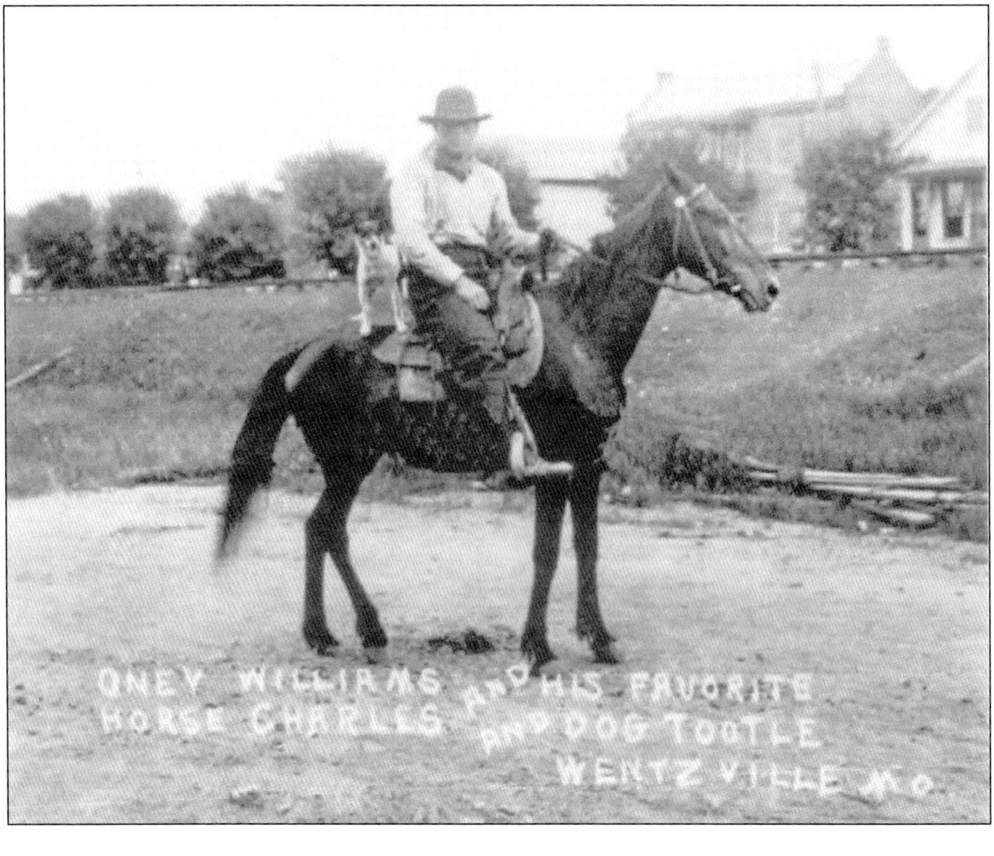

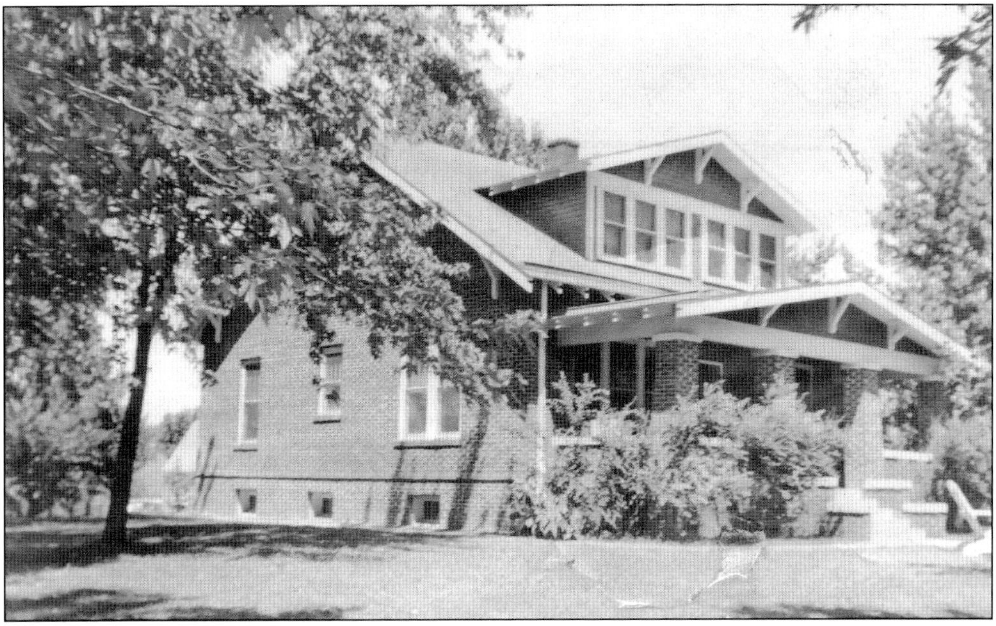

Charles "Charlie" Richards's home was built by his father-in-law, Charles E. Musick, in 1916. Charlie and his wife, Alma Lee Musick Richards, inherited the home in 1929. This photograph, taken in 1935, was part of a series of photographs taken by the city to illustrate the more prominent homes and landmarks in Wentzville.

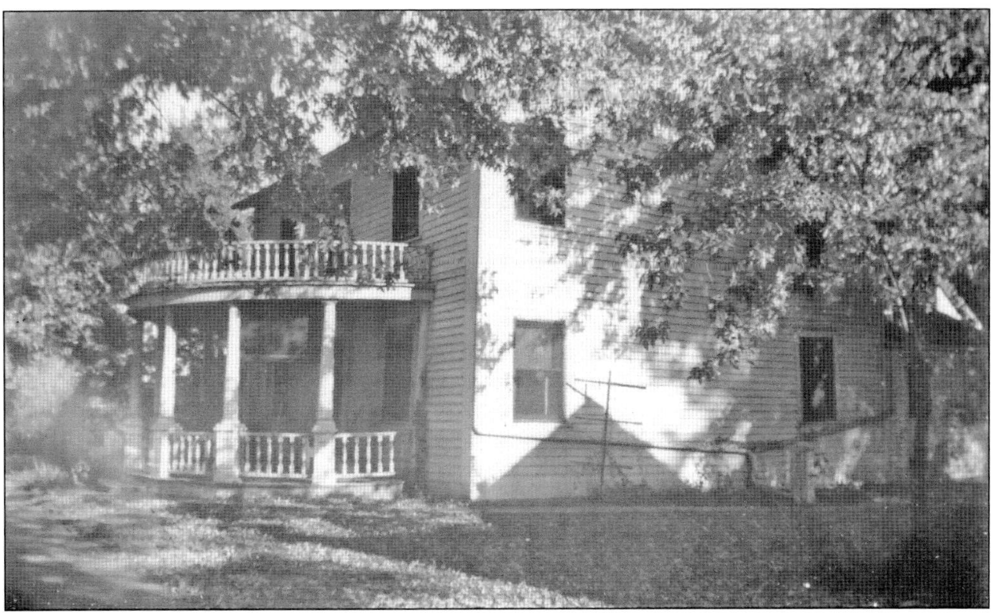

The home at 408 East Main Street is the only remaining structure from the original seven-block plat laid out by town founder William Allen in 1855. It was owned by Robert B. Dula of the Dula and Carr Tobacco Company until 1885. Judge John C. Brown lived there until the 1920s. Brown was the only six-term mayor in Wentzville, serving from 1908 to 1914 and again from 1920 to 1926.

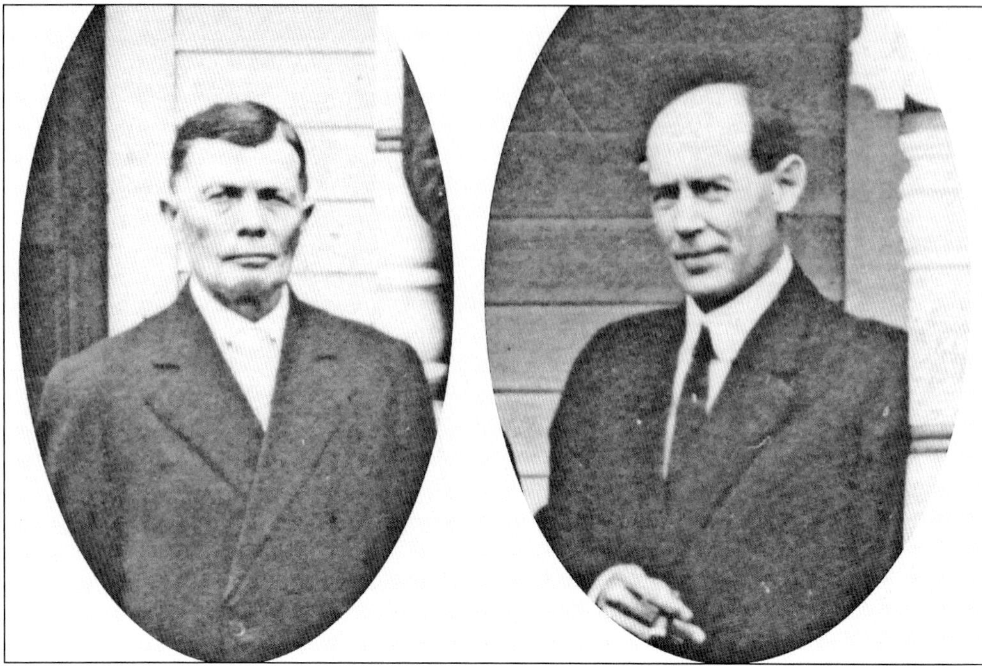

Charles Musick (left), owner of Musick Livery, Feed, and Stable, was councilman in 1890, mayor from 1904 to 1906, and city marshal from 1914 to 1918. He was killed by a train in 1929. William Karrenbrock (right), born in 1872, owned the Karrenbrock Flour Mill and Elevator, and founded the Wentzville State Bank in 1905. He died in 1952 at the age of 80.

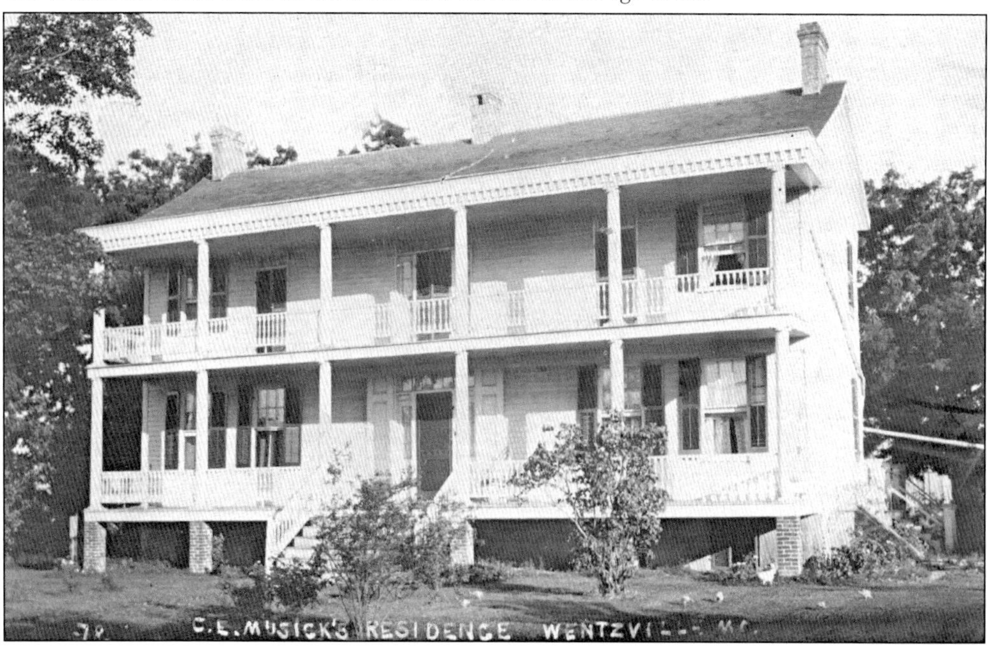

The Musick mansion was located on West South Main Street in an area that used to be known as Musick's Grove. Owned by Charles Musick, the grove was the location of town picnics and Fourth of July celebrations. The home was sold in 1916 and then became a rooming house. This park-like farm was acquired by the Wentzville Community Club in 1962 for its new facility.

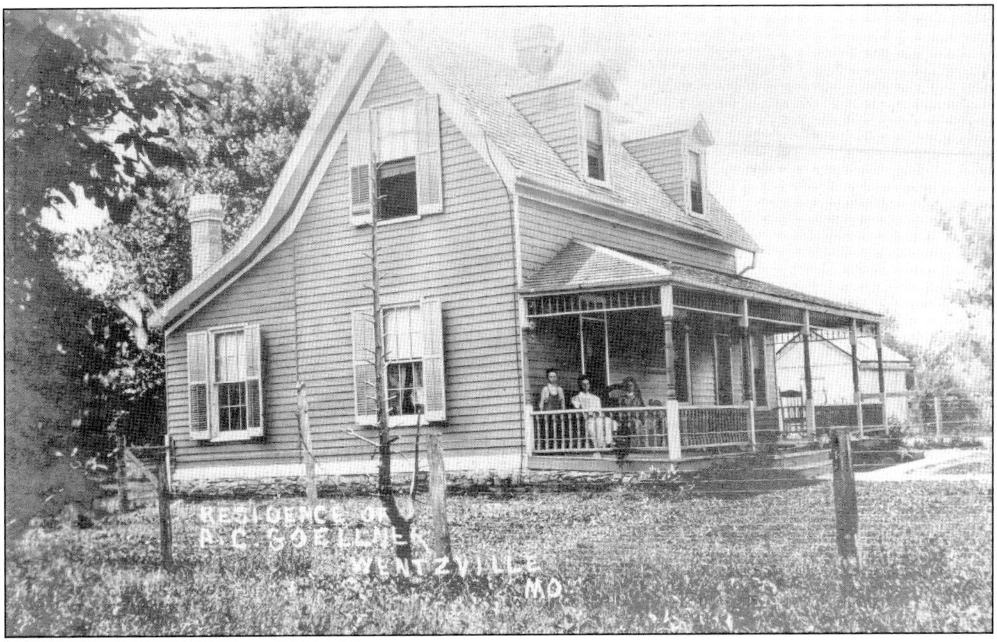

These two 19th-century homes, which still stand in the Village Center of Wentzville, have been integrated into neighborhoods and have become show places. The home pictured above was the residence of A.C. Goellner, who owned the City Meat Market in 1903 and was a partner in the Wentzville Mercantile. Below is the home of Gus Knippenberg, pictured around 1915. (Both, Mayme Dierker Ball.)

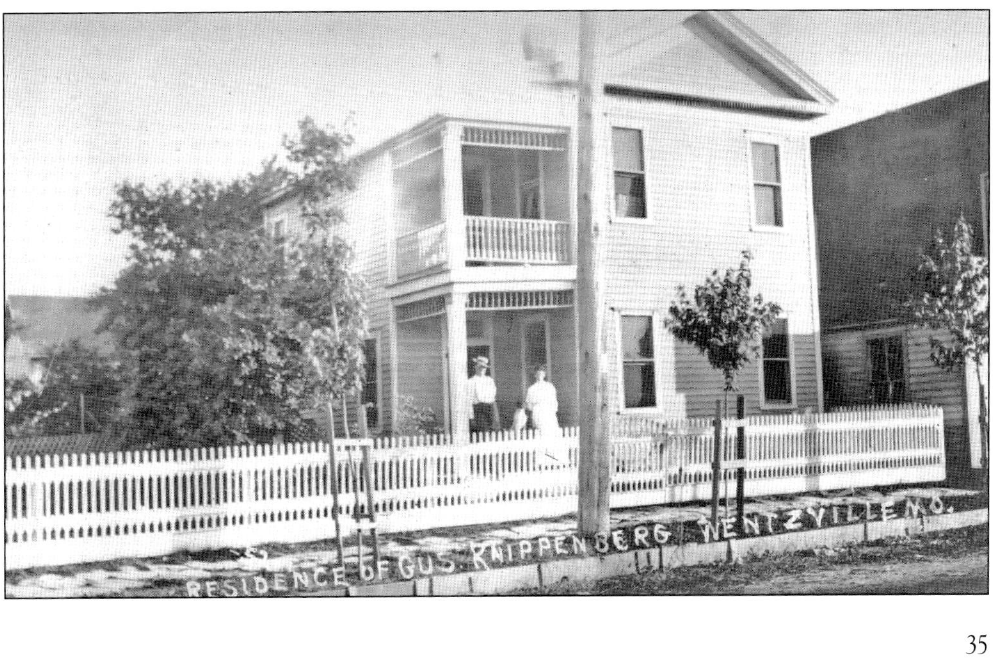

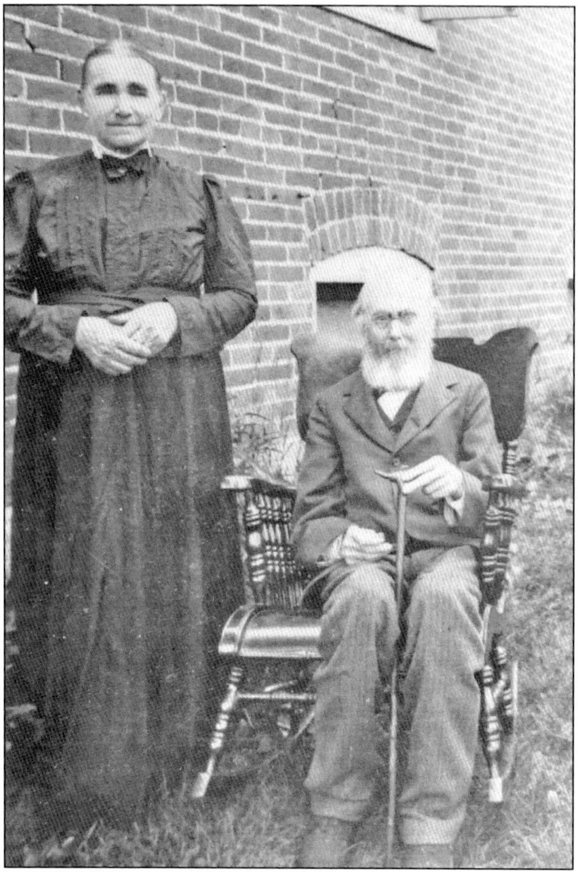

Clara Elizabeth and Henry William Karrenbrock, both age 73, are pictured in 1908. Henry's family emigrated from Westphalia, Germany, in 1829, and he settled in Wentzville in 1892. He founded the Karrenbrock Milling Company. Its leading flour brands were White Cream and High Patent. After he retired, Henry's sons Charles F. and William F. assumed control of the mill.

Charles Ruebling and family kept their Wentzville home in pristine condition. This photograph was taken in 1908. Ruebling was listed as a county councilman and alderman of Ward 1 in 1916. (Mayme Dierker Ball.)

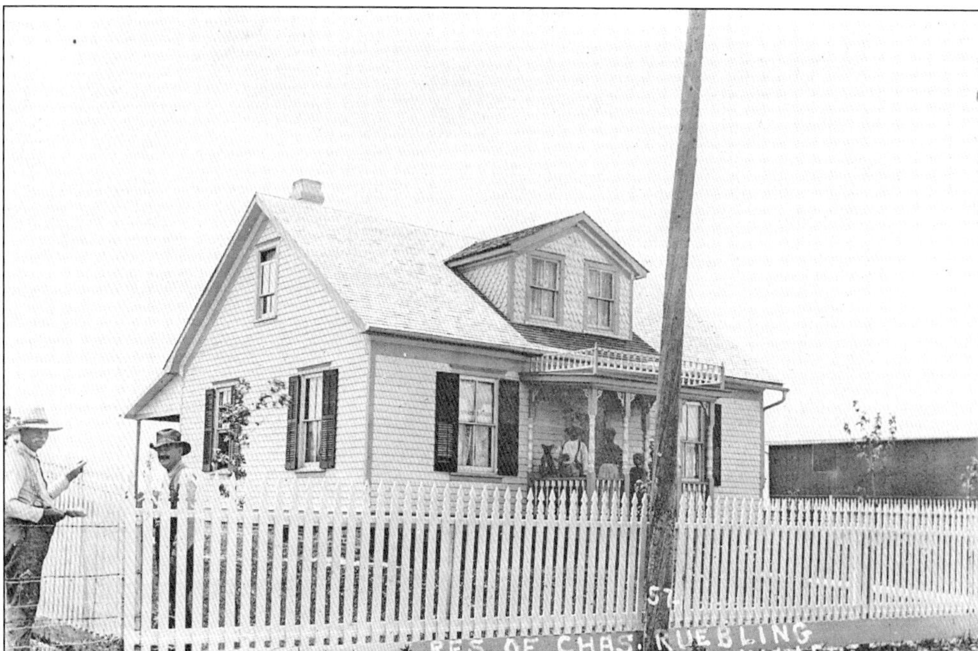

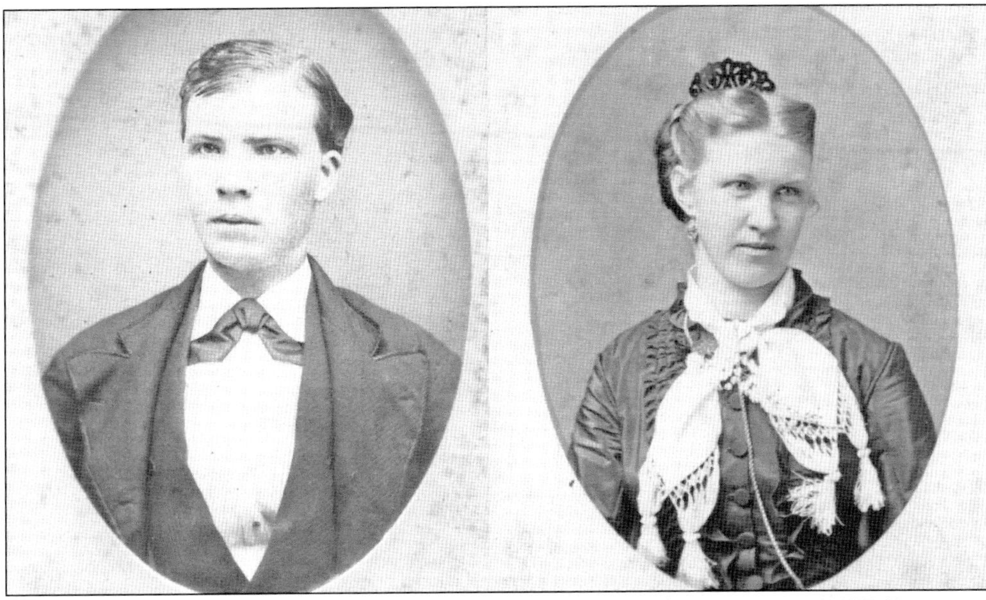

Fritz Schierbaum and Marie Heitgard Schierbaum were married on January 4, 1877. Fritz was a blacksmith when he arrived in Wentzville in 1878. He went on to be an alderman in 1894, and built the largest store in St. Charles County, Schierbaum's Implement and Wagonmakers. It manufactured wagons, buggies, wheat binders, and other farm machinery. Marie died on March 27, 1919, and Fritz followed on August 20, 1924.

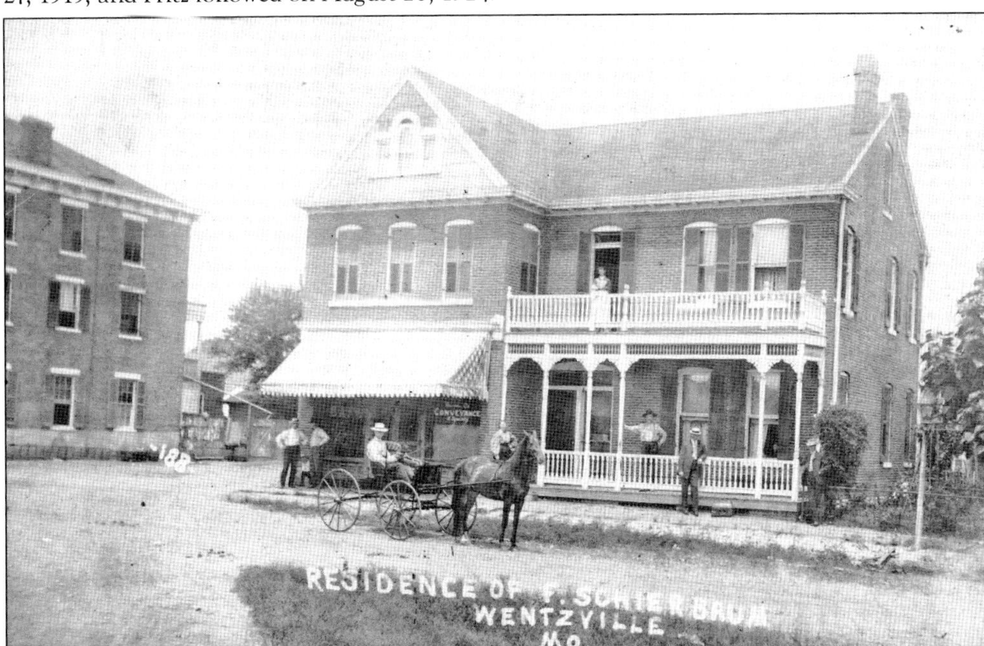

The Schierbaum home, shown here around 1878, is a Wentzville landmark, still standing on the corner of East Allen Street and Linn Avenue. The left part of the building has been occupied over the years by many shops, ranging from hardware to clothing, donuts to paint, a bank, and Wentzville's post office. Fritz Schierbaum was a community leader and was influential throughout Missouri. (Bill Schiermeier.)

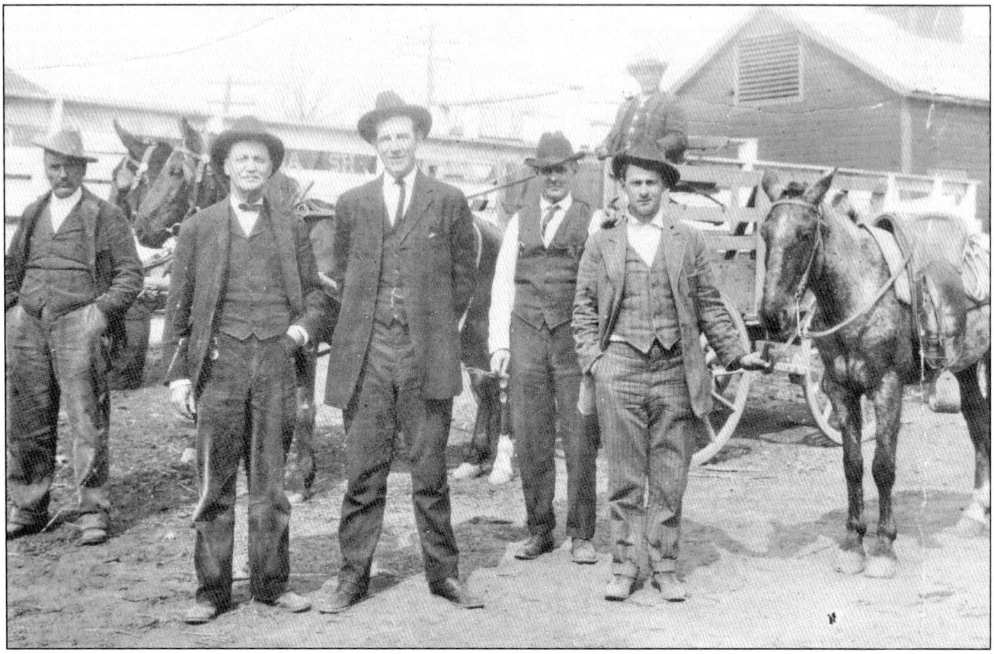

Stock traders were men who rode horseback through the country to find farmers with stock for sale. This Wentzville group, pictured in 1912, includes, from left to right, Mr. Strunk, Bob May, Murray Foristell (feed dealer and judge), William "Billy" McCoy, Richard "Dick" Anselm, and Charles Ruebling in the wagon. Herds of cattle and hogs were often driven through the streets of Wentzville. (Rick Anselm.)

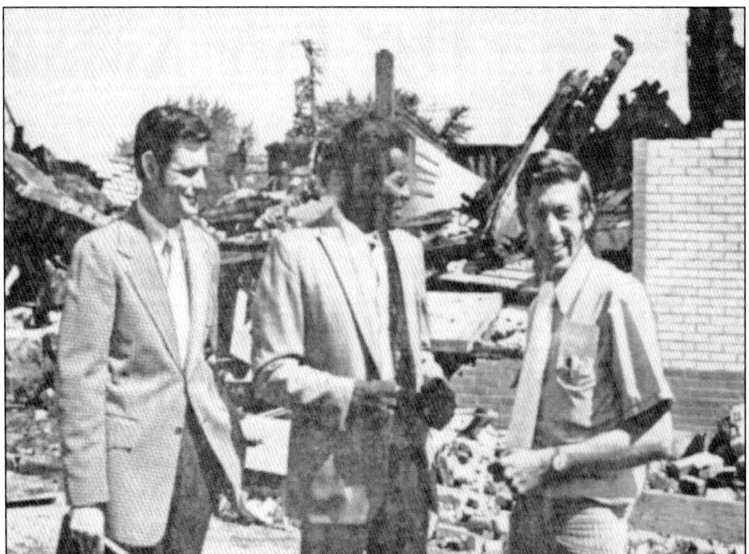

WENTZVILLE CLEANUP: Conferring on removal of fire-damaged buildings in the Wentzville central business district (from left) are insurance adjuster Gregory M. Geil, rock singer Chuck Berry and Mayor Meade Foster. Berry owns the building. Foster said that in the course of an "extremely amicable" discussion, Berry agreed to remove the debris and level the remaining walls this week. (Post-Dispatch Photo by Lloyd Spainhower)

Berry Park is a ranch in Wentzville where rock legend Chuck Berry lived beginning in the late 1950s. Berry owned several buildings in town, one of which, the American Theater, burned to the ground in 1973. This clipping, dated June 27, 1973, relates the post-fire discussion concerning the removal of debris. Chuck Berry passed away in 2017 in his home at Berry Park. (*Post Dispatch*.)

Four

SERVICES, CHURCHES, AND SCHOOLS

Wentzville has faced many challenges through the years. From 1855, when it was founded, to 1872, the town went without a charter, in part because the community was divided by the Civil War. Most business owners were Confederate sympathizers, whereas many who lived in the rural area, mostly of German descent, were on the side of the Union. The war seemed to last longer in Wentzville than in the rest of the country, and Wentzville suffered from the division.

Finally, in 1872, the citizens petitioned the county court; 83 citizens were in favor of creating a charter, and 17 were against. The court recognized the overwhelming majority and granted the charter on March 5, 1872; Wentzville was officially proclaimed a town. The new town's board of trustees worked feverishly to build infrastructure, meeting in the back rooms of businesses and in the parlors of leading citizens' homes. During the 1880s, several major fires caused the loss of many homes and businesses and all public records from 1872 to 1890. Wentzville was off to a rocky start.

The early 1890s were not much better. The city election of 1892, which was supposed to be held in April, was not held until May—the town simply forgot. In 1894, Wentzville cleaned house; the mayor and aldermen were all replaced. No explanation has ever been found.

While the government was busy figuring out how to govern, Wentzvillians were building schools and churches, some of which have lasted more than a century. The various church denominations all did their best to be the spiritual compass for Wentzville. A two-year high school was built in the 1890s and was elevated to a four-year school in 1933. That building still stands on Linn Avenue.

It has been a long journey from a few dedicated men and women in the 1850s to the present-day fourth-class city of over 40,000 citizens. The city government is showing strong interest in reinvigorating Wentzville's Village Center, and the past is coming nearer every day.

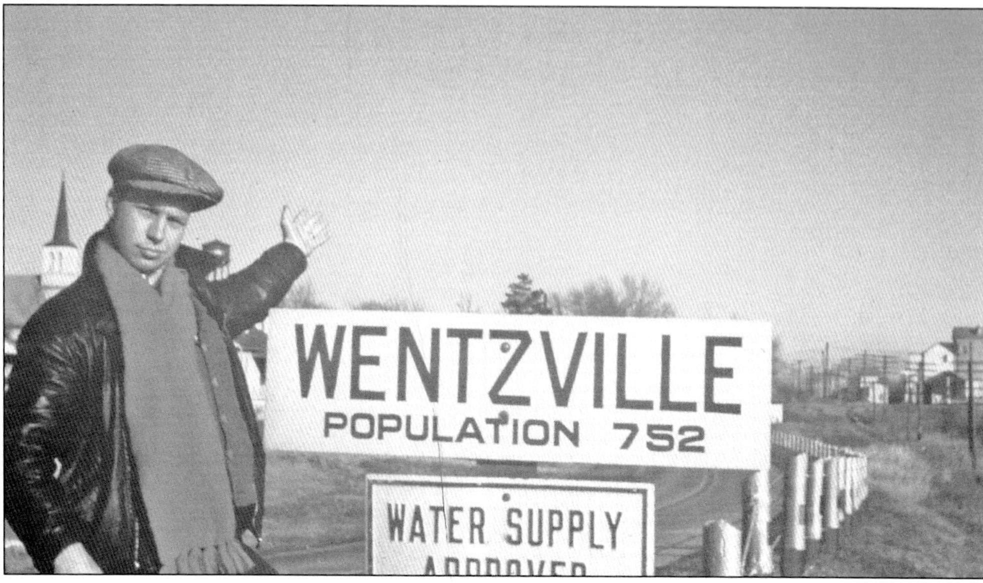

A *Look* magazine photographer, Larry Wentz, came through Wentzville on December 12, 1941, looking for information on his great-grand-uncle and the town's namesake, Erasmus Livingston Wentz. Unfortunately, the historical society was not founded for another 35 years. He did, however, take several high-resolution photographs and brought this one to share in 1982 when he returned to be presented the key to the city.

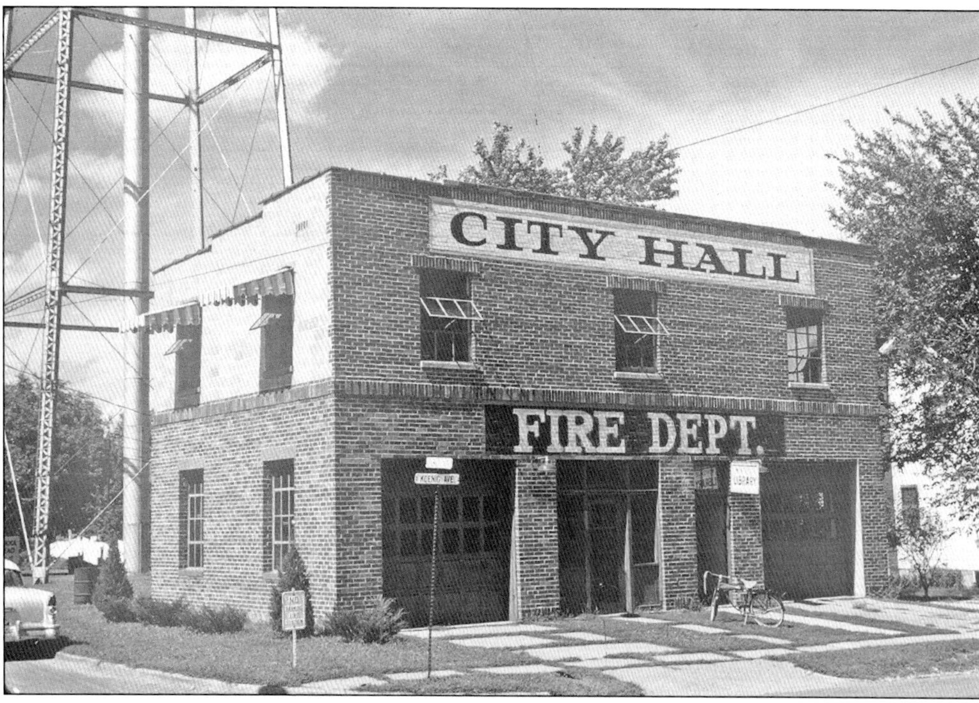

The city hall, fire department, police department, and library occupied this building in the 1940s and 1950s. The lower level was built in 1935 and was used as a pumping station for the new water tower. Later, the second floor was added to house city hall and the library. By the time this photograph was taken, a new fire department was under construction on Pearce Boulevard.

The first permanent library in St. Charles County was located in Wentzville on Wall Street. The first librarian was Jennie C. Lewis (shown in 1917), a teacher who later became Mrs. Murray Foristell. The idea for a library began in 1907 when 12 women, led by Mrs. J.W. Burd, formed the Wentzville Library Association. For the first 10 years, a portion of the library was housed in the public school; members joined for $1. In January 1942, the Athenian Club officially transferred the library to the Wentzville Library Association. In February 1942, the Work Progress Administration (WPA) took over the library, which by then was housed in the Freese building. It was moved to the top floor of the city hall/firehouse (page 40) in August 1944. Below, a young Kevin Pyatt checks out books from the second-floor library in 1958.

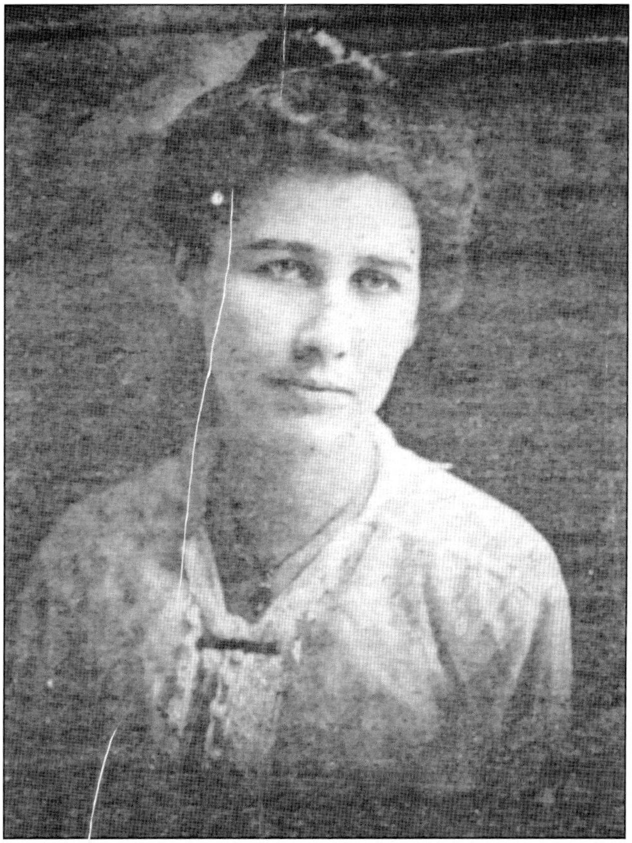

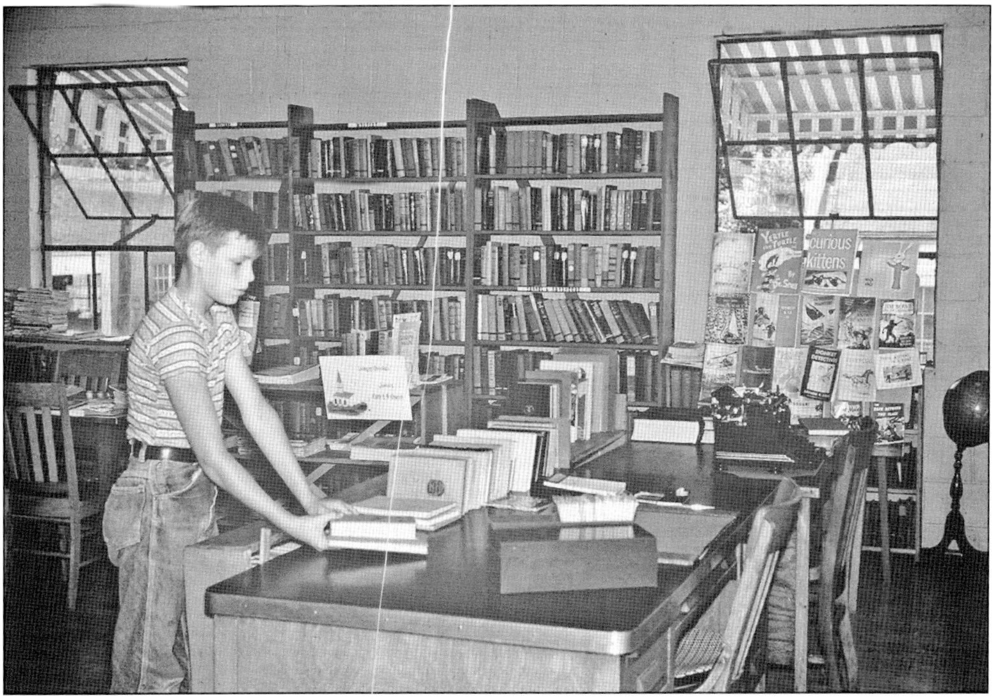

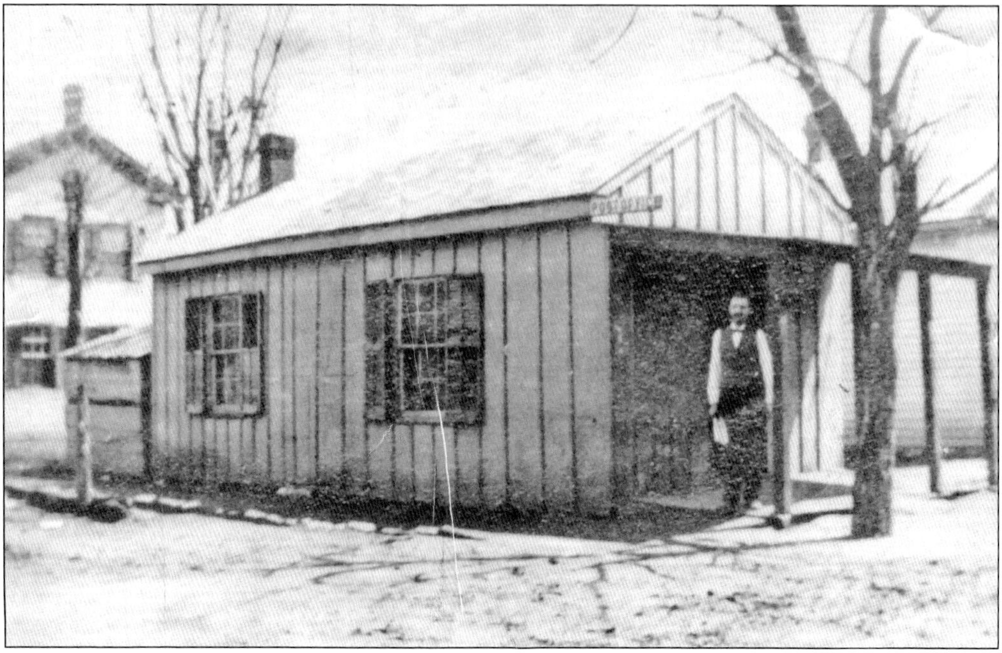

John F. Bornhop, seen in front of his post office building on Linn Avenue in 1900, came to Wentzville in 1880. He originally worked for the Savage and May Tobacco Company but became assistant postmaster in the early 1890s. He then applied for and was awarded the title postmaster in 1897, consequently moving the post office from within the Thompson Hotel to his building, shown above. Bornhop was Wentzville's postmaster from 1897 to 1914, at which time he lost his bid, and the post office moved into the lower left level of the Schierbaum building on what is now East Allen Street (seen below in 1919). There it stayed until it was moved up the street in 1960. Bornhop, never one to stay idle, bought the *Wentzville Union* newspaper in 1917, becoming owner, publisher, and editor.

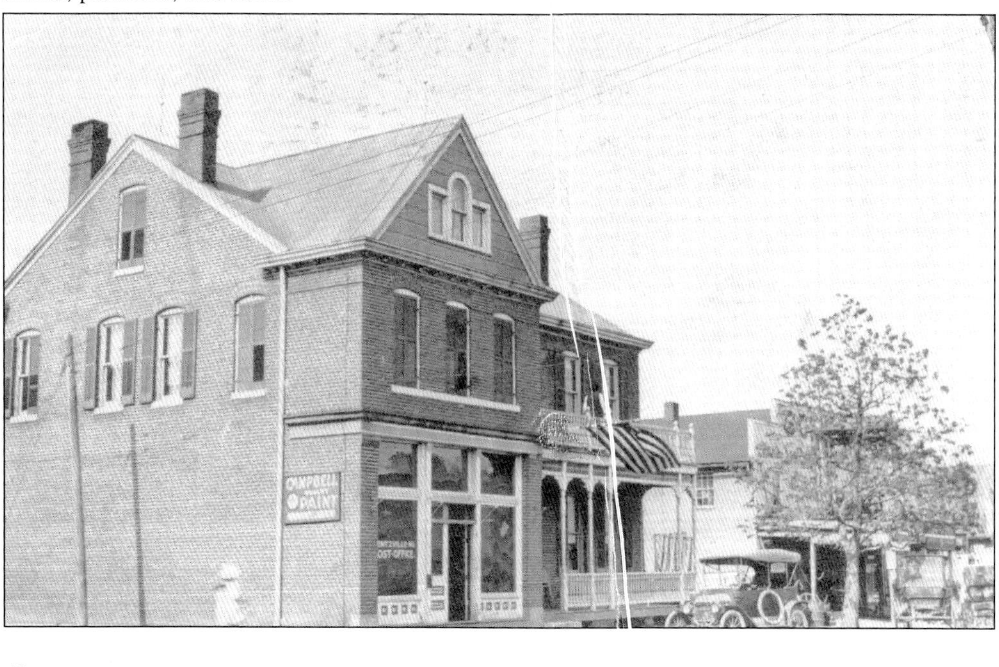

Marshal Samuel Slayback Anselm was a hometown hero. After city marshal James Schmidt died in office, Sam was appointed by the board of aldermen in 1958, and was re-elected by the people for the next 27 years. He was the longest-serving city marshal in Wentzville and the last elected in the county. He is shown here having his morning coffee and donut at a Wentzville landmark, the Y Café. (Rick Anselm.)

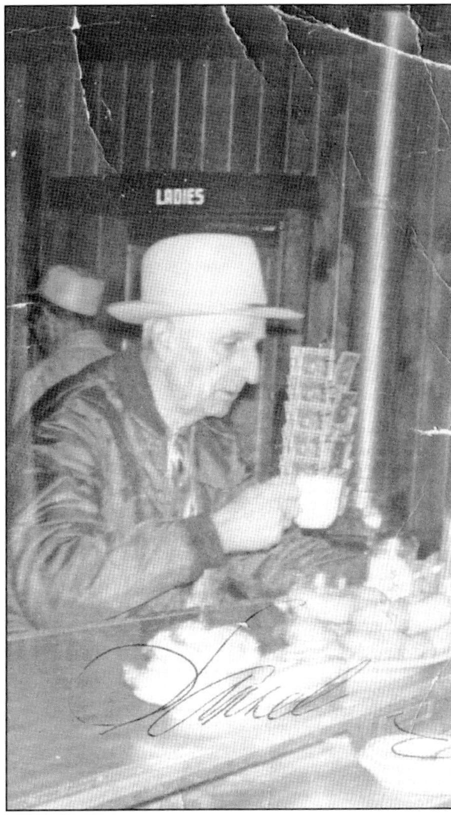

This rickety-looking building was the old jail, used to incarcerate Wentzville's rowdy citizens from 1904 until more suitable accommodations could be built around 1940. The structure was originally an outbuilding, located on the property of marshal Clevelend S. Sidebottoms, who is shown here locking the door on another outlaw. Wentzville's two-year high school can be seen in the background.

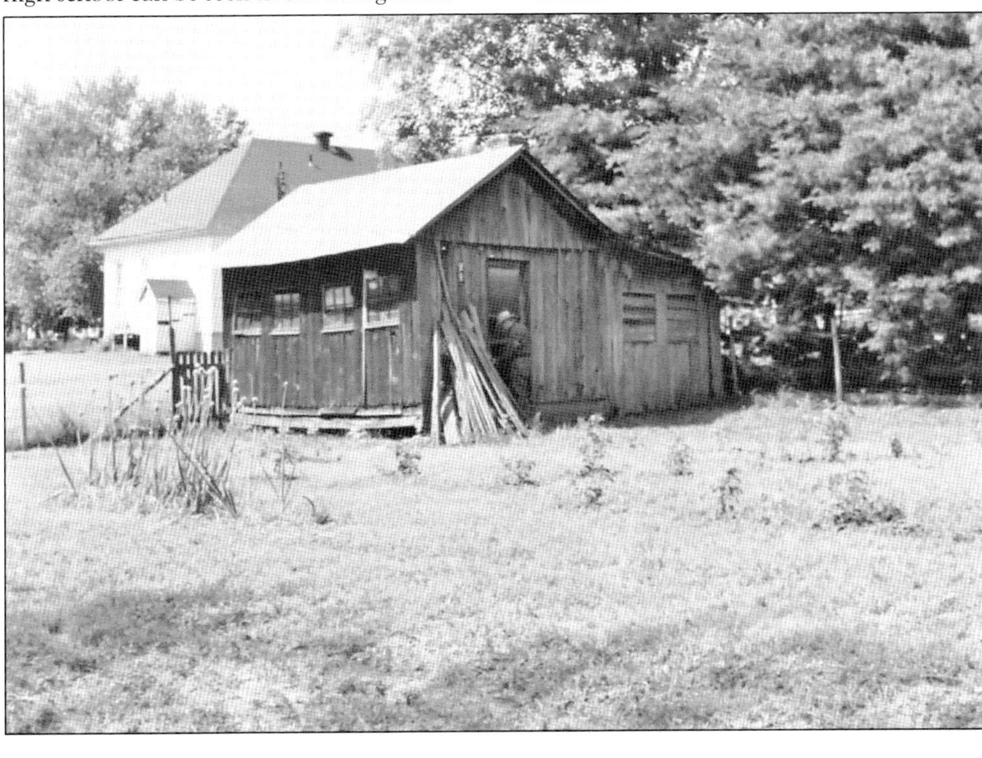

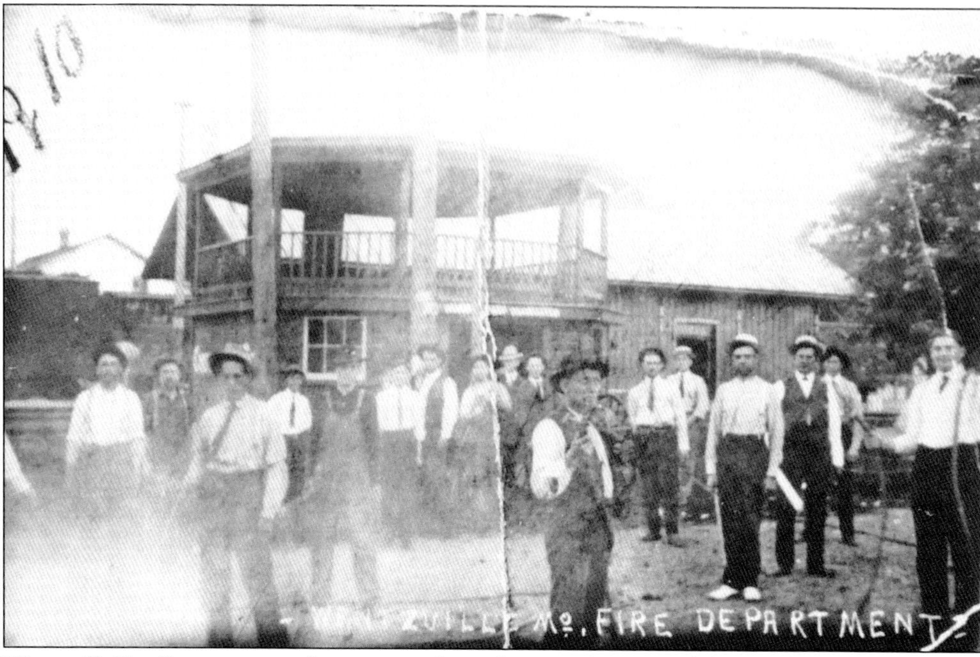

Wentzville Fire Department volunteers are shown here in 1910 around the combination bandstand/chemical firehouse, which housed the hand-pumper, buckets, and axes. The earliest records of the fire department date to October 19, 1883, when two fires nearly destroyed the town. Robert Dula, a prominent tobacco man, acted as fire chief and saved the day. A larger department was organized in the 1920s, after the bandstand/firehouse was razed in 1916 because it blocked the view of oncoming trains. In 1928, a Model T without a cab was purchased and fitted with a small water tank, a limited amount of hose, and a pump to lift water from cisterns, wells, and ponds. The equipment was housed in a garage on Linn Avenue. In 1931, a fire broke out directly across the street, burning half the block and threatening to take the whole town.

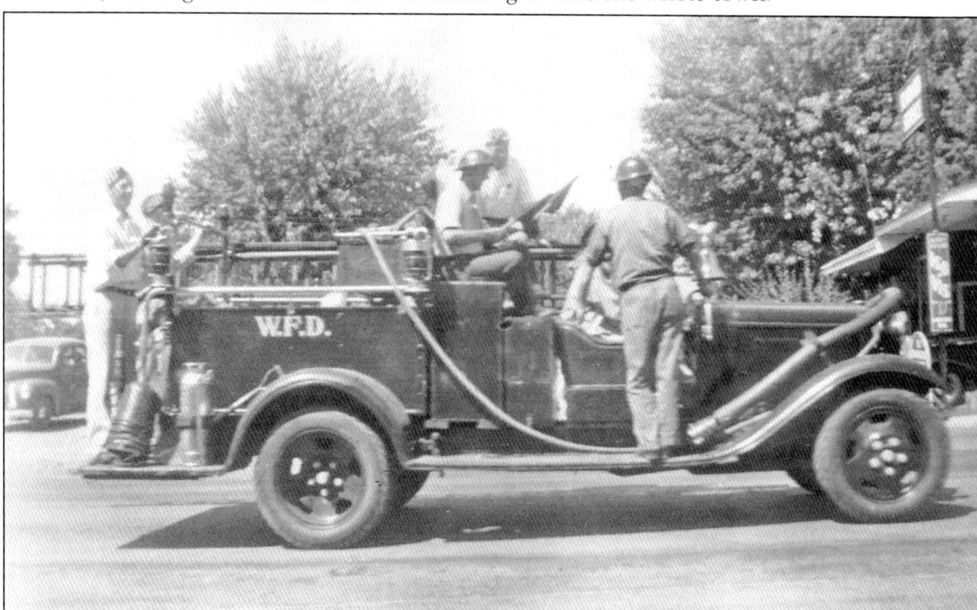

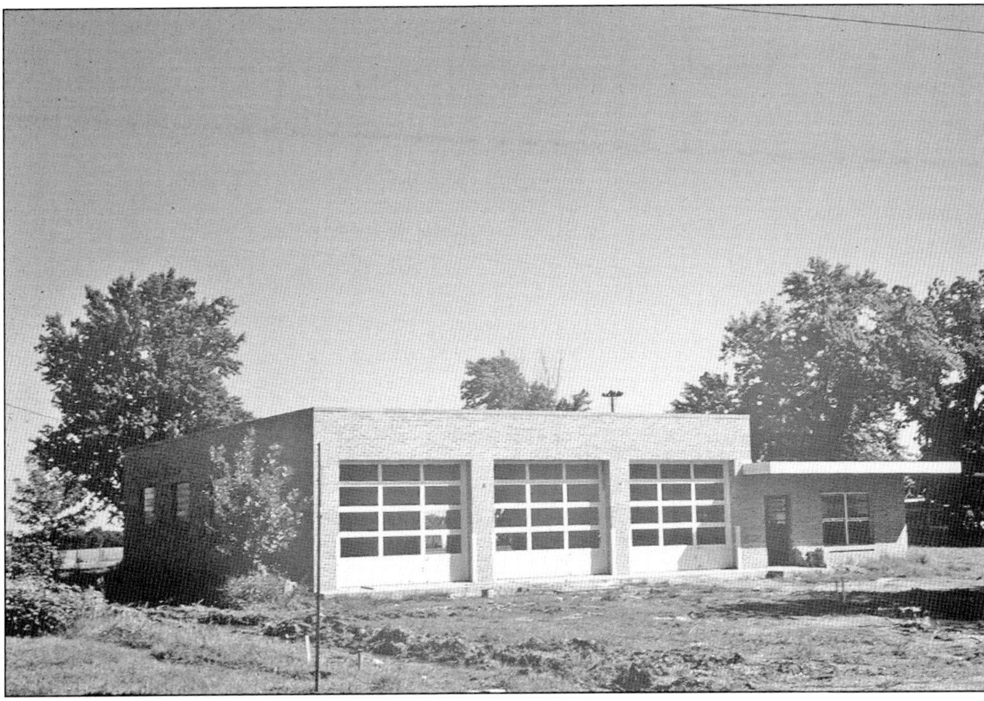

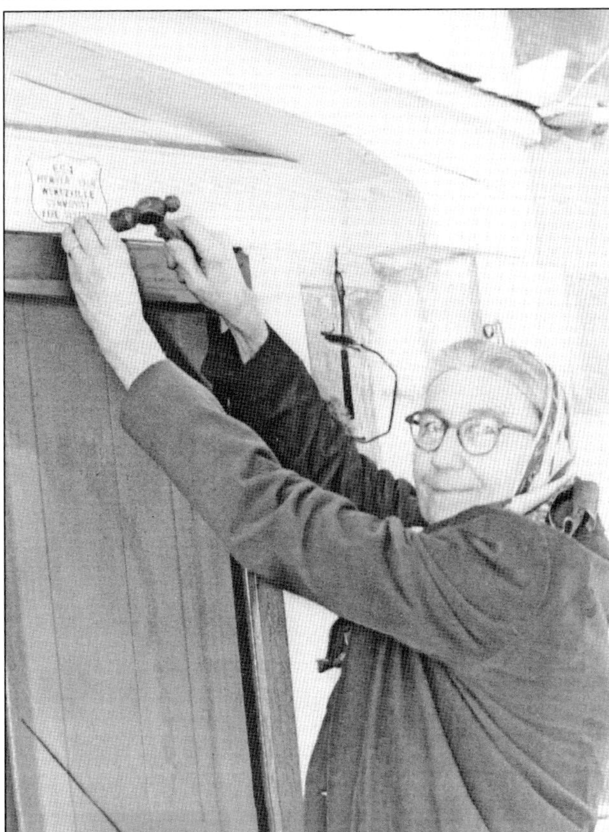

The Wentzville Fire Department held fundraisers beginning in the 1930s for equipment and a more modern firehouse. In 1934, a waterworks was built, including the first tower and pump house, and the fire truck and equipment were moved from the garage on Linn Avenue to the new pump house. Sharing the building with city hall, the police department, and the library left no room for expansion, so in 1958, the fire department built a new three-bay firehouse on Pearce Boulevard. Still operated by the volunteer fire department, funding was in constant need. One fundraiser was the sale of fire tags. At right, Martha Pallardy is shown nailing her tag onto her home in 1958. At that time, the fire department would not put out a fire unless the owner showed a tag. In 1971, the Wentzville Fire Protection District No. 13 was voted into existence.

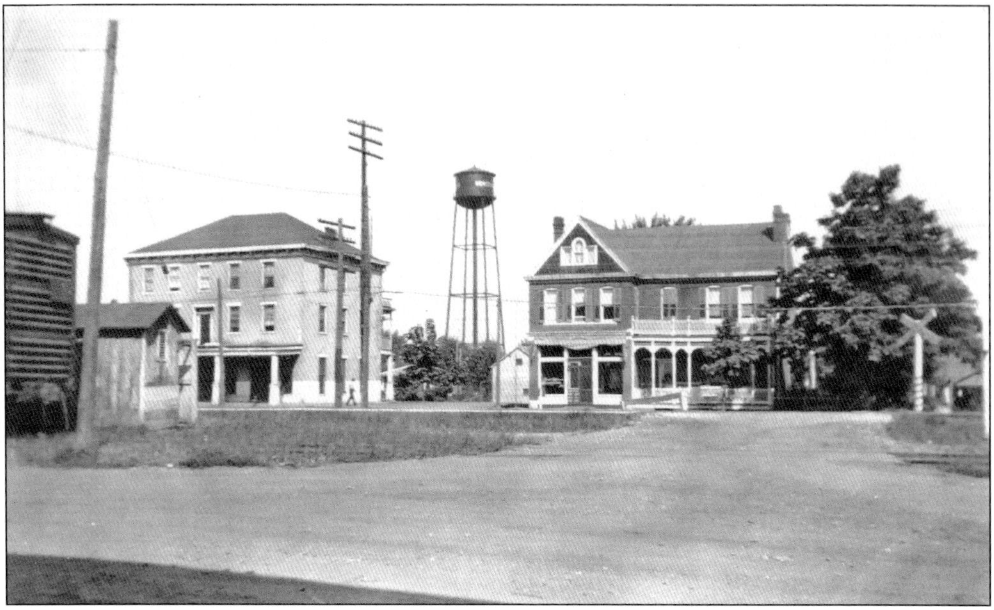

During the Great Depression, the WPA made it possible for Wentzville to build and install a water and sewer system. In 1935, a new water tower was completed, shown here from the south side of the railroad tracks between the Heady Hotel and the Schierbaum building. Because of the new waterworks, the last town-threatening fire occurred in 1931.

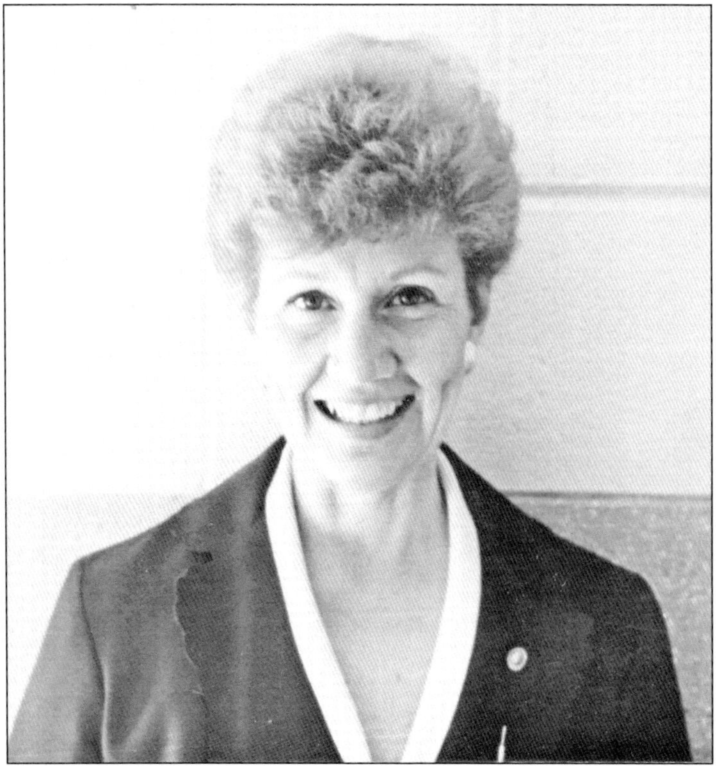

Nancy K. Reynolds, a grade-school teacher, was approached in 1974 to run for mayor. Laughing, she declined, believing it was a joke. As the election approached, she was told that friends had signed her up as a candidate. She refused to campaign, but the morning after the election, she was told that she had just become the first woman mayor of Wentzville and, in fact, of St. Charles County.

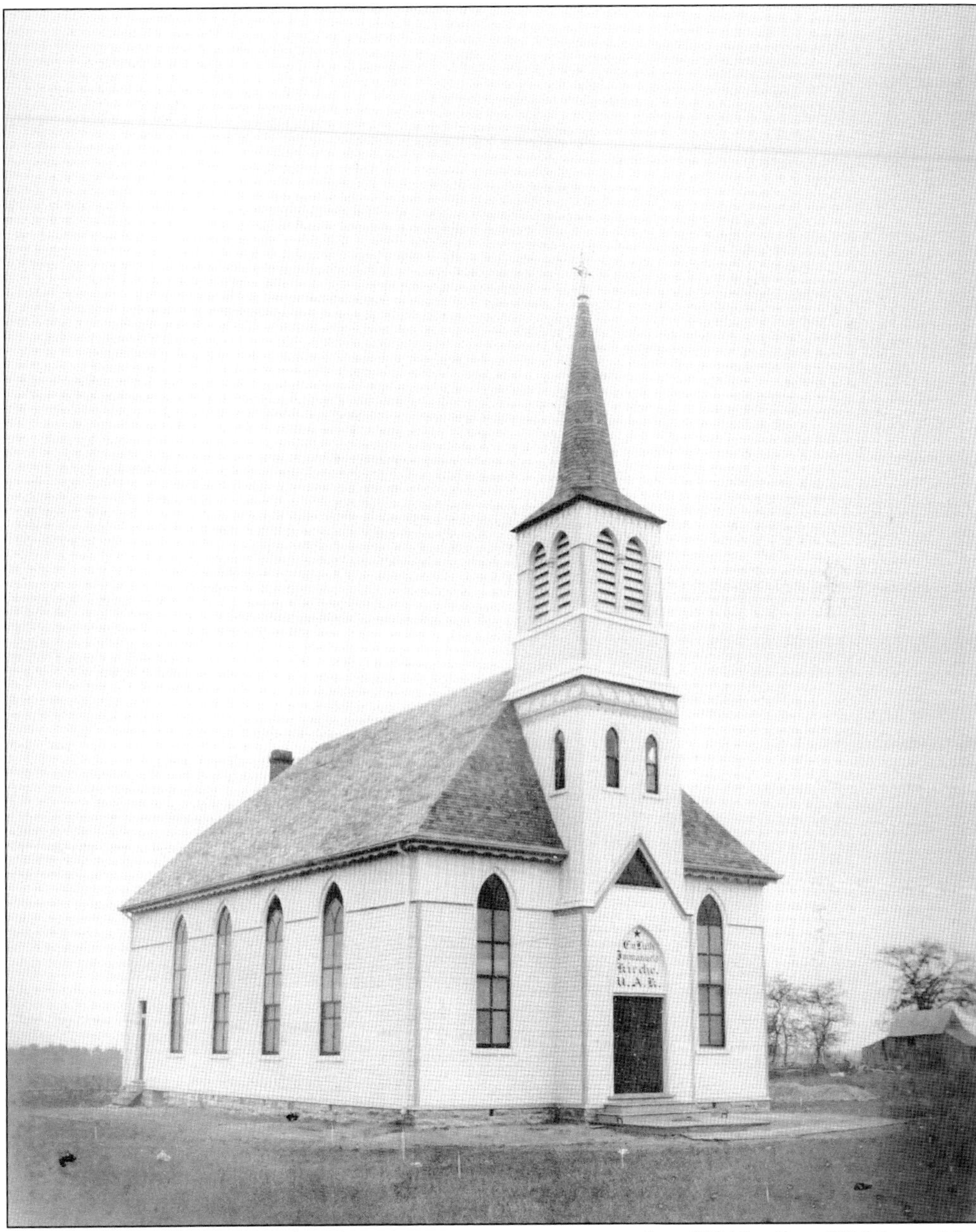

The Immanuel Lutheran Church congregation was organized in 1874 by Rev. W. Matuschka, then pastor of the congregation at New Melle. The first church was built in 1874 and was a brick building at 406 Second Street. The church lot cost $60; the total cost of the church was about $1,600. A new structure, shown here with its classic design upon completion in 1899, still stands as a landmark in Wentzville. The dedication of the church took place on November 12, 1899. The congregation met in front of the new church, where Rev. H.J. Mueller delivered a short address before they entered for worship. The following year (1900), the congregation built a new parsonage and its first school building. In 1921, electric lights were installed. The concrete state highway (Highway 40) was laid through the five-acre church property in 1923. This highway gave the church a splendid front and great accessibility.

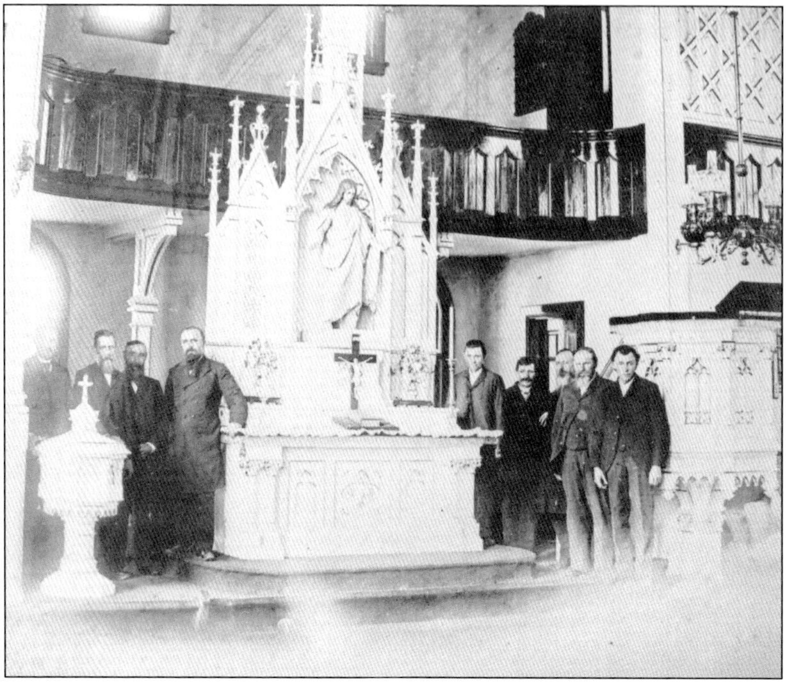

This photograph of the inside of the Lutheran church is believed to be from 1899. Rev. H.J. Mueller is to the left with his hand resting on the magnificent altar.

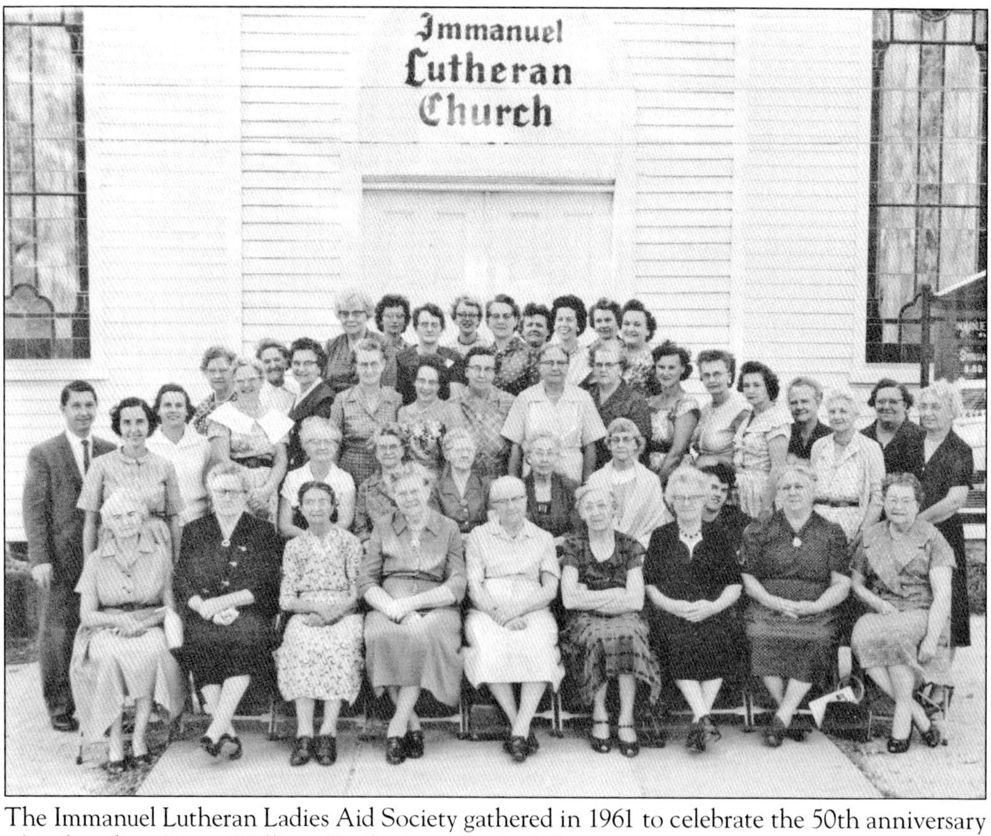

The Immanuel Lutheran Ladies Aid Society gathered in 1961 to celebrate the 50th anniversary of its founding. Pastor William Gerike is on the far left.

Immanuel Lutheran's first schoolhouse, built in 1900 to the right of the church, is seen around 1910 with Rev. H.J. Mueller and the schoolchildren. Reverend Mueller resigned on April 11, 1915, due to ill health. The church soon outgrew this school, and a new one was built and opened on August 12, 1917. Later, the original schoolhouse was moved to George Freese's junkyard, where it was used for storage.

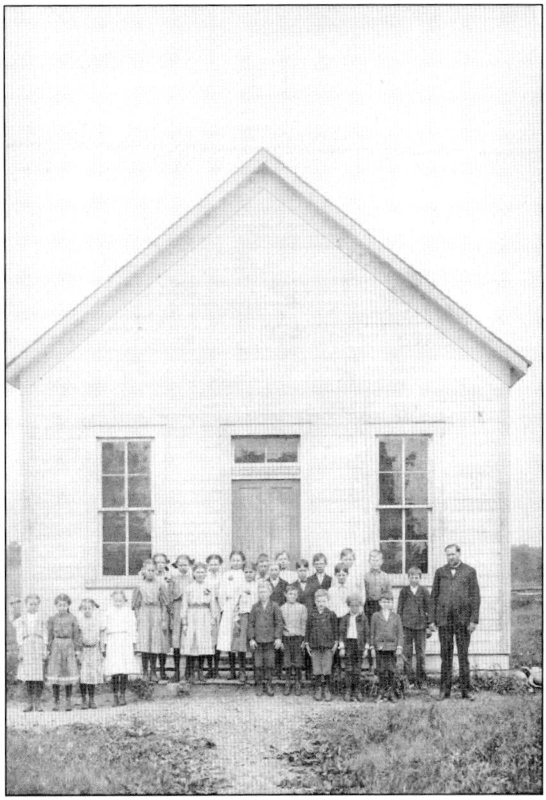

No records of public schools in Wentzville exist before the Civil War (1861–1865), but in 1866, a three-story building at East Main Street and Linn Avenue became the school. The school was on the first floor, the second floor housed a church, and the Masonic lodge was on the third. A three-room brick building on Linn Avenue was the first permanent school in 1883.

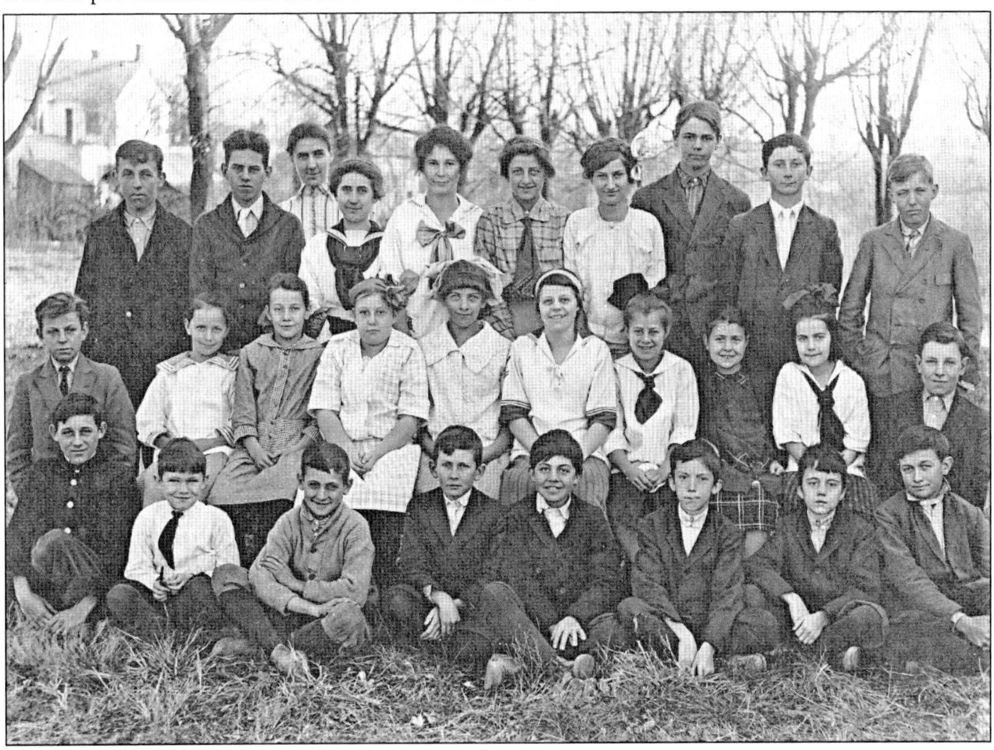

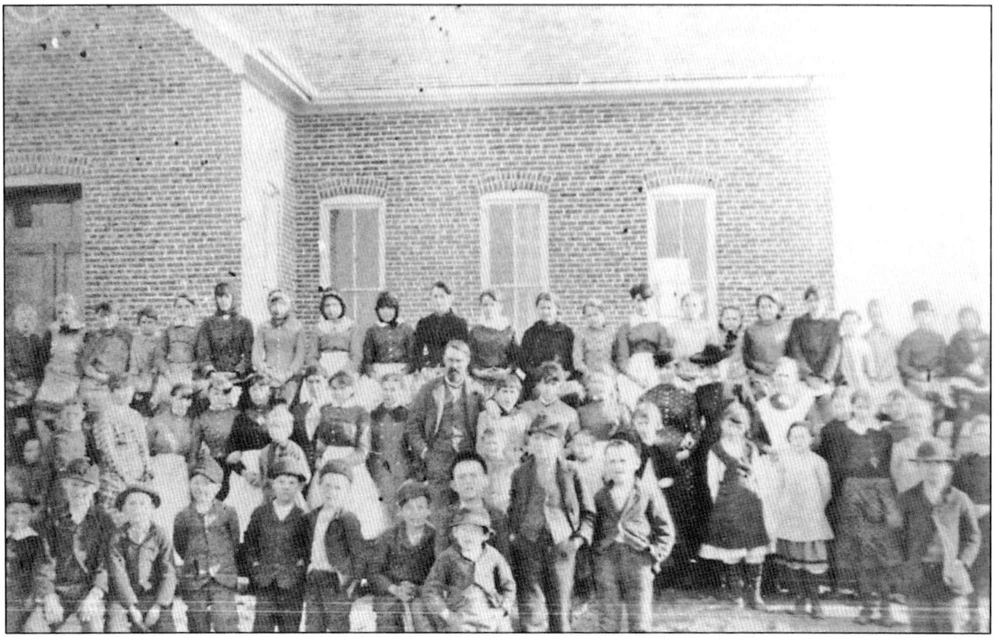

This photograph of Wentzville schoolchildren was taken in 1887 in front of the school on South Linn Avenue. Ed Gannaway, the bearded man at center, was the schoolteacher. He was born near Wentzville in 1853 and was appointed deputy assessor in 1878. (Octavia Evans Sigman.)

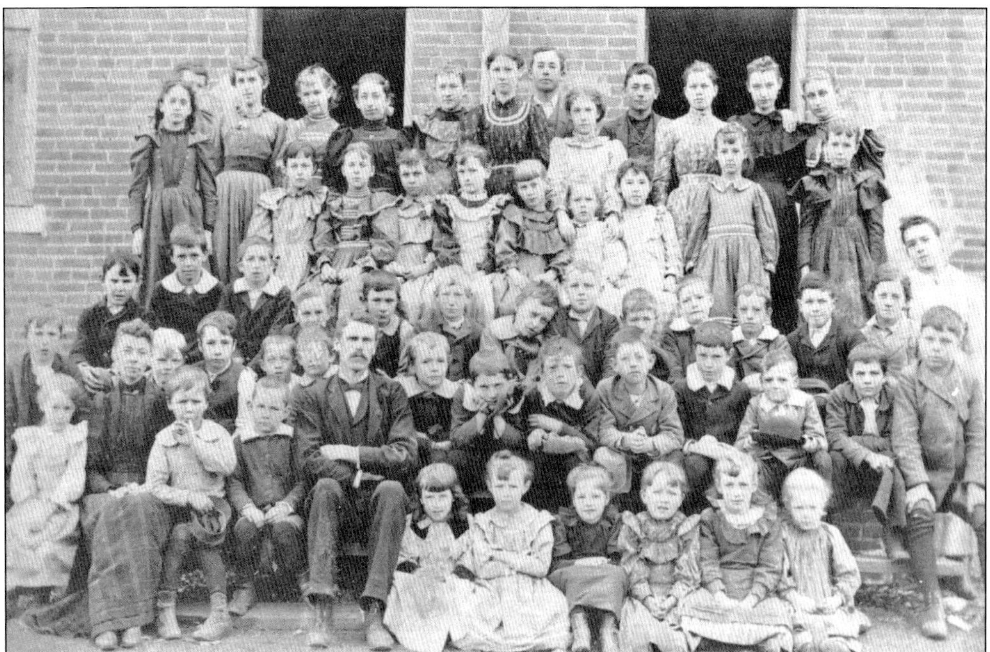

Students pose in their finest on November 7, 1894 in front of the two-year high school on Linn Avenue. (Dave Hagen.)

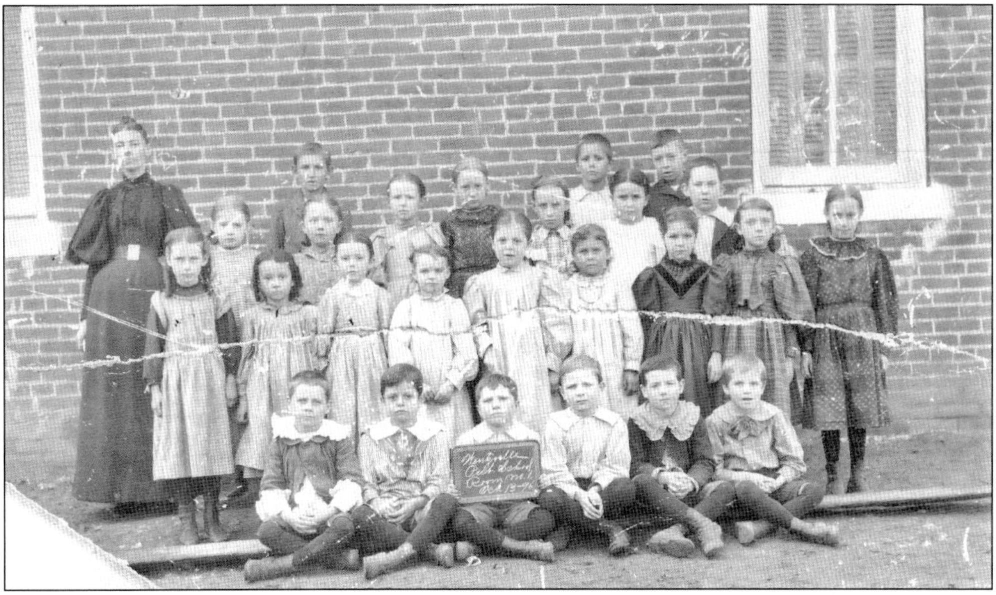

These sweet children pose before their school in 1896. From left to right are (first row) Cecil Fry, Lee Walker, Tom Dula, and Edgar Bostler; (second row) Rossie Moran, Eda Penn, Emma Sherman, Bertie Williams, Pearlie Fry, Minnie Woods, Addie Ball, and Clara Karrenbrock; (third row) teacher Allie Jenkins, Carrie Bornhop, Louise Penn, Alma Sherman, Cora Karrenbrock, Virgie Wade, Hilda Neirdling, and Murray Dyer; (fourth row) Bill Dudley, Lloyd Allen, and Clarence Lee. (Dave Hagen.)

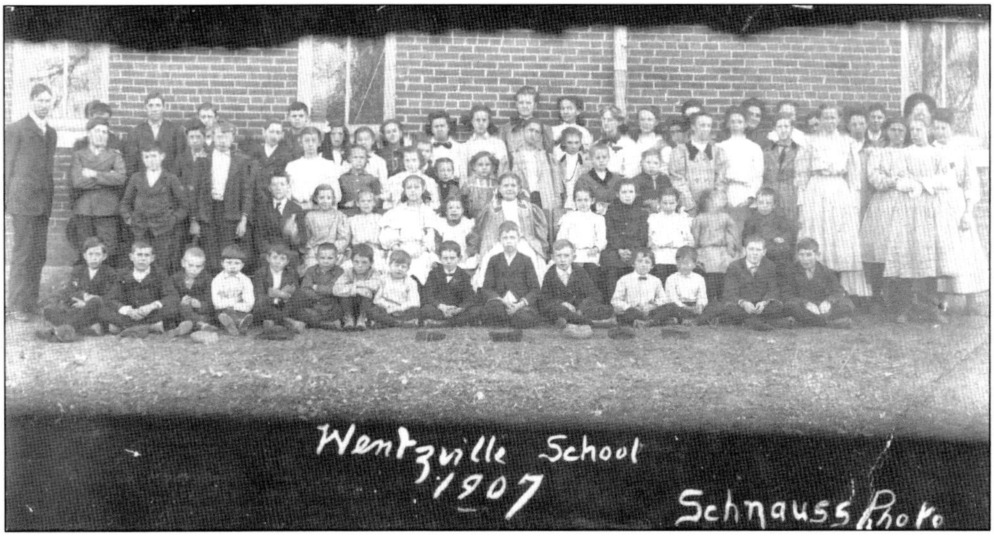

This photograph of Wentzville's schoolchildren was taken in 1907. Children attended this school from first grade through two years of high school. In 1939, the two-year high school was accredited as a four-year school. (Mary Moritz.)

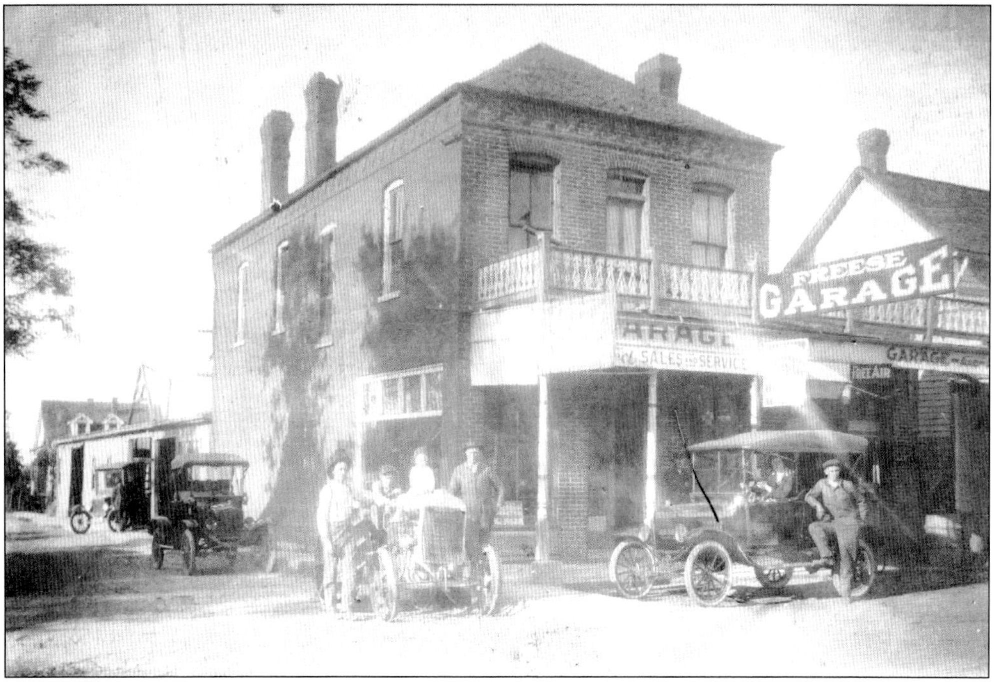

The corner of West Allen Street and Blumhoff Avenue was home to Wentzville's first automobile dealership, Freese Ford. This photograph was taken in 1914, when George Henry Freese first moved to Wentzville and began running a garage and selling Hupmobiles (see page 15). Freese sold and repaired Hupmobiles for two years before selling Fords out of this building, which he did until 1928. Below is an early invoice to Freese from the Ford Motor Company. Freese was born on May 16, 1885, and married Ida Schemmer on January 2, 1913. He died on October 13, 1979. They are both buried in Cappeln, Missouri.

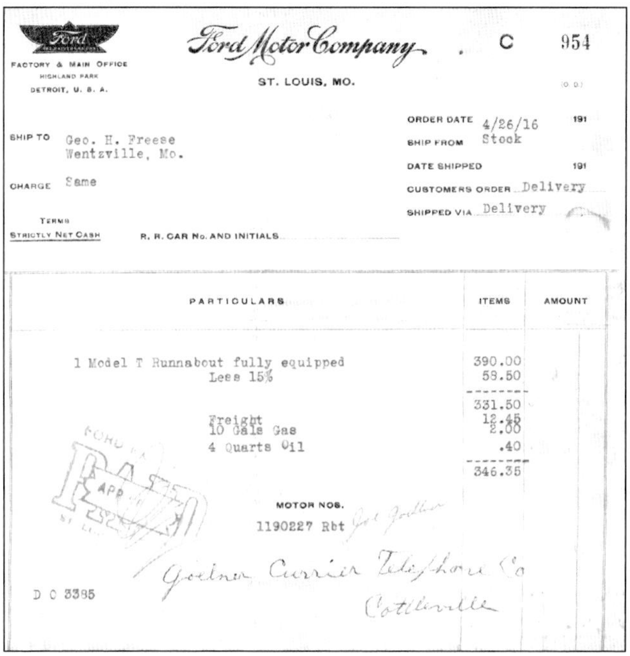

Ford Motor Company. C 954

FACTORY & MAIN OFFICE
HIGHLAND PARK
DETROIT, U. S. A.

ST. LOUIS, MO.

ORDER DATE 4/26/16 191
SHIP FROM Stock
DATE SHIPPED 191
CUSTOMERS ORDER Delivery
SHIPPED VIA Delivery

SHIP TO Geo. H. Freese
Wentzville, Mo.

CHARGE Same

TERMS
STRICTLY NET CASH

R. R. CAR No. AND INITIALS

PARTICULARS	ITEMS	AMOUNT
1 Model T Runnabout fully equipped	390.00	
Less 15%	58.50	
	331.50	
Freight	12.45	
10 Gals Gas	2.00	
4 Quarts Oil	.40	
	346.35	

MOTOR NOS.
1190227 Rbt

Goetner Currier Telephone Co
Cottleville

D O 3385

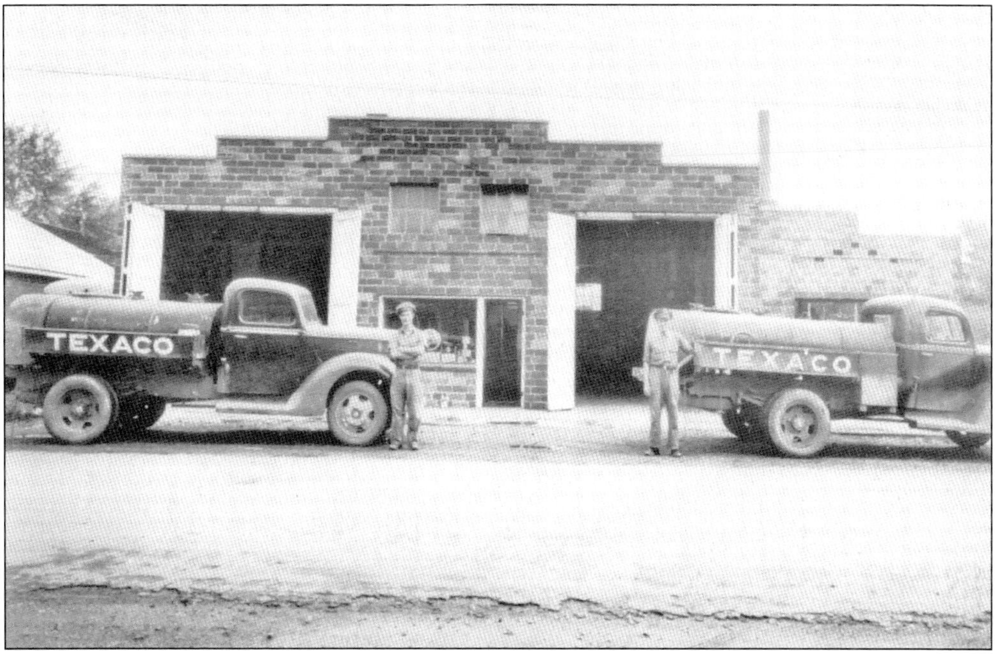

The National Petroleum Company (NPC), established in 1930 by Melvin Moritz, supplied gasoline and other petroleum products to service stations and farms in Wentzville. Moritz opened his first gas station in the same year, selling White Rose gasoline. Moritz soon became a distributor for Texaco products, converting his station around 1933. In the photograph above, railroad tank cars deliver gasoline and heating oil trackside to NPC trucks. When demand for gasoline grew, Moritz built three large reservoir tanks downhill on Church Street. Running a gravity-fed pipeline from the railroad tracks to the tanks allowed him to serve his customers without delay. NPC became the largest supplier of gasoline and heating oil in all of western St. Charles County. After Melvin's death, his son Norman took NPC into the 21st century.

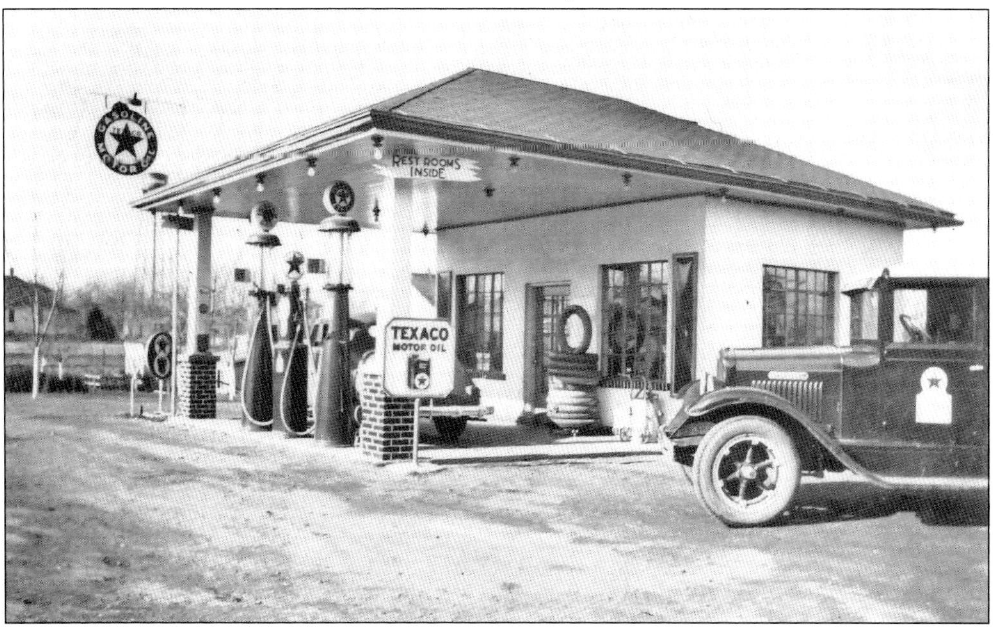

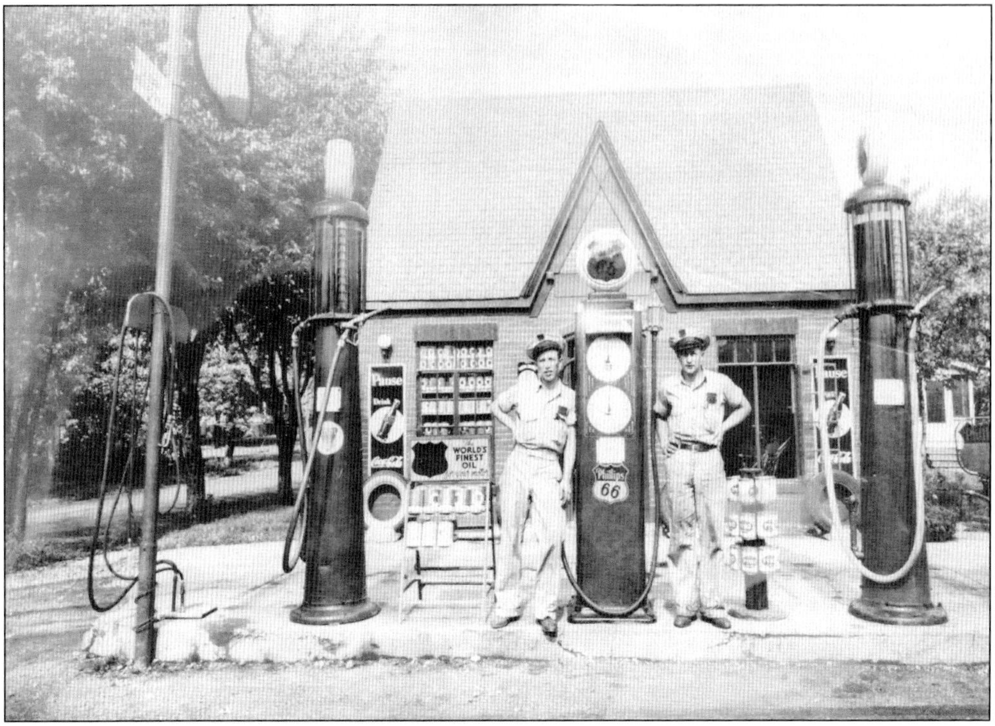

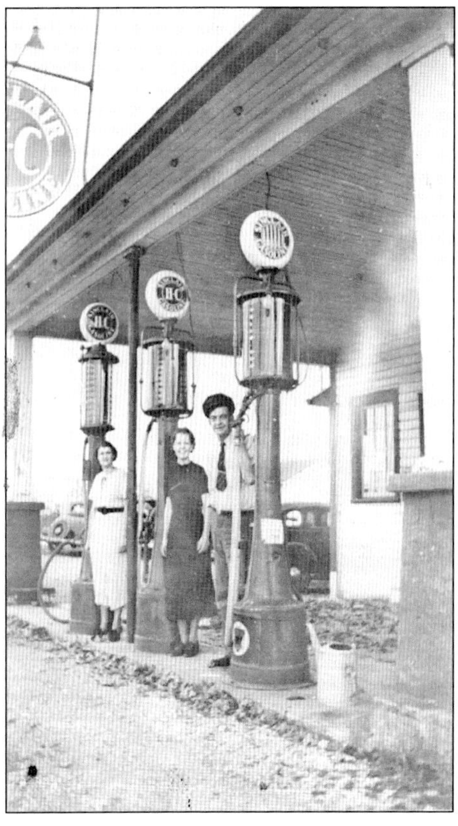

This Phillips 66 gas station was one of Wentzville's first. Located at the four-way stop of old Highway 40 (now Pearce Boulevard) and North Linn Avenue, this station is the epitome of small-town America. On the left is the owner, Ed Matlock, with Clark Matlock. Linn Avenue can be seen on the left.

The White House Inn operated from the 1930s to about 1960 and was located on old Highway 40 by Point Prairie Road. The inn was a small resort that offered cabin lodging complete with dining, swimming pool, and Sinclair gasoline. This was one of several gas stations and motels that sprang up when Highway 40 was built through Wentzville in 1923. (Maxine Anselm Haynes.)

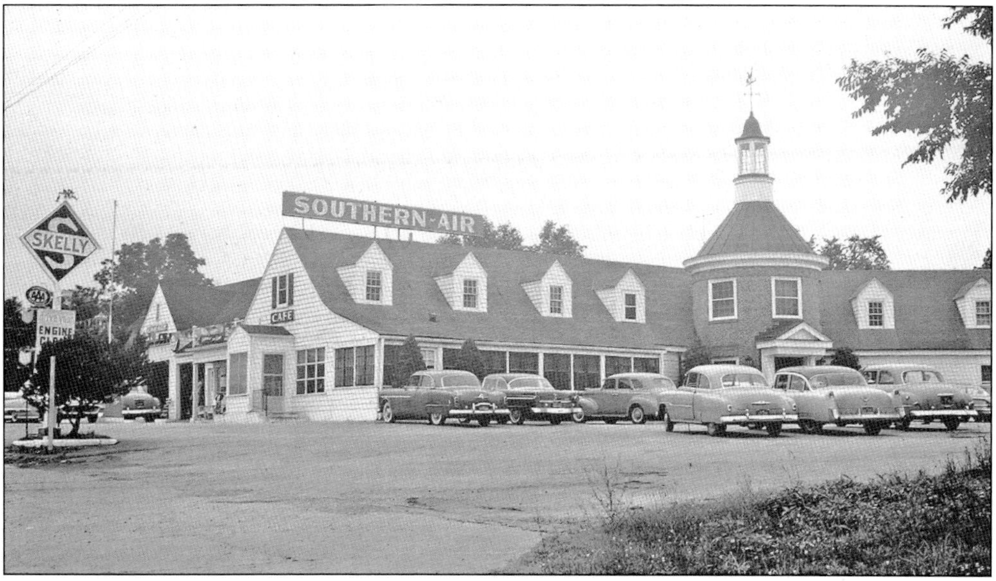

The Southern-Air building stands today as a branch of Lindenwood University, but this restaurant and service station was built in 1937, strategically placed to be near Highways 40 and 61. The 24-hour garage, food counter, and gas station became known nationwide because of its accessibility and great food; multiple billboards on the highway ensured a steady flow of customers. Russell Lewis ran it as a diner in 1941. In 1948, a dining room and lounge were added. In 1962, Bob Robertson bought it, removed the garage, and added three banquet rooms. Because of health issues, Bob sold it to Edward Fries in 1968. Fries eventually sold it to rock and roll legend Chuck Berry, who turned it into a lounge and nightclub. Below is opening day in the diner as Nadine Lewis (manager, left) and Viola Mispagel (later Boland) await their first customer. (Above, Larry Wentz; below, Viola Boland.)

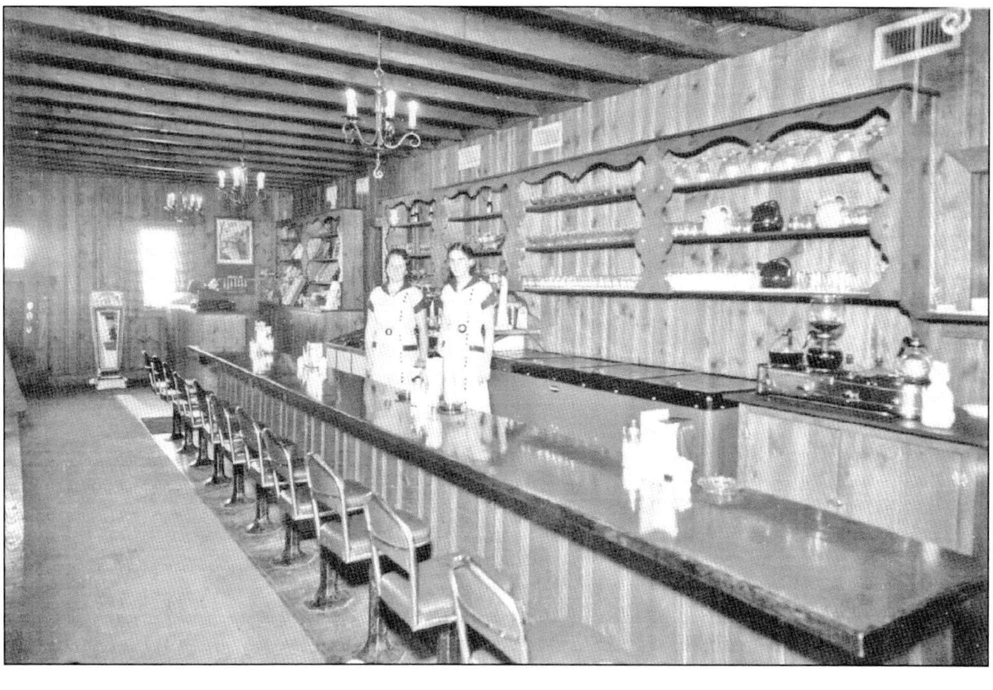

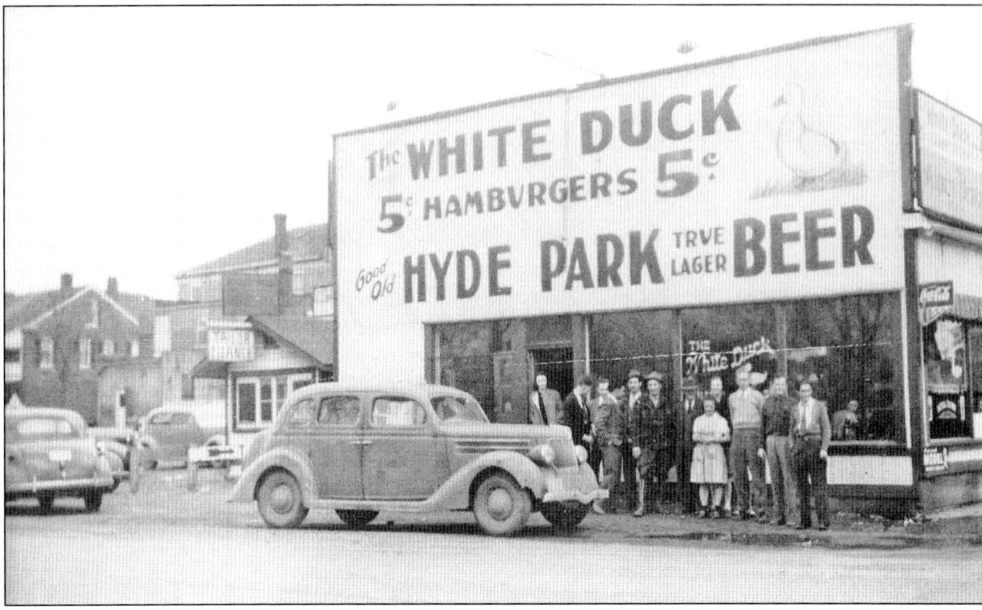

The White Duck bar and café was owned by Charles Willerding for many years. Wentzville locals frequented "the Duck," and with the newly built Highway 40 frontage, out-of-towners stopped for its excellent hamburgers. Unfortunately, this local landmark burned to the ground during one of the many fires that plagued Wentzville through the years. Seen below at the White Duck's bar and back bar around 1935 is a young Charlie Willerding, proprietor. Charles Joseph Willerding was born on August 18, 1914. He served four years in the US Army with a tank division in Okinawa, Japan. Charlie died on December 21, 1968. Longtime Wentzville residents still talk fondly of their White Duck memories. (Both, Nancy Frei.)

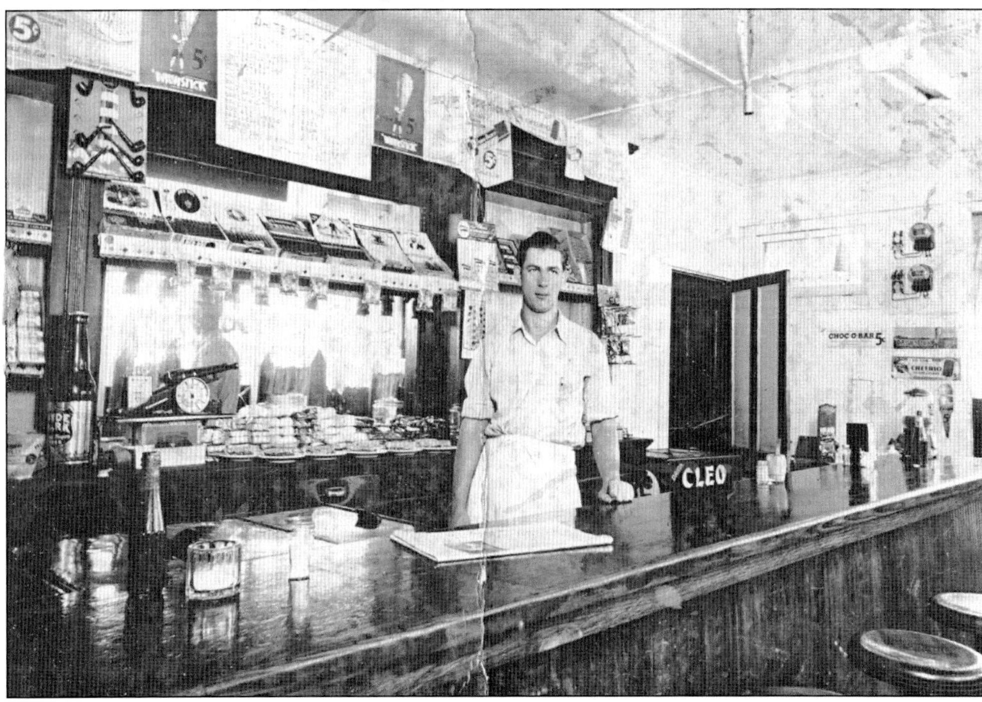

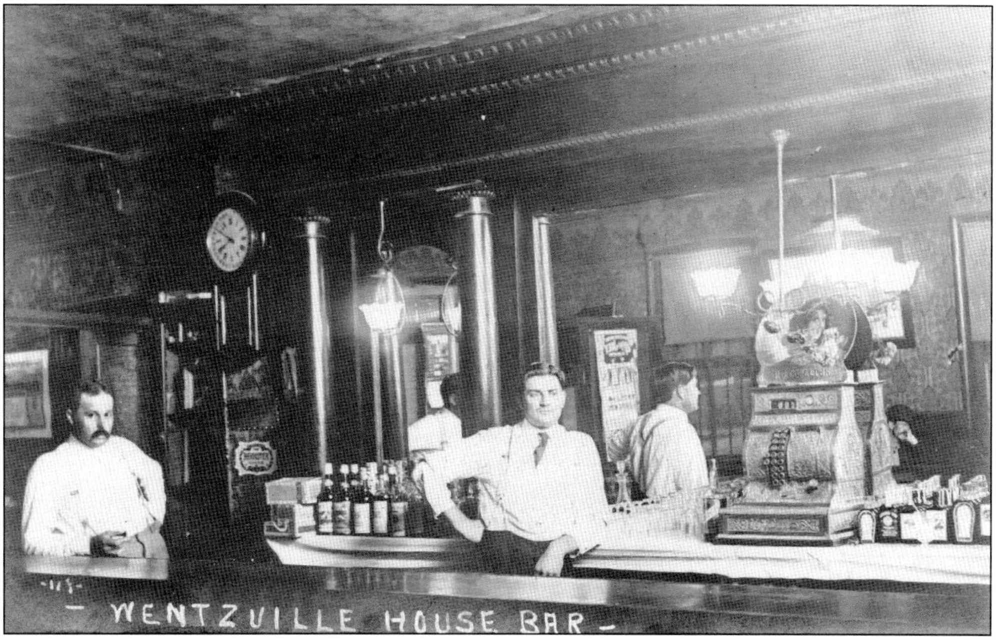

The Wentzville House Hotel's ornate barroom is seen around 1910. Bartender Chris Goellner and proprietor Peter Willerding pose in front of their massively mirrored back bar, giving a glimpse of early times with gas lights and a beautiful bronze cash register. According to the clock, it is 8:00, probably p.m., because just right of the cash register is the reflection of a customer getting an early start before the crowd.

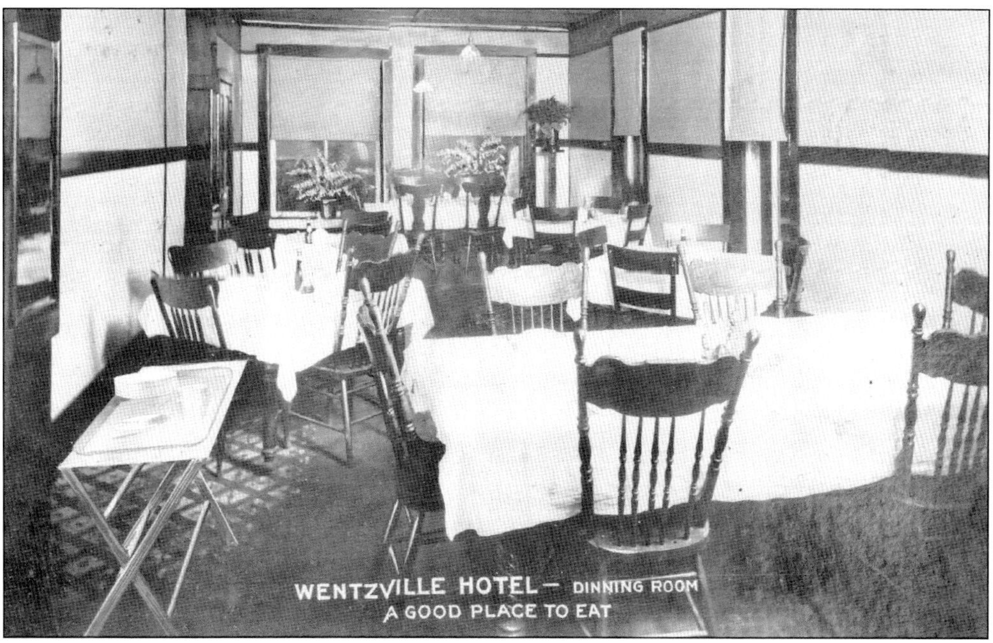

Both guests and townspeople could enjoy fine dining in the Wentzville House Hotel dining room. The sound of a player piano coming from the lobby added to the atmosphere. To look even more elegant before the meal, customers could enjoy a shoeshine in the lobby from Bill Jones, nicknamed "Flick Rag."

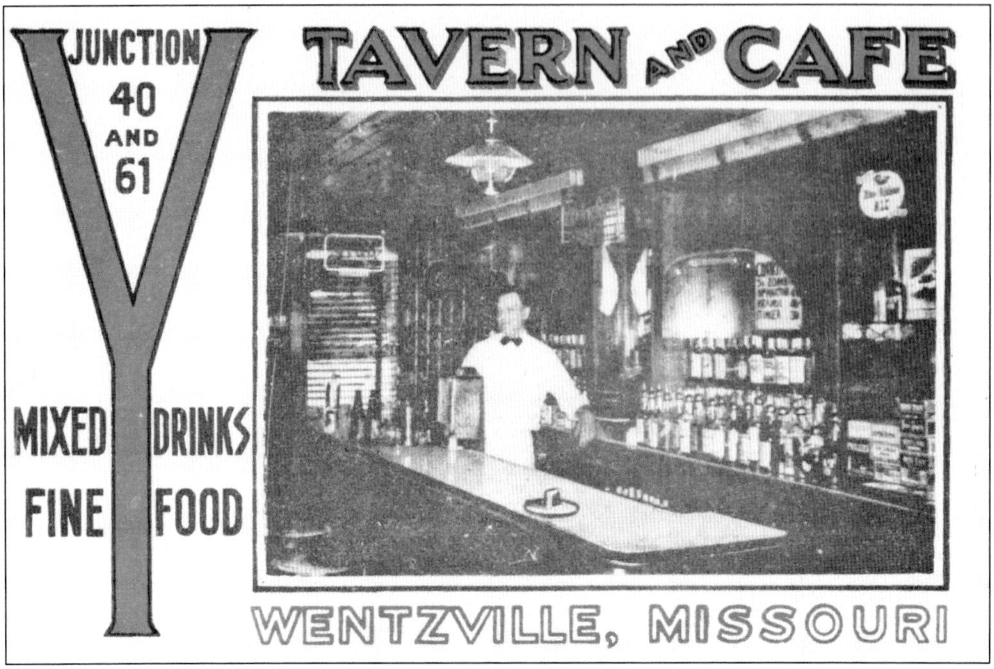

The Y Café got its name from its location in the middle of the intersection of Highways 40 and 61. Like the Southern-Air, it was strategically located. Business was always good, but in the early 1930s, an incident raised the notoriety of the café. When the FBI was hunting John Dillinger, the agency got word that he was on his way from Chicago to St. Louis, so they called all of the authorities along Highway 61, including the state patrol. Fred Hagen, a Missouri state patrolman who lived in Wentzville, received the call. He waited at the Y Café and exchanged shots with Dillinger as he raced by. Machine-gun bullets were left lodged in the walls of the Y Café. This amazing confrontation became a legend, and locals talked about it for years.

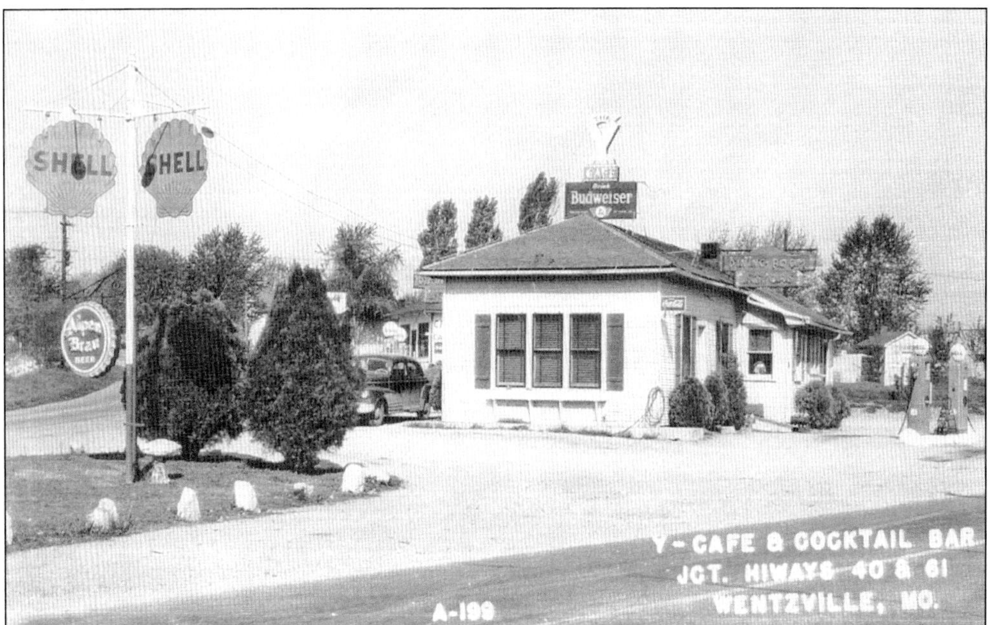

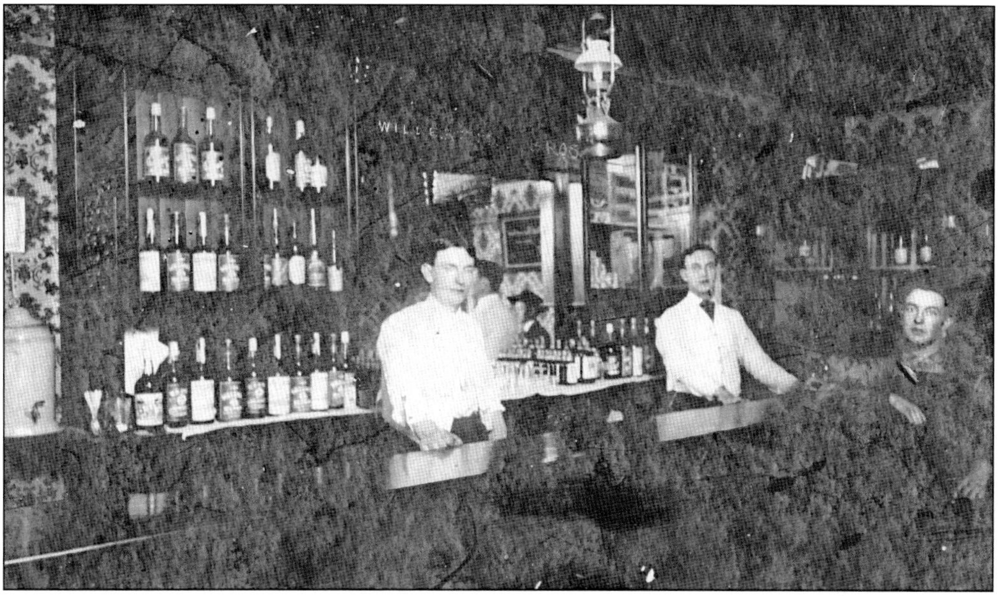

John Willerding operated the Willerding Brothers Bar in the Thompson Hotel building, which, ironically, was never a hotel. Although it was originally built to be a hotel, it housed instead several businesses, including the Muzzy and May Tobacco Company and the post office. Shown here are the Willerding brothers around 1908 behind their bar. (Nancy Frei.)

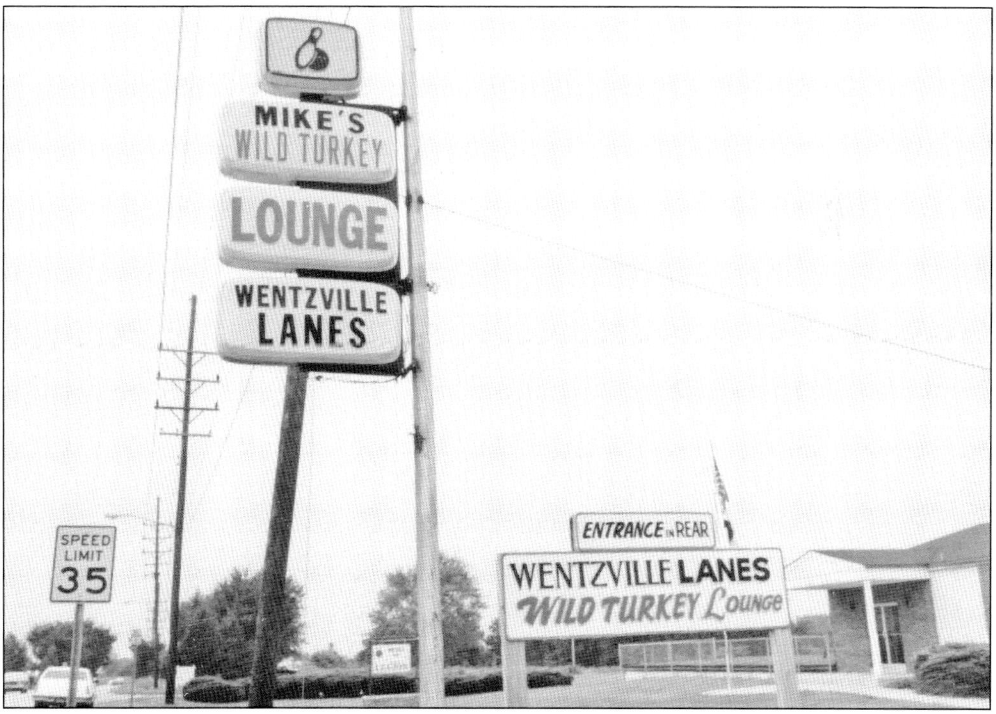

Most Wentzville citizens do not realize that the city ever had a bowling alley; in fact, they would be surprised to learn that at one time the town housed two bowling alleys. The one shown here, Wentzville Lanes, was on old Business Highway 61 (today Luetkenhause Boulevard) in the basement of the American Legion along with Mike's Wild Turkey Lounge. (Jerry Matlock.)

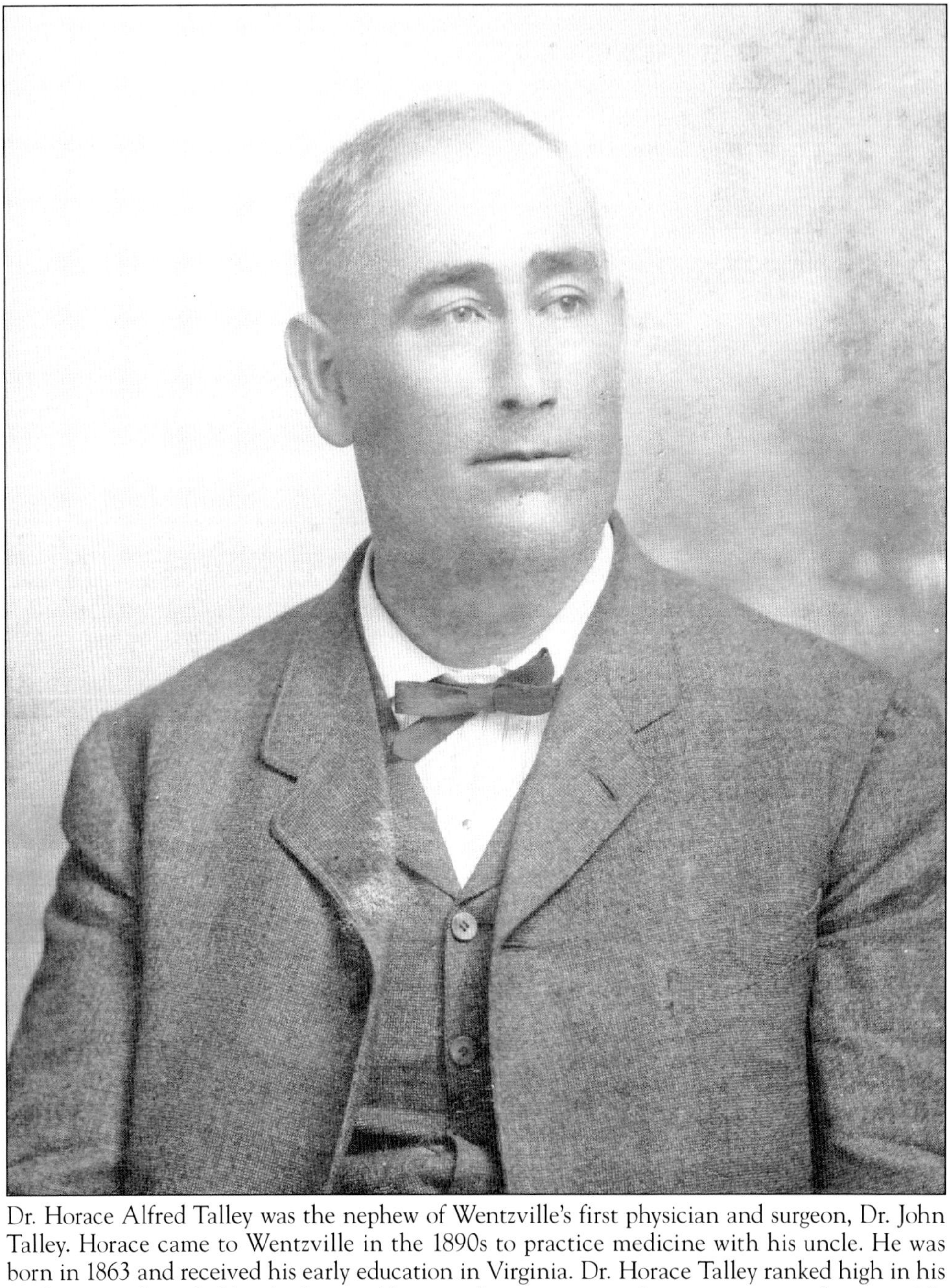

Dr. Horace Alfred Talley was the nephew of Wentzville's first physician and surgeon, Dr. John Talley. Horace came to Wentzville in the 1890s to practice medicine with his uncle. He was born in 1863 and received his early education in Virginia. Dr. Horace Talley ranked high in his profession and was held in high regard by countless patients in the community and county. He was elected mayor in 1896 and again in 1902, and was instrumental in helping Wentzville attain the designation of fourth-class city in 1903. Dr. Talley was killed on January 30, 1917, when fast Wabash passenger train No. 20 crashed into his new Ford Runabout at the crossing east of the Karrenbrock elevator. He had been called to dress the wounded hand of William Kleimerer at the Schierbaum blacksmith shop. In his haste to get to his patient, he either did not see the train or thought he could beat it.

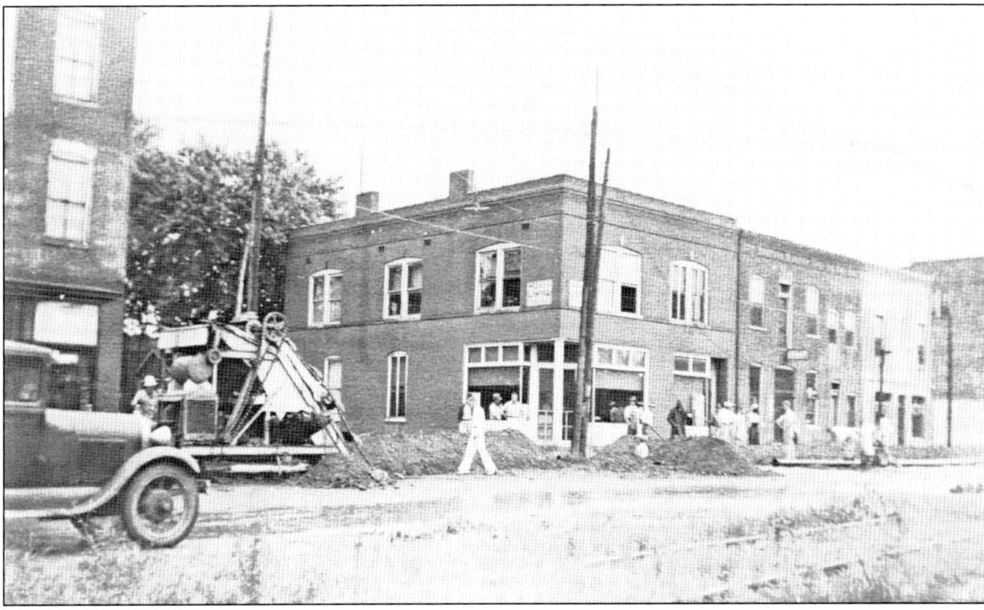

In July 1935, most of Wentzville's streets were a mess, but the citizens, though inconvenienced, were happy because they were about to get a public water system. For the first time, homes and businesses would have running water and could begin building water closets, abandoning their outhouses. Wentzville had gotten a new highway in 1923, electricity in 1926, and now water and sewers in 1935. That meant it was a bit behind other fourth-class cities of that time, but Wentzville was finally ready for the 20th century. Shown above on South Main Street and Linn Avenue is the Wentzville Bank, along with various other businesses, all staying open while the water pipes were installed. Even advertising continued as usual, as seen with the flyer at right from Dr. J.H. Kelley's dental office. (Above, Ruth Bechtold.)

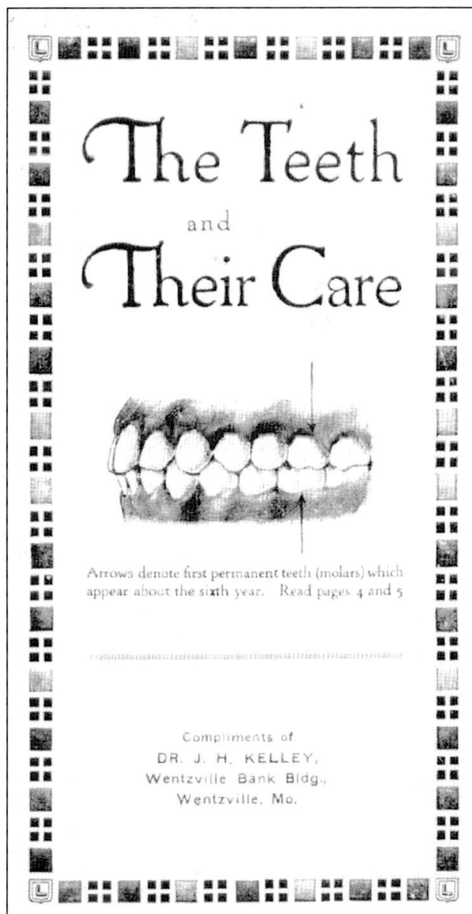

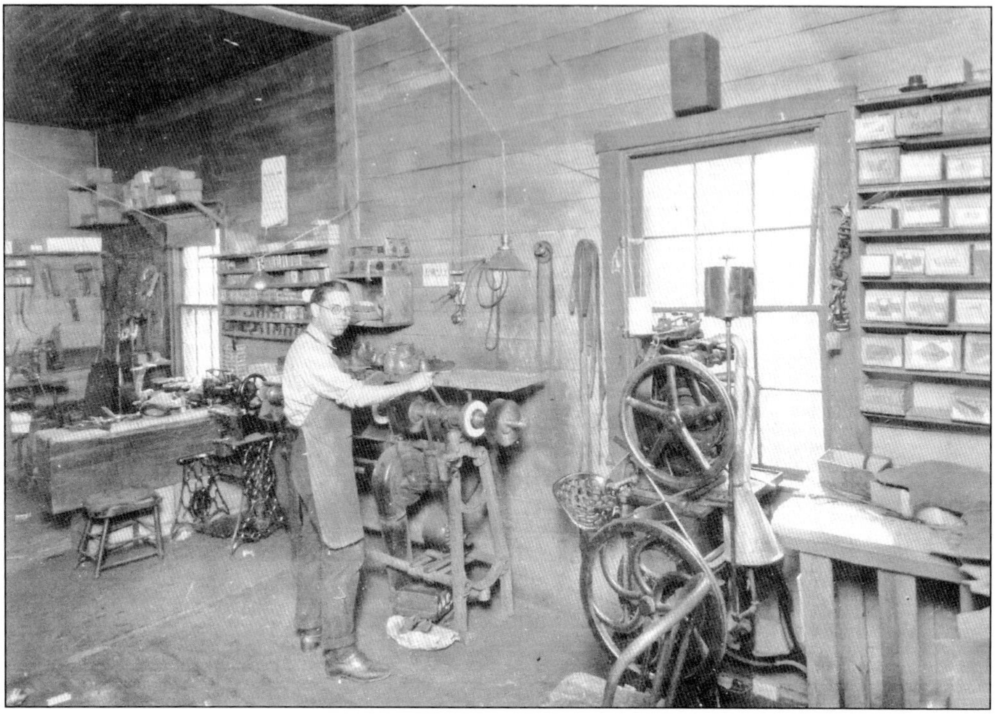

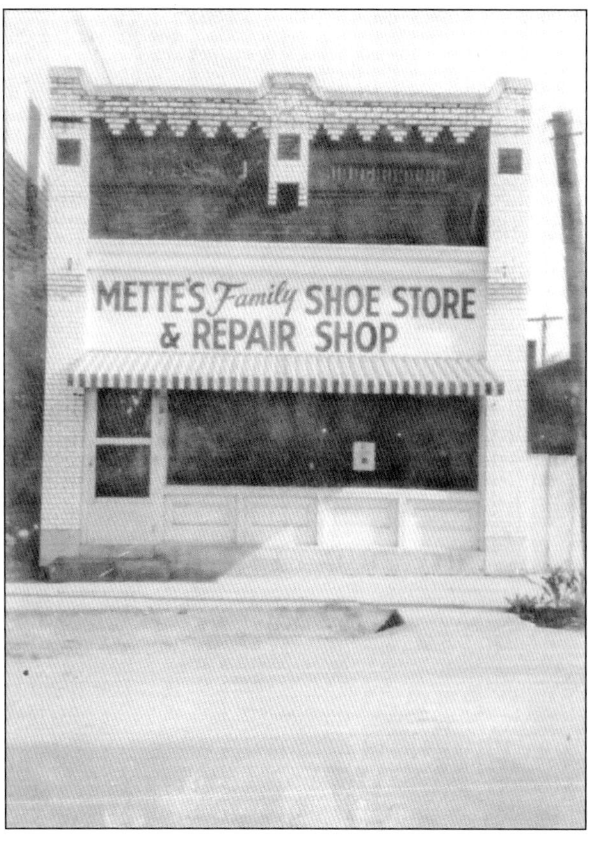

Gus Temme, a shoemaker and repairman, is seen in his shop on South Main Street around 1925. Temme was a well-respected businessman in Wentzville for many years, garnering the trust of the citizens, who elected him mayor in 1964. He was a civil servant for many of his later years, serving as city collector in the 1930s and justice of the peace in the 1940s. (Roland Temme.)

Mette's Family Shoe Store & Repair Shop was one of the many family-owned businesses on West South Main Street that closed when the big-box stores came to Wentzville in the later half of the 20th century. Clarence "Tink" Mette learned his trade under Gus Temme, and in October 1941, he bought Temme's Shoe Repair Shop and started selling shoes to Wentzville citizens.

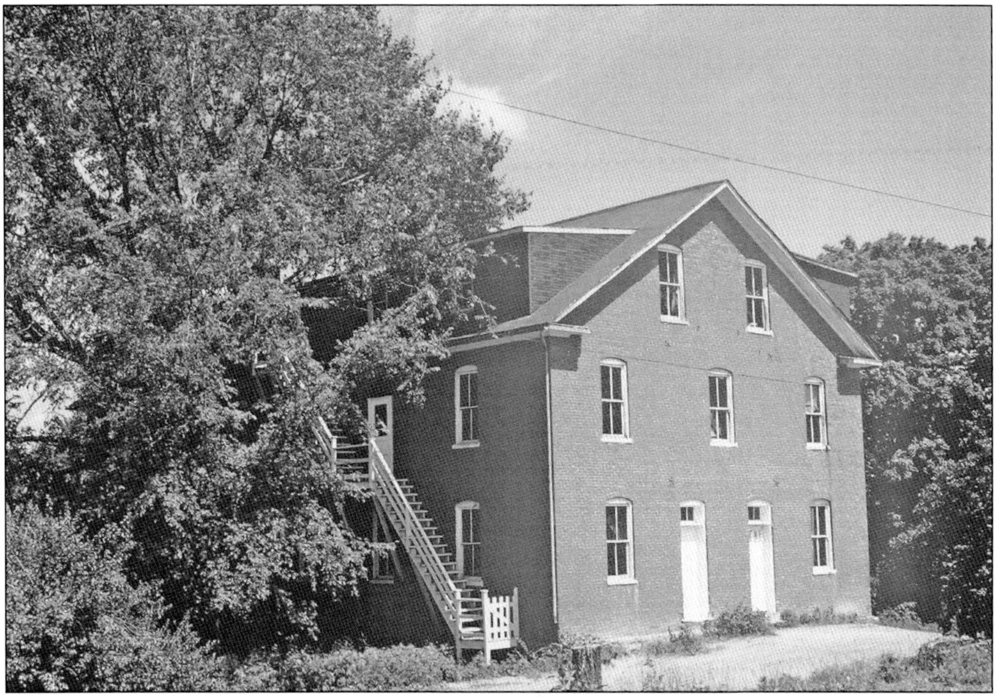

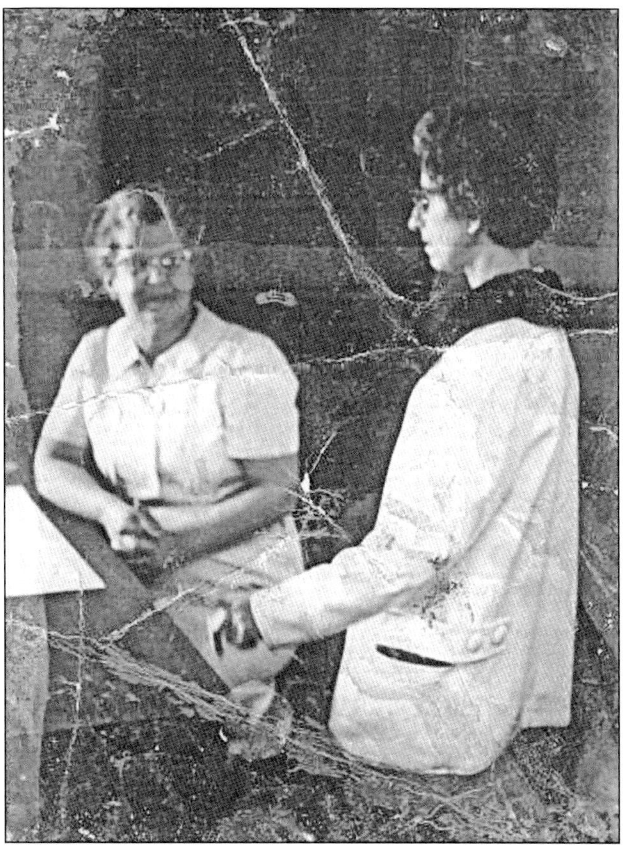

The old tobacco factory ran from the 1860s until it was purchased by the Karrenbrock Flour Mill in 1892. In 1932, it closed and was abandoned, but the Wentzville Community Club stepped in to save this landmark building. The club loaned it to the Acme Garment Factory, the "Best Undergarment Company," thereby bringing jobs to Wentzville during the Great Depression. The new factory opened in September 1936 and initially hired 12 operators. Minimum wage was 20¢ per hour in the beginning and increased to $1.05 by the 1950s. The building was again abandoned, and the city gave it to the historical society, which tried to save it but could not. In January 2002, the building was razed. At right are two Acme Garment Factory employees in 1940. Seated is second supervisor Mrs. Noel (Florence) Hughes, talking with one of her operators. (Above, Larry Wentz.)

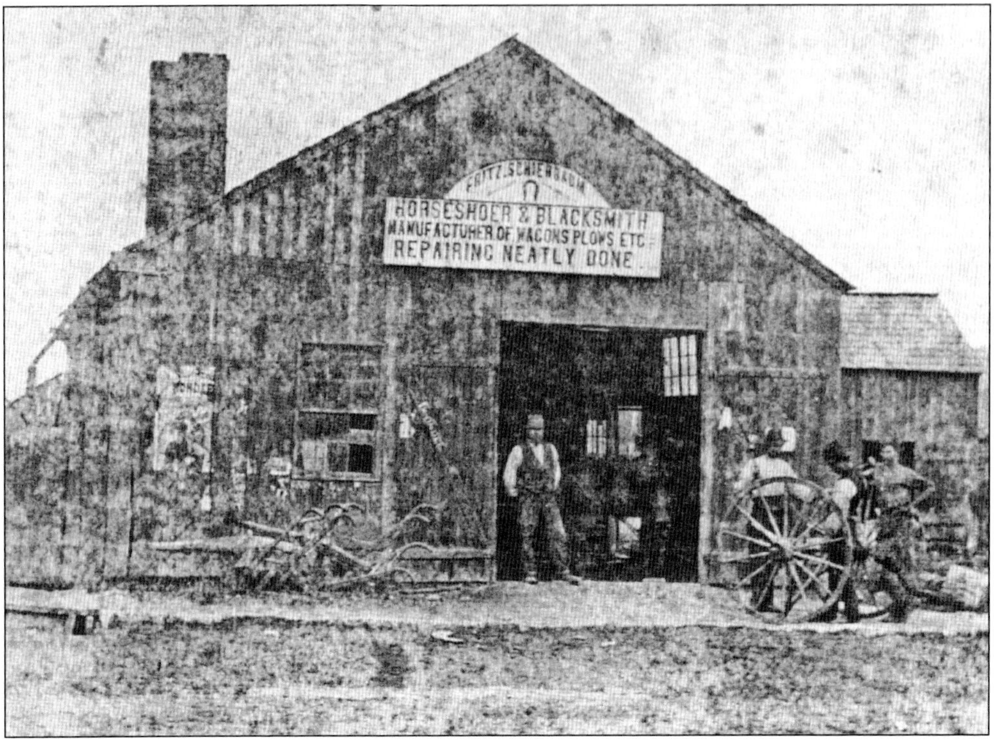

Fritz Schierbaum's first blacksmith shop is seen on North Main Street around 1880. He was a quality wagonmaker, so his fame spread countywide. Soon he needed more room to fill his orders of binders and other farm equipment, so he built a massive Western-style shop in the mid-1880s (see page 20).

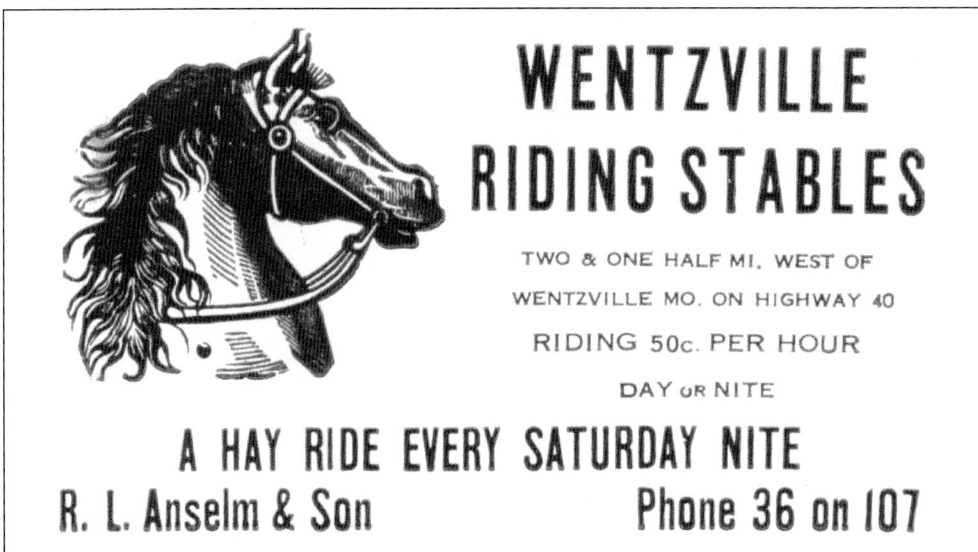

Stock trader and riding stable owner Richard L. Anselm was in business from the late 1880s to the turn of the 20th century. His son Samuel became city marshal and served in that capacity for 27 years, longer than any other city marshal in the history of Wentzville. (Maxine Anselm Haynes and Rick Anselm.)

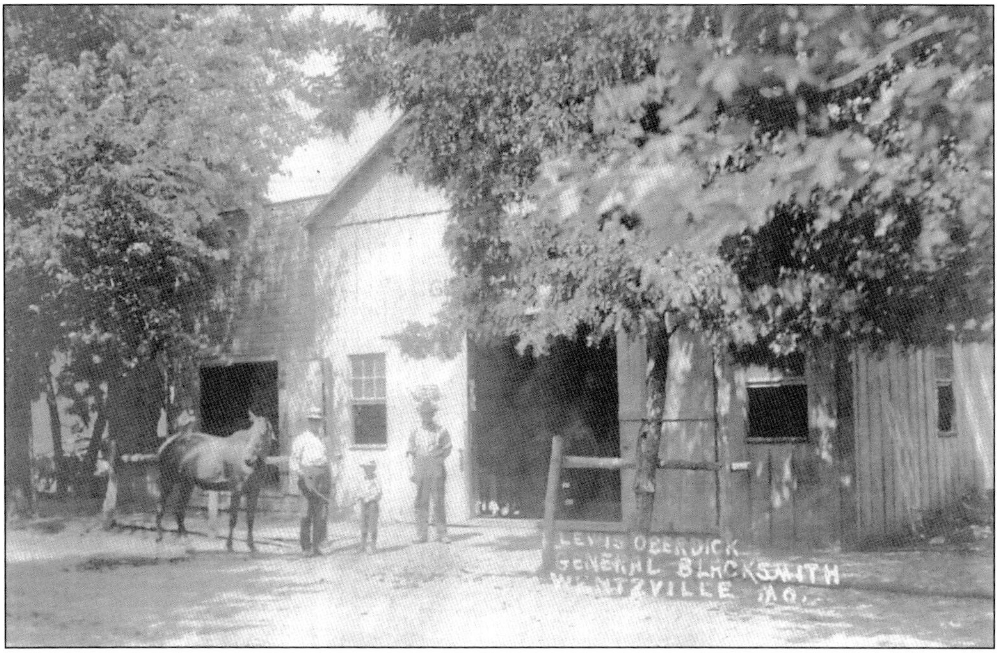

Lewis Oberdick stands in front of his General Blacksmith shop. One of several blacksmith shops in Wentzville, Oberdick's is believed to have been on Second Street (now Pitman Avenue), facing Elm Street. This shop was next door to the Wentzville Creamery and Ice Company (see page 78).

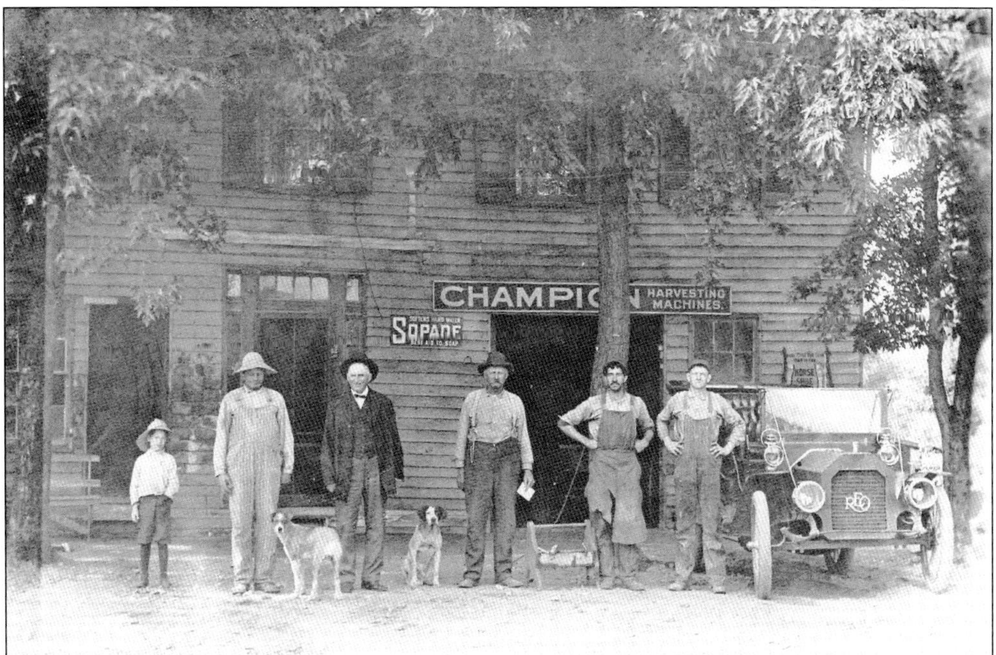

These men, dogs, and boy are pictured before a Wentzville shop around 1905, judging by the REO Runabout on the far right. The owners serviced harvesters and automobiles and even, according to the sign, sold "Sopade," which softened hard water. Automobiles were not sold in Wentzville until 1916, so the chance to work on a car was cause for a photo opportunity.

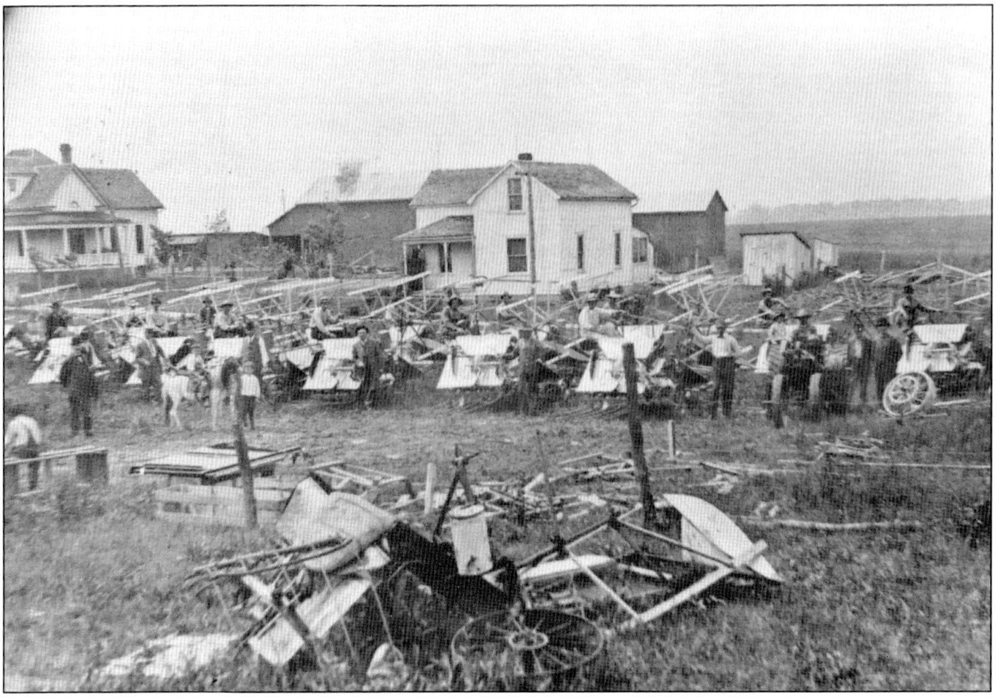

Wheat binders manufactured by Fritz Schierbaum are seen lined up behind his wagonmaker shop around 1900. The dirt path occupied by a boy on a pony was actually a road between fields that appear to be filled with junk and binders. That road was later old Highway 40 (now Pearce Boulevard). The small home in the center still stands today on Koenig Street and Linn Avenue.

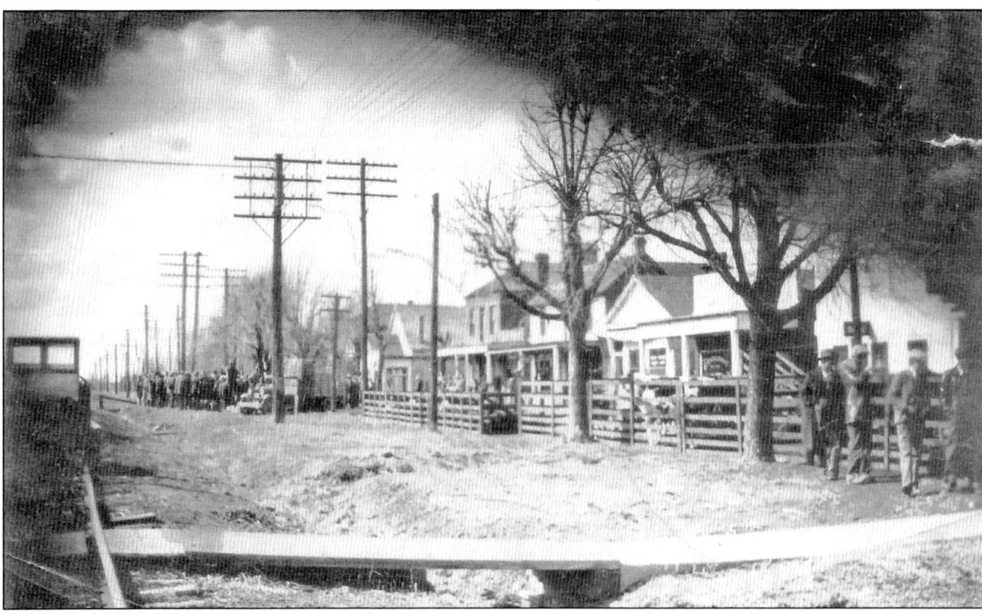

Livestock pens, homes, and businesses lined the area adjacent to the railroad tracks. This photograph barely survived one of the many fires that plagued Wentzville over the years. Later, the dirt path to the left of the pens became West Main Street (now West Allen Street), but it would be hard to drive on in this condition.

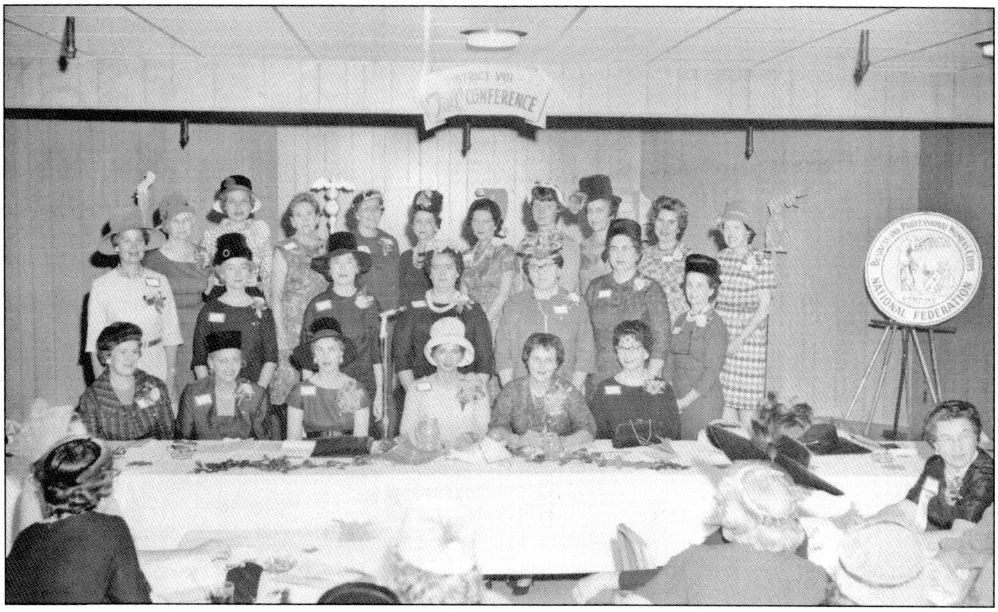

Wentzville held its first district conference of the Eighth District Business and Professional Women's Clubs in 1962. Hosted in the new banquet room of the Southern-Air Restaurant, nearly 200 women were present from 13 different clubs from the area, including many from St. Louis. Pictured are the women who shared the speakers' table. The meeting was a who's who of influential women.

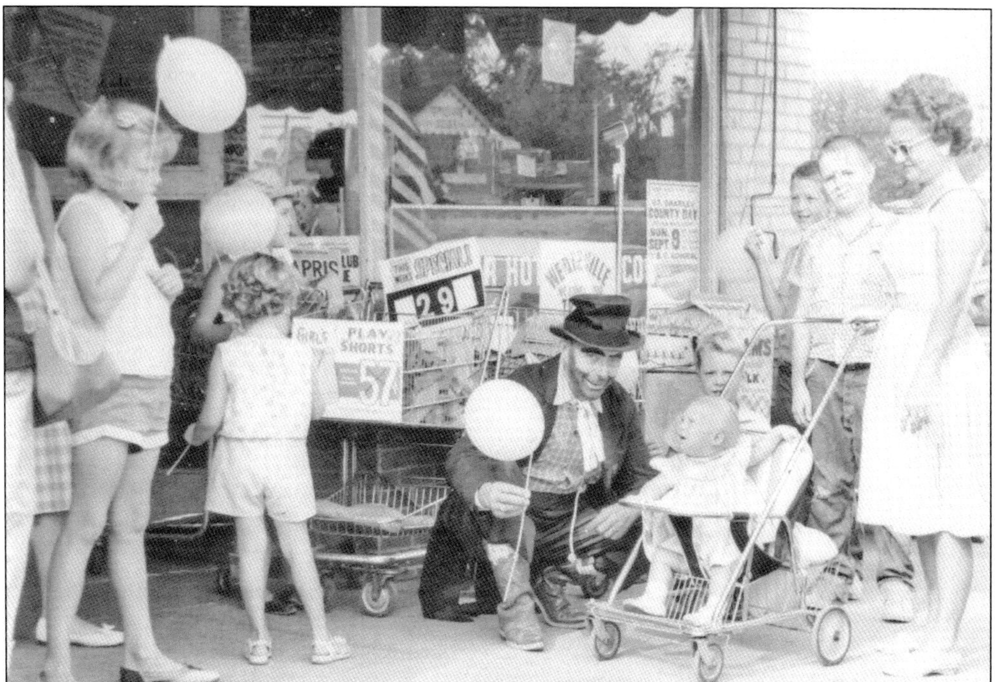

A typical summer Saturday in 1962 might find business owners dressed up in costumes to give away balloons on a stick to the town's children, enticing their mothers to come to the sidewalk sale. The baby in the stroller looks skeptical as she sizes up that hobo clown on South Main Street.

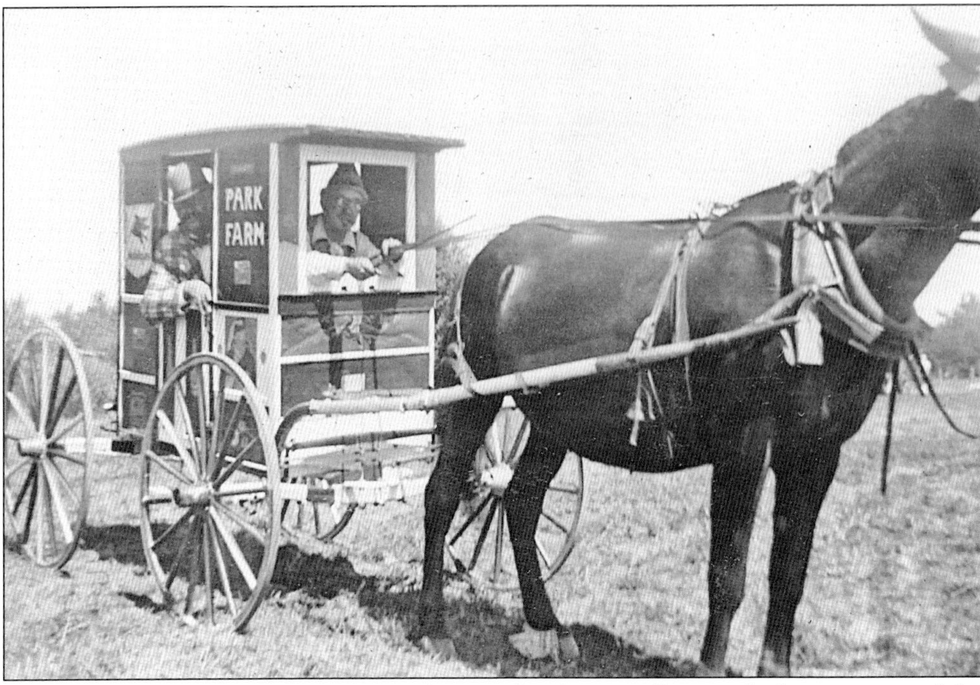

The old mail delivery wagon was sold to Park Farm after the post office switched over to automobiles. Many Wentzville residents still remember this horse-drawn wagon, because it was used in several town parades over the years. (Mary Moritz.)

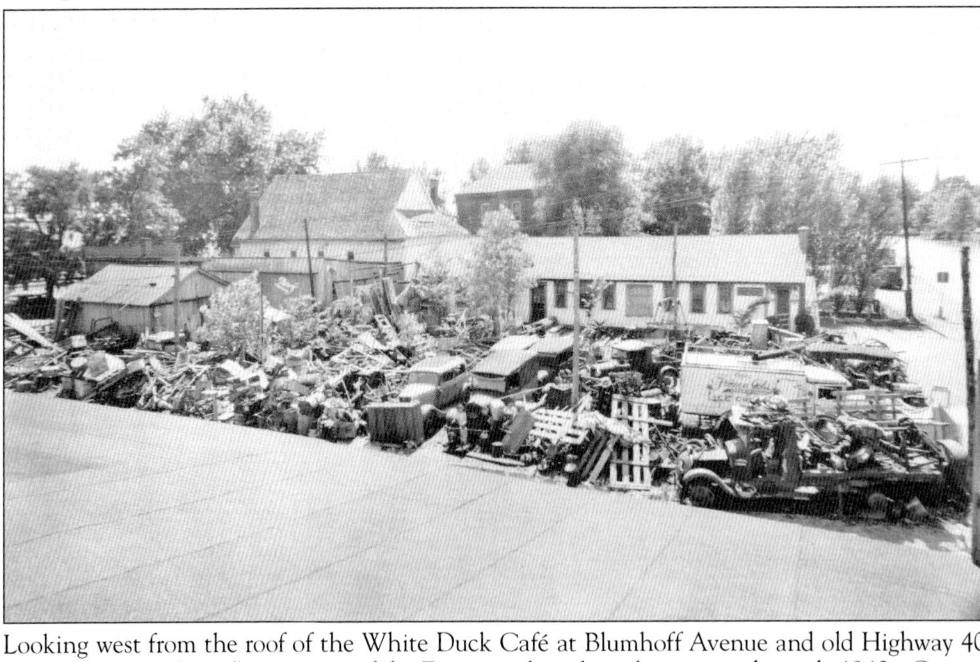
Looking west from the roof of the White Duck Café at Blumhoff Avenue and old Highway 40 (now Pearce Boulevard), a portion of the Freese junkyard can be seen in the early 1940s. George Freese, the Ford dealership owner, collected anything and everything, and stored his treasures in several buildings and junkyards along the highway. The city tried in vain for many years to get him to clean up the junk.

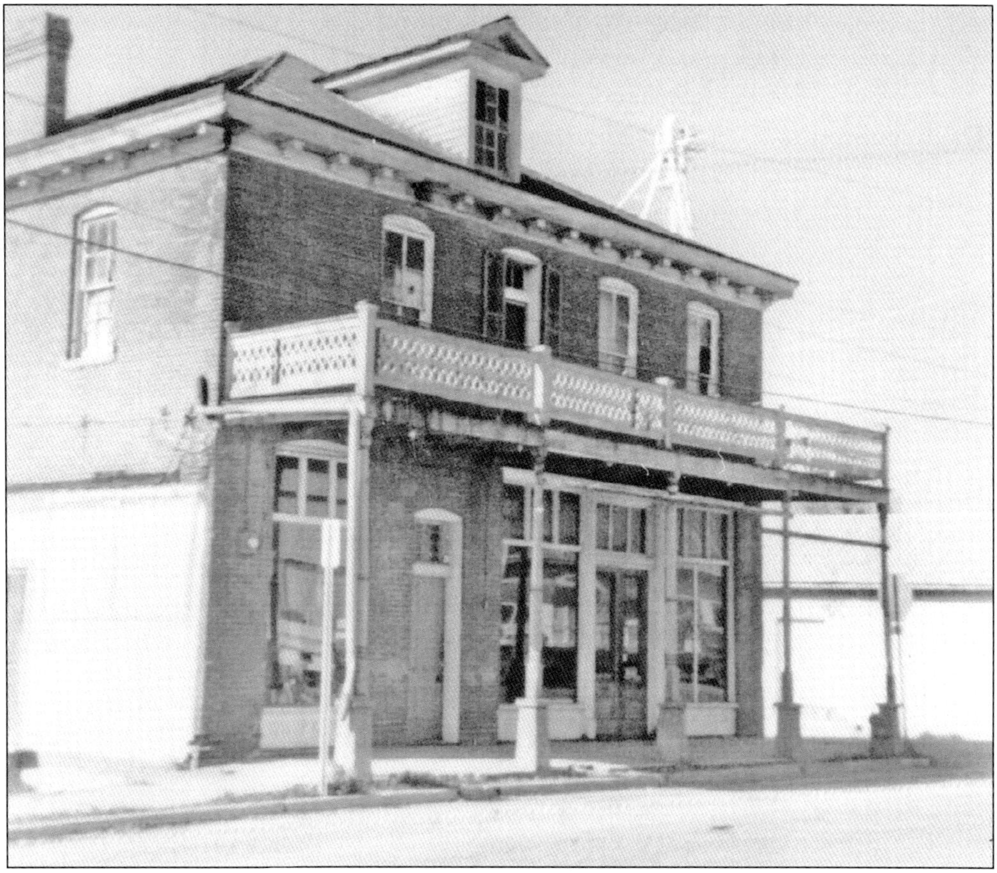

Originally built and operated by Wentzville founder William M. Allen in 1858, the Wentzville Mercantile, pictured above shortly before its demolition, was purchased by Henry Michel in the 1870s. A group of Wentzville men formed the Wentzville Mercantile Company in 1905; John Brueggemann was the president. In 1924, stockholder Tarlton Pitman and his wife, Annetta, bought the business. They owned and operated the "old time" store for 45 years, but after her husband's death, Annetta found it difficult to wade through the stacks of insurance and tax forms. "I feel like I'm working for the government," she said in 1969. The 120-year-old store soon closed. The Mercantile Smokehouse, shown at right in 1962, cured tons of meats that were sold in the store. (Right, Susan Licklider.)

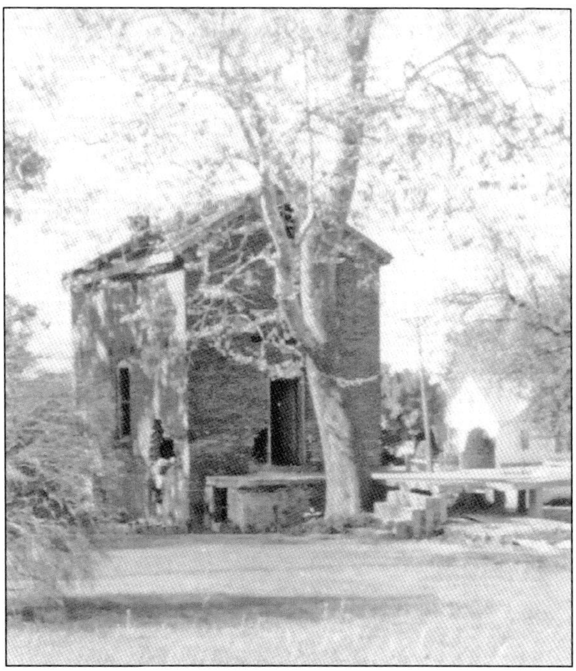

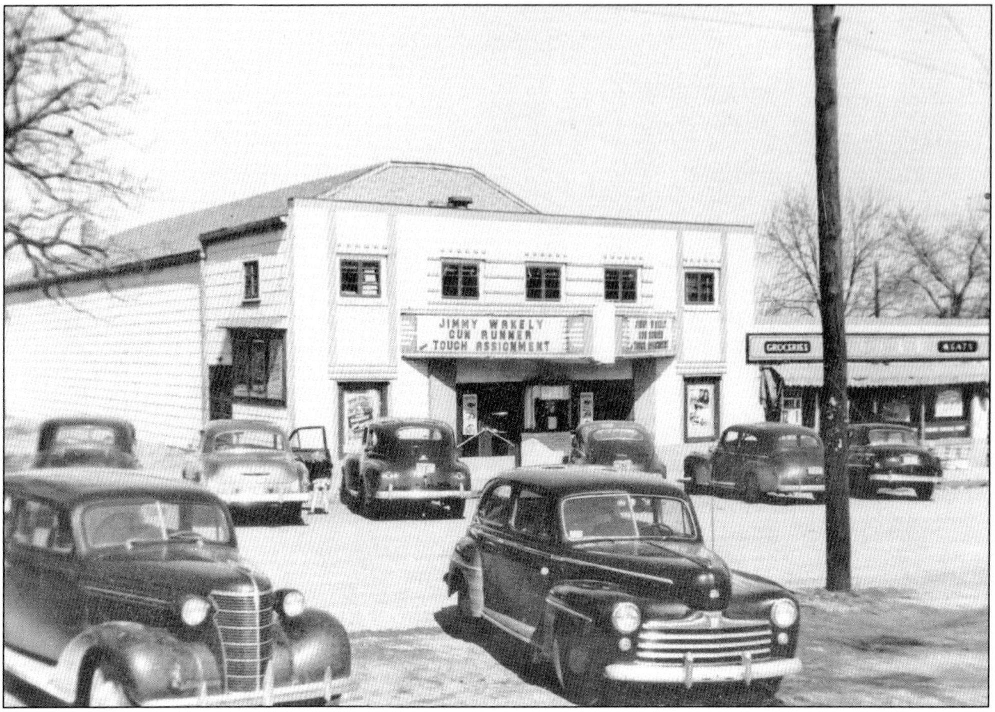

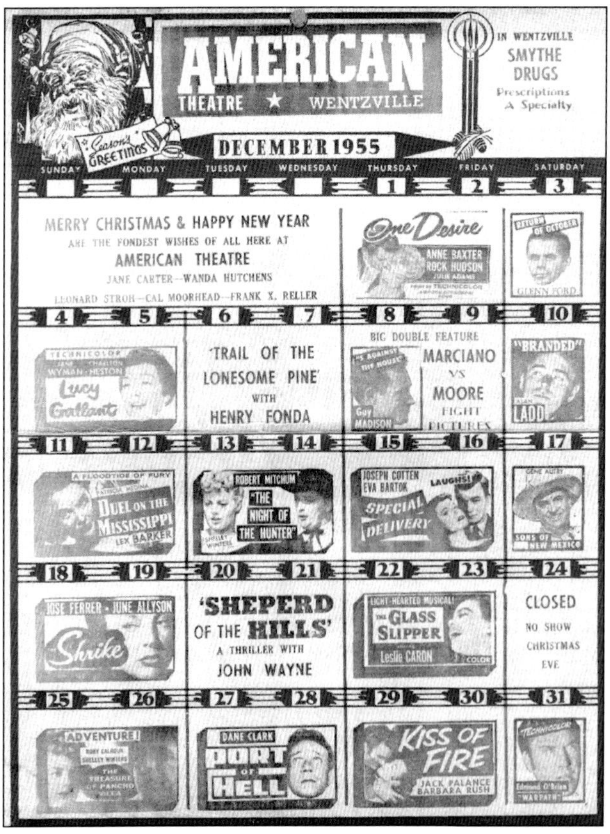

Today, Wentzville has a shiny new movie theater, but it is not the first. Several decades ago, the American Theater sat on what is now East Allen Street. It was first owned by Sen. Frank X. Reller. Shown above in 1953, young and old flocked to the theater to see Hollywood's latest. Family movies were shown until it was sold to Wentzville's famous resident, rock and roll legend Chuck Berry. After the sale, the theater began showing a more risqué type of entertainment. The citizens of Wentzville complained to city government regularly, and the American Theater mysteriously burned to the ground in 1973. At left is a typical monthly schedule of movies in 1955.

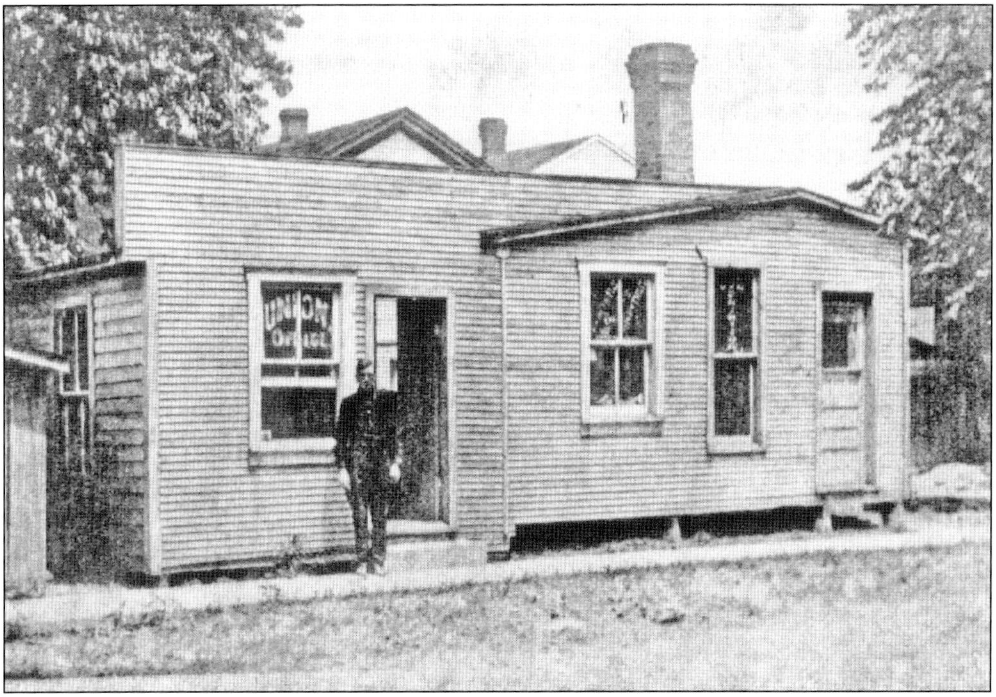

The *Wentzville Union* newspaper was founded in 1890. The owner and publisher, William McCracken, poses above in front of his office in 1916. In 1915, John F. Bornhop built the structure shown below to serve as the new post office. When Bornhop lost his bid to retain his postmaster position, he leased the building to the *Wentzville Union* and to a doctor who used the second floor for his office. When McCracken joined the Army to serve in World War I, he sold the newspaper to Bornhop. This building, which was located on Linn Avenue and Second Street, was lost in September 1931 to the last multi-building fire in Wentzville. The fire consumed seven businesses and homes on Linn Avenue. The *Union* served Wentzville for over 80 years before being sold and absorbed by another paper.

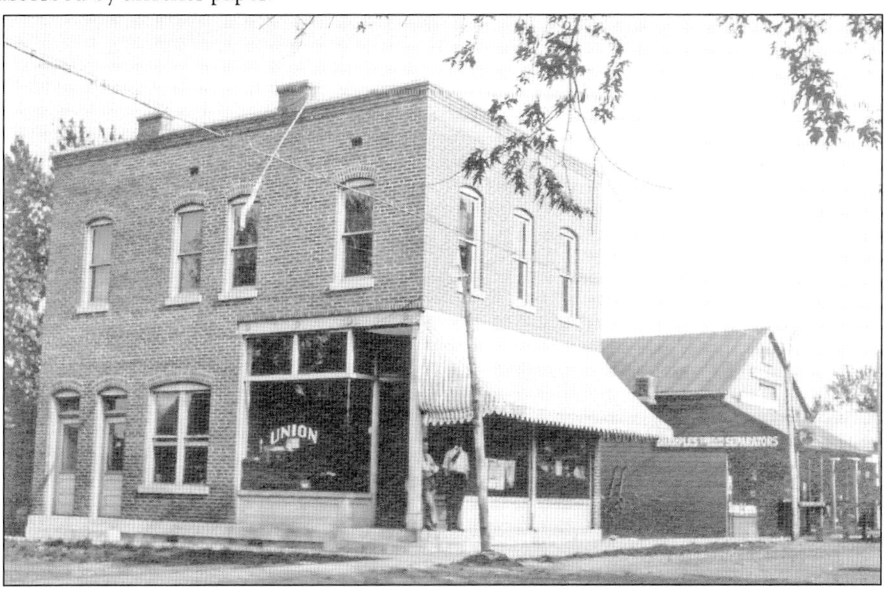

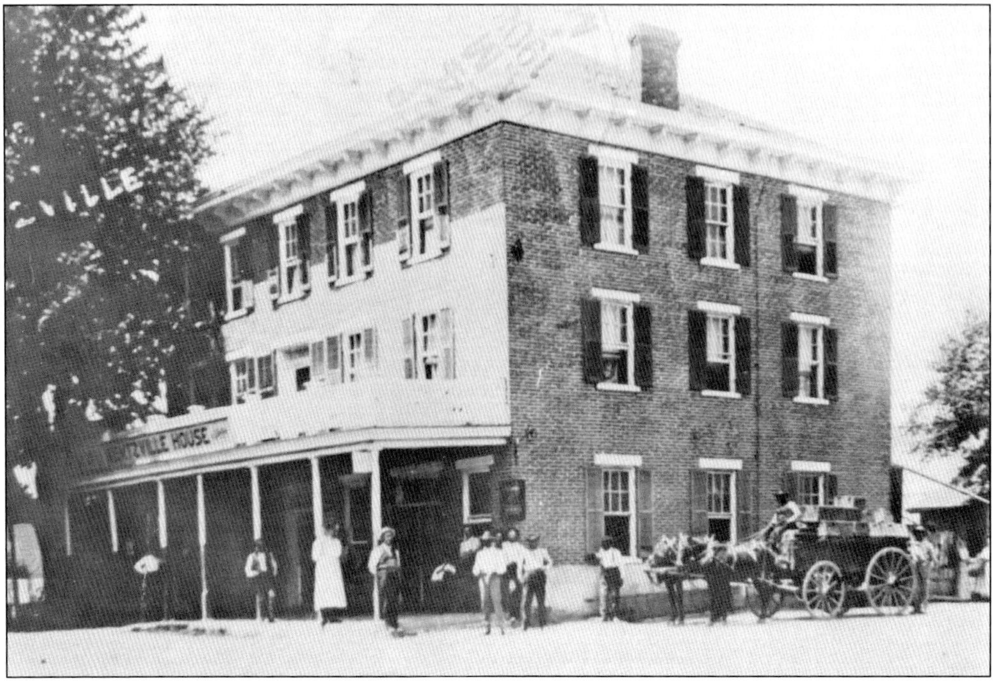

With the railroad came growth, and a hotel was needed. George and Henry Dierker built the Wentzville House Hotel in 1861. Soon after that, the Civil War battle known as the Battle of Wentzville occurred, and wounded soldiers from both sides were brought to the hotel. The next night, the hotel was set on fire and destroyed. Six years later, the Dierkers rebuilt the hotel, this time in brick 14 inches thick. The main floor held an ice cream parlor, a luxurious dining room, a coffee shop, and a "tonsorial parlor." The dining room was known for its country-fried chicken, served with seven vegetables: all one could eat for $1. Below is the Wentzville Dry Goods store, shown with Henry Michel in December 1924. Henry started the store with his brother-in-law E.H. Dierker. It later became the Koenig-Buscher Store.

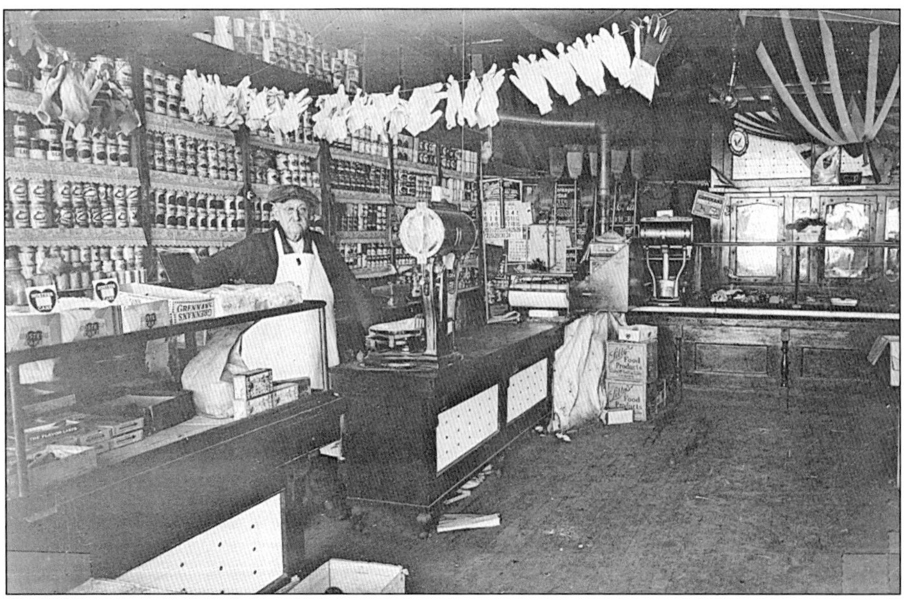

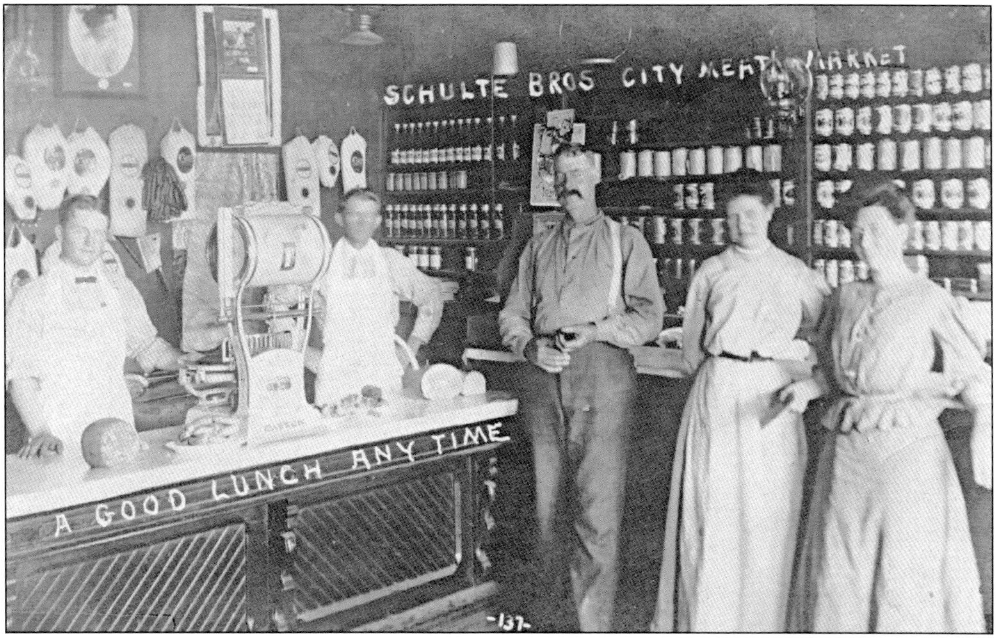

This postcard from around 1910 shows the Schulte Brothers' Meat Market. Charles C. Schulte, proprietor, is seen in the center. They guaranteed home-killed meat and a full line of fresh and salt meats and canned goods. They also offered homemade lard and home-cured ham and bacon. In a 1913 ad, they proclaimed "Positively no credit!"

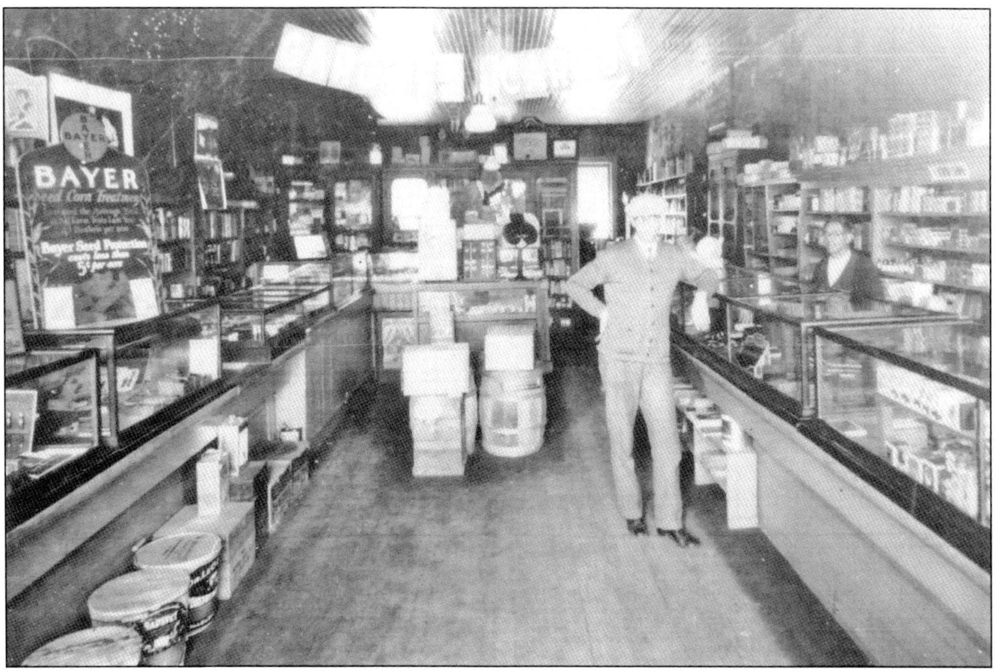

The D.B. Van Huffle Drugstore was located on the corner of Linn Avenue and South Main Street. It was the only drugstore in Wentzville for many years. Van Huffle was a shrewd businessman who believed in advertising in every possible outlet. He is shown behind the counter in 1910, with Mr. Kersting leaning against the counter. (Mamie Sommer.)

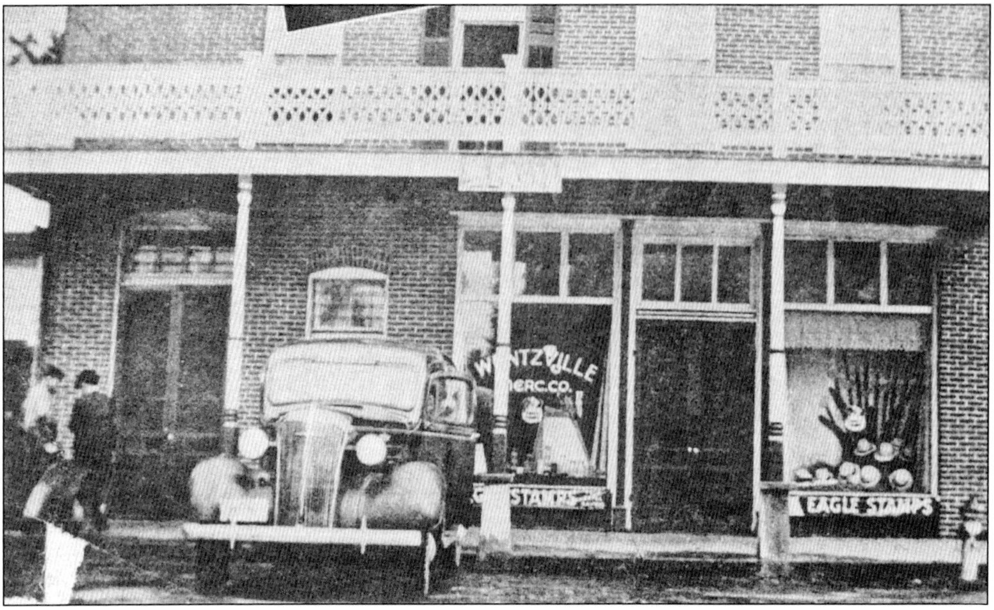

The Wentzville Mercantile, shown just before its destruction on page 71, is shown here open for business in 1940. The mercantile panel truck is being loaded with groceries and assorted goods to be delivered to customers throughout the Wentzville area. A 10-year-old Jim Pitman used to help load the truck.

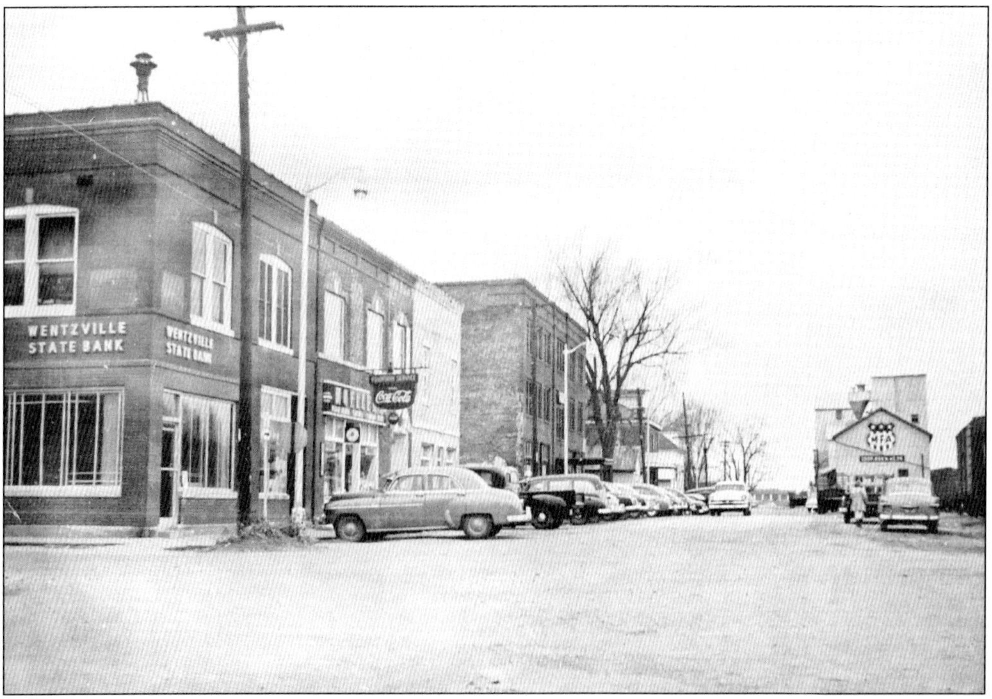

West South Main Street, looking from the intersection at Linn Avenue, is seen in the 1940s. Wentzville State Bank and Mueller's Drug Store are clearly seen as the first two businesses from the corner. The Wentzville Mercantile can be seen on the end with its white second-floor balcony. The Missouri Farmers Association is almost directly across the street.

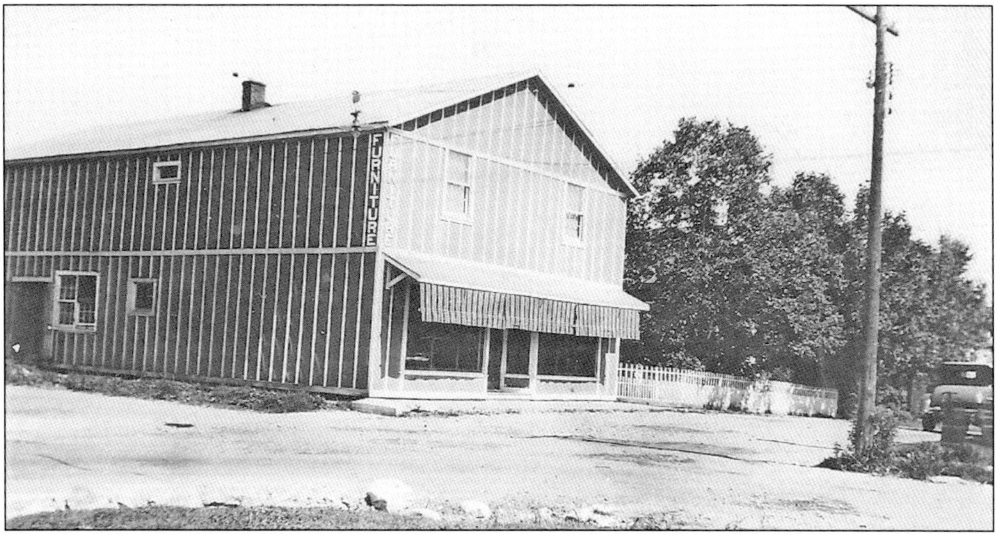

Niederjohn Furniture Company occupied the northeast corner of Second Street (now Pitman Avenue). Omar Niederjohn was a master craftsman who created hand-carved walnut furniture. His furniture was known nationwide and is still highly sought after today as antiques. This photograph was taken on July 17, 1935.

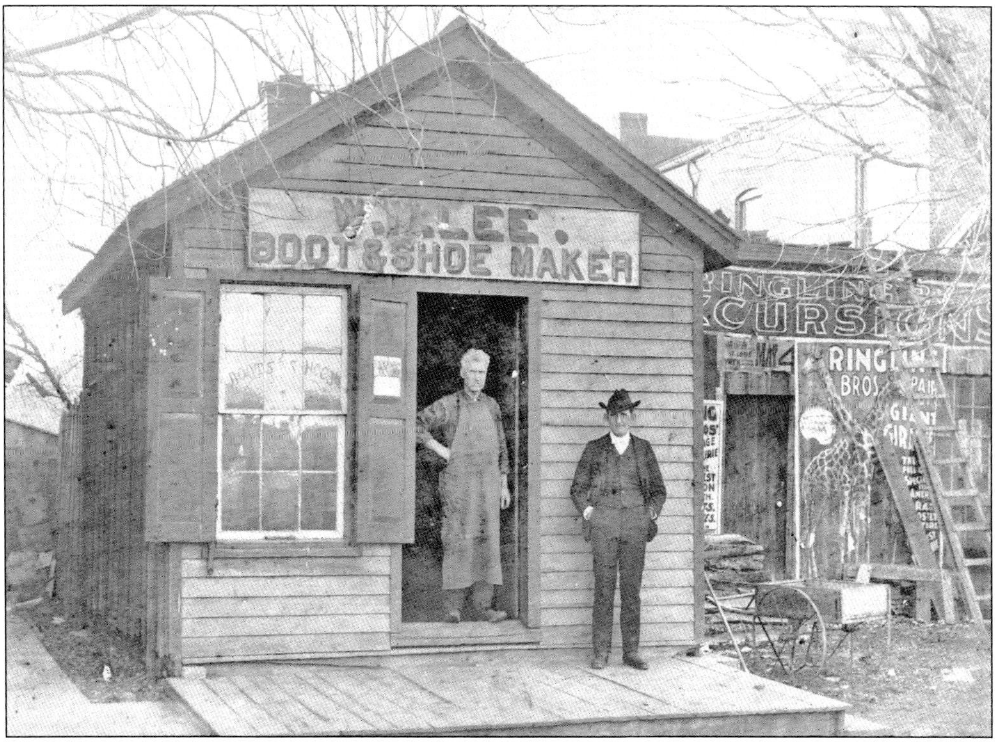

W.W. Lee Boot and Shoe Maker, shown around 1880, was located on Linn Avenue across the street from the Van Huffle Drugstore. Lee served in the Civil War with the 178th Ohio Infantry. He married the widow of William Owen, who also served in the war but as a Confederate under Stonewall Jackson. Mrs. Lee was the only woman in Wentzville to have been married to both a Confederate and a Yankee.

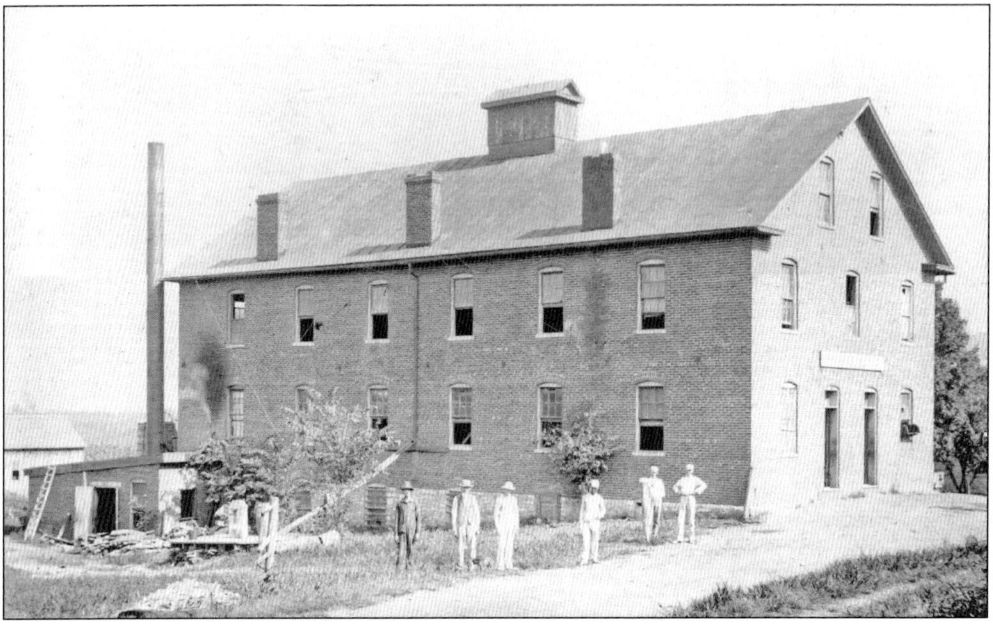

The Karrenbrock Flour Mill was founded in 1892 by Henry W. Karrenbrock. Some of his products were Davis' Golden Sheaf flour, White Cream, and High Patent. The building was erected before the Civil War and was used as a tobacco factory until 1885. When Karrenbrock retired, he left his sons Charles and William in charge. William sold his interest to his brother in 1907, and the mill operated until 1932.

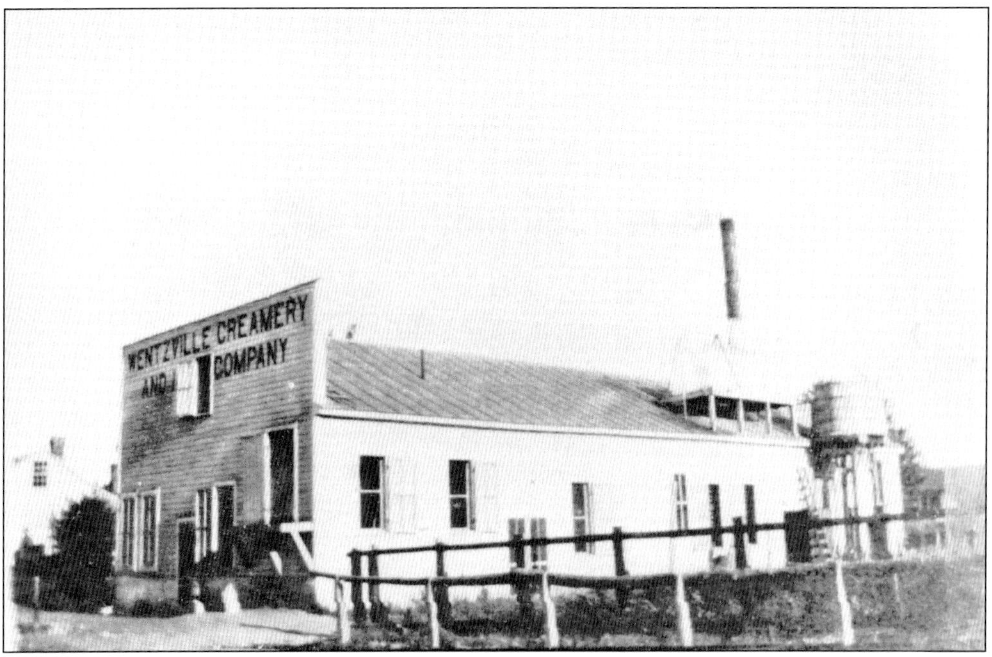

Ed Karrenbrock founded and built Wentzville's first creamery and ice house on Second Street (now Pitman Avenue) and Whitehead Avenue in 1915. Wentzville Creamery and Ice Company was best known for Frozen Gold Ice Cream. This building still stands and houses Wentzville's Friendship Brewery.

Six

Bad Times

When the first trains arrived in Wentzville in 1857, people began building homes and businesses. Those structures were usually built with wood, making them prime targets for fire. The volunteer fire department did its best with bucket brigades, but several major fires in the 1800s destroyed much of the town. A story in the *St. Charles Journal* in November 1882 read, "A Destructive Conflagration: The fire fiend has again visited our town, this time with great destruction of property and large pecuniary loss." The fire took a lumberyard that occupied nearly a city block, the Methodist church, the Masonic hall, and the school. Numerous homes and outbuildings were damaged or destroyed.

Another large fire was reported in 1886, and a 1907 fire once again took the school. The last major fire destroyed seven buildings on both sides of Linn Avenue on September 21, 1931. After that, the town came together with one common goal: to build a waterworks system.

Gilmore, the tiny township two miles east of Wentzville, was once larger and more prosperous than its neighbor. It had a post office, hotel, train station, and roundhouse at the Wabash-Shortline intersection. Gilmore was destined to become "the city" in western St. Charles County, but that all changed at 3:30 p.m. on July 1, 1915, when a cyclone destroyed the town, leaving only the hotel and saloon. The village of O'Fallon was flattened, along with parts of Dardenne and Wentzville. It destroyed the Peruque Creek train trestle and blew Wabash train No. 9 (with passenger cars) completely off the track. The destruction of Gilmore led to the current prosperity of Wentzville.

The serial husband-killer Emma Sarana Hepperman was arrested in Wentzville in July 1940 for killing her husband, Tony Hepperman. The investigation uncovered that she had killed at least five husbands from 1923 to 1940. Emma was found guilty of first-degree murder of her seventh husband by feeding him arsenic-laced potato soup and was given a life sentence at age 46. The story about Wentzville's "Death Angel" made national headlines and was highlighted in the magazine *Actual Detective Stories*.

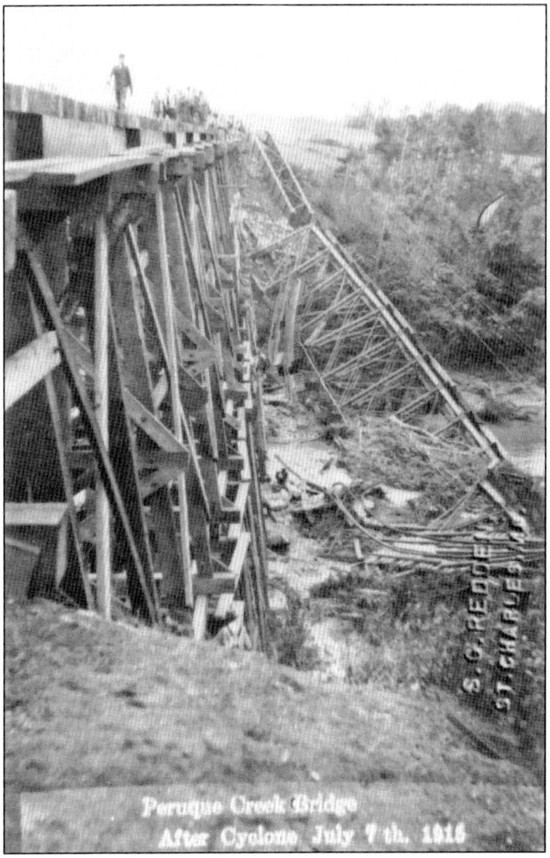

The Peruque Creek Bridge was heavily damaged by the tornado of July 7, 1915. The bridge carried the only trains coming to the western part of St. Charles County from St. Louis, so it was a crucial structure for commerce and passengers. Impressively, it took railroad workers only four days to put it back into service after the tornado.

The tornado was powerful enough to throw a train off the tracks. This photograph shows a locomotive and boxcars before they were removed after the storm. Although Wentzville has survived many tornados during the spring months, the one in July 1915 was rare and unexpected.

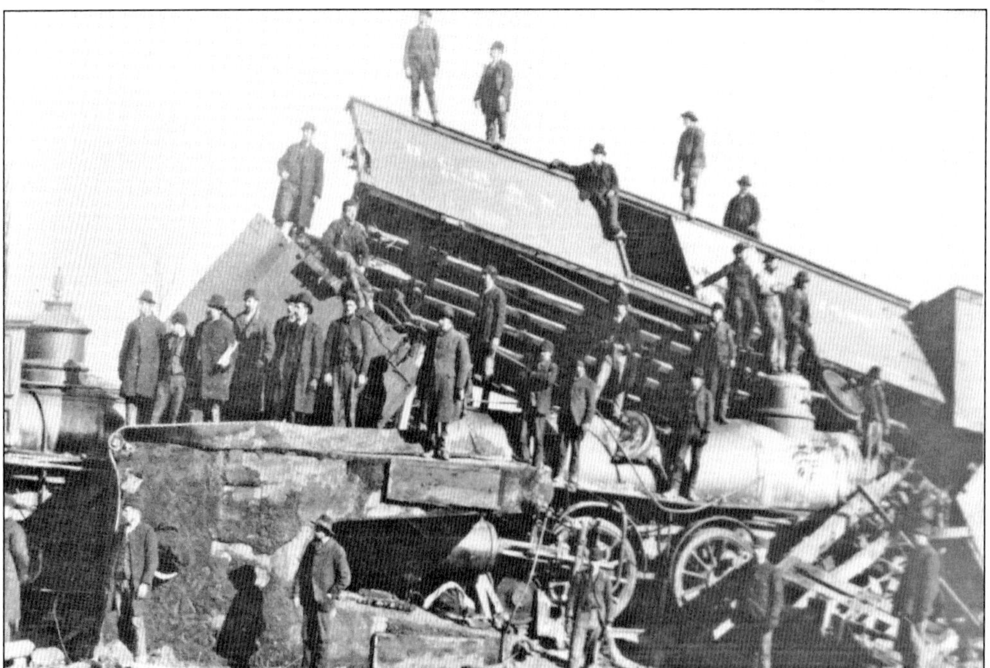

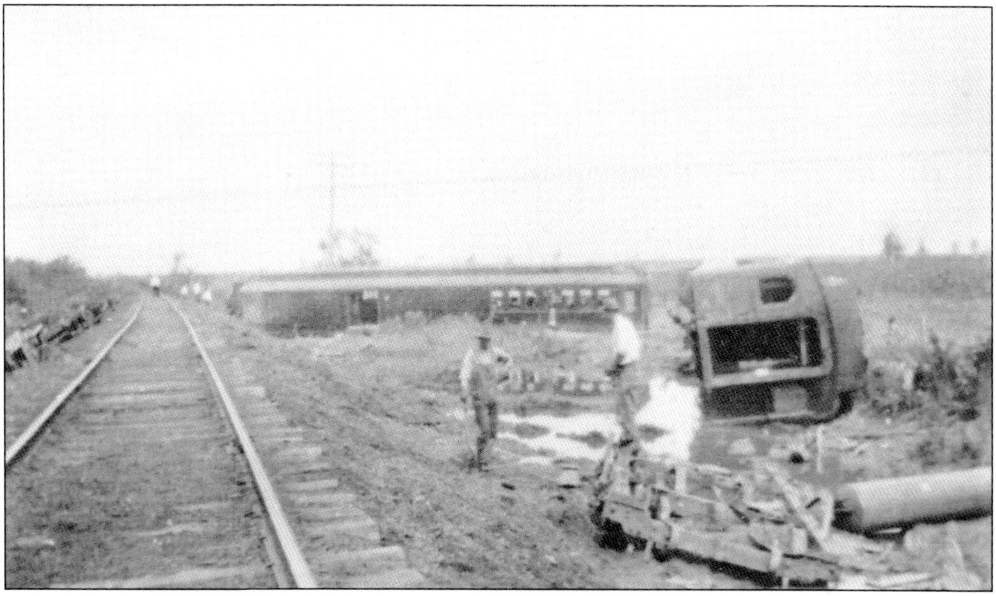

Above is a photograph looking west from where the tornado blew the Wabash passenger cars off the tracks. Railroad workers and farmers work together to remove debris from the tracks. Looking east below is another view of the damage. This shows some of what was left of the town of Gilmore, Missouri. Gilmore, which is just east of Wentzville, was assumed to be the community that would grow while Wentzville would stay a sleepy little village. After Gilmore and its train station were destroyed by the 1915 tornado, attention shifted to Wentzville, and it began to grow. Gilmore barely survived, and many Wentzville citizens today do not even know it is there.

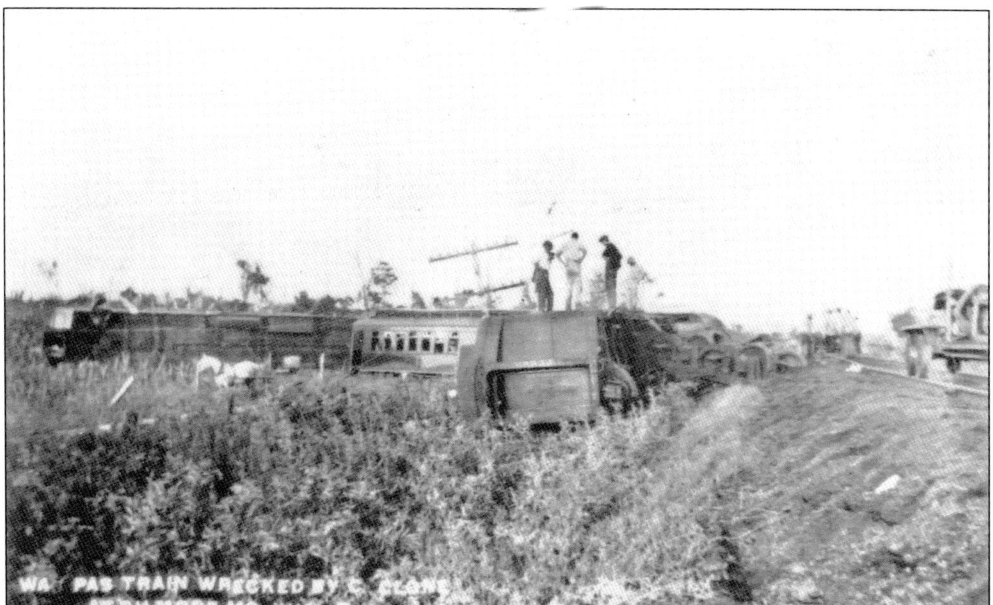

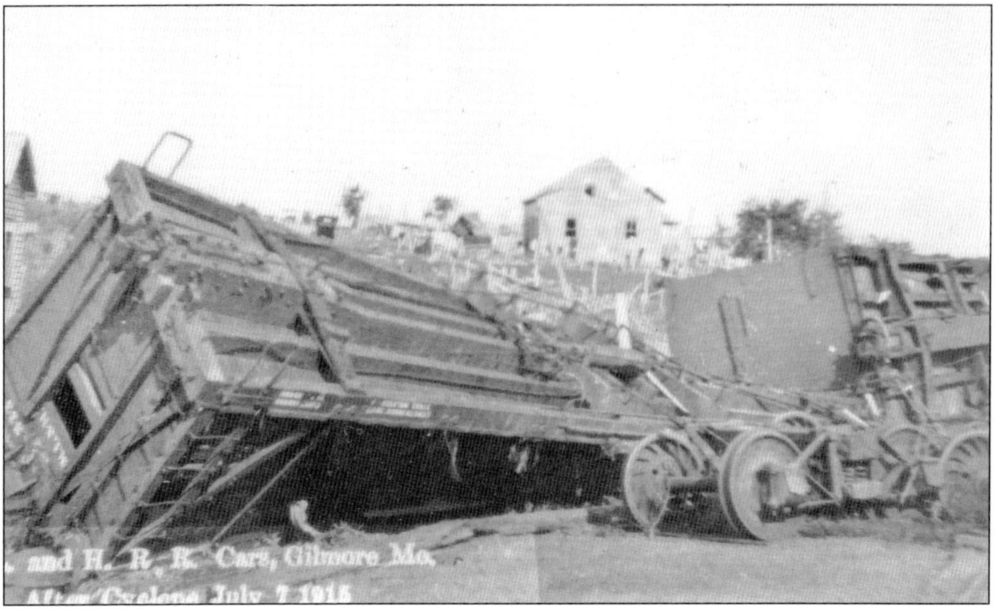

Behind the wreckage of boxcars is a portion of what remained of Gilmore. The destruction was devastating. Below stands a woman, perhaps a passenger, on one of the Pullman cars that blew off the tracks. Another cyclone hit Wentzville on May 18, 1883. A newspaper article says that a family tried to get into their cellar for safety but could not open the door; the cyclone demolished the building, so their lives were saved by being unable to enter. Another news story tells of a man who was in bed asleep when the storm hit. When he awoke, he found himself and his bed in a fence corner, safe and sound.

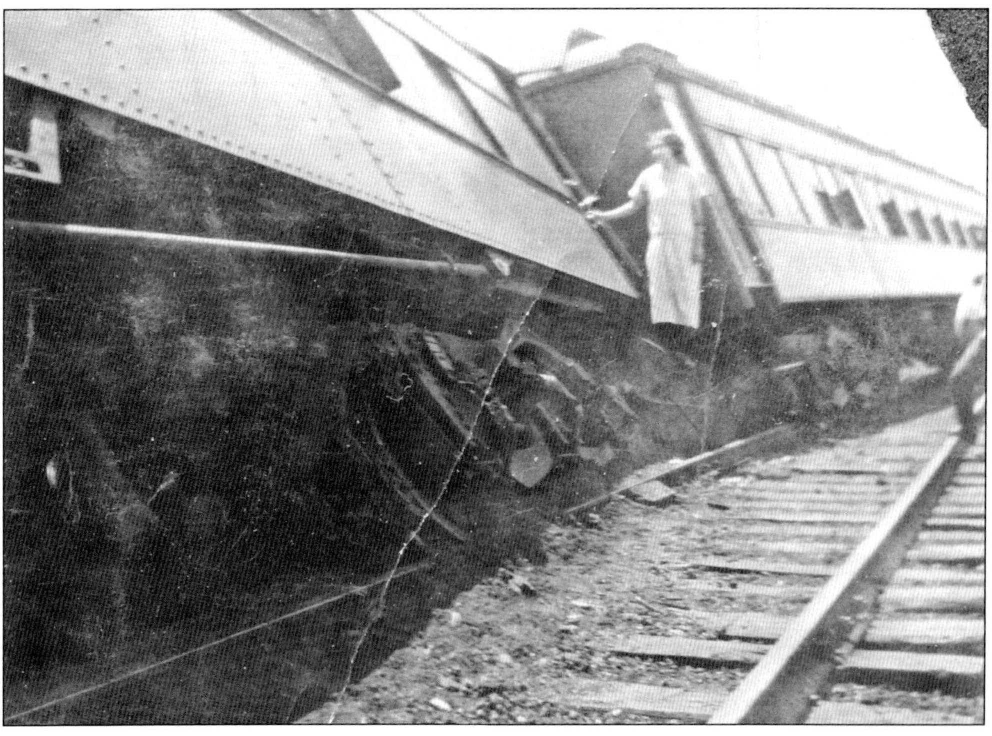

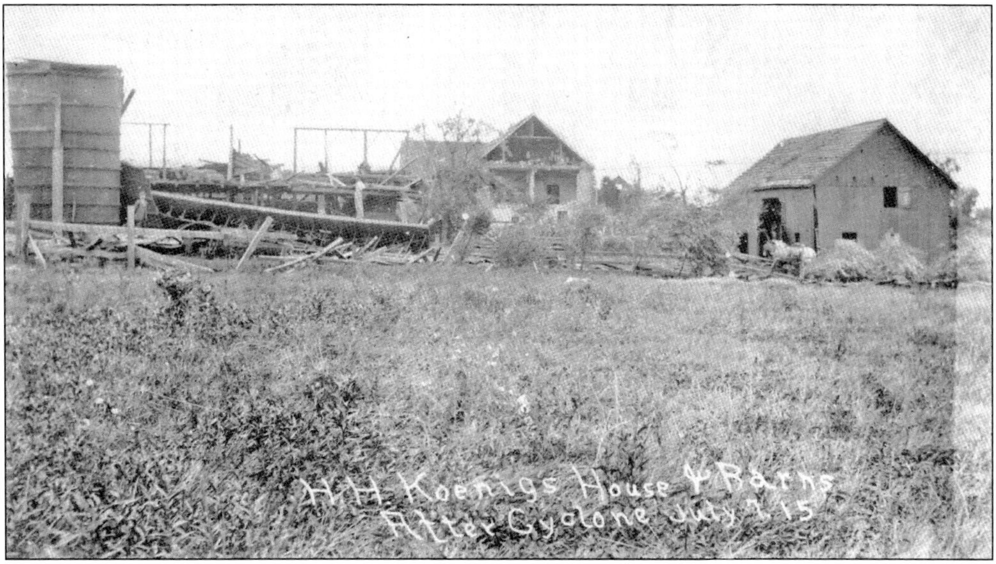

The tornado of 1915 damaged the home of H.H. Koenig in Wentzville, and his barn was leveled. The home of his relative Harry Koenig was destroyed. Both Harry's wife and infant daughter were in the home when it was hit. Martha Koenig was fatally injured when she was struck by debris. Her daughter and husband made it out alive.

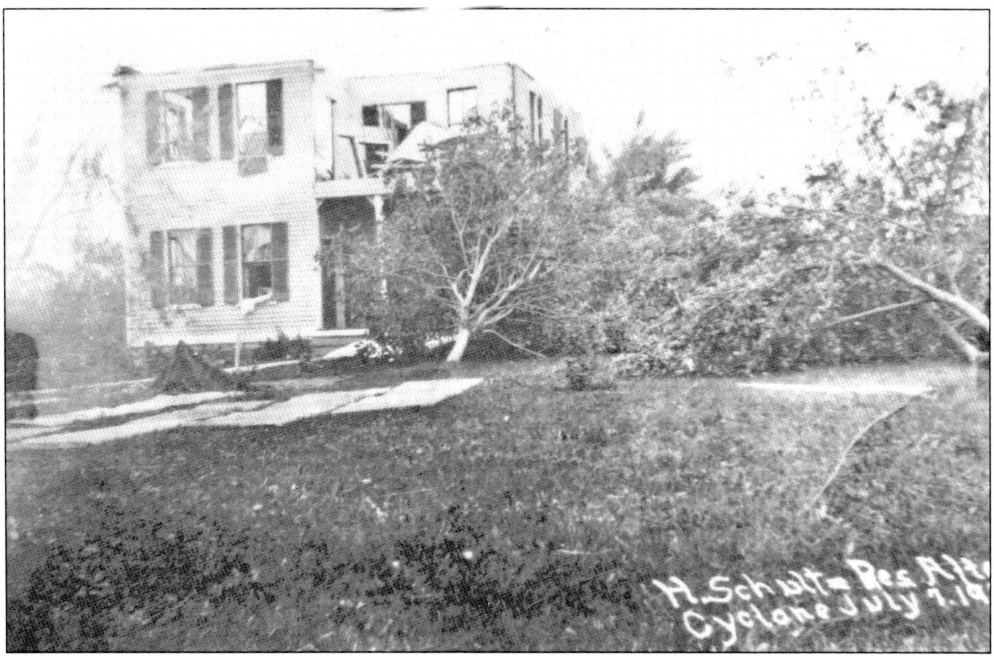

About 15 Wentzville homes were damaged during the 1915 tornado. Before this, the last tornado to hit St. Charles County was in 1883. This is what was left of the home of Henry Schulte and family in July 1915.

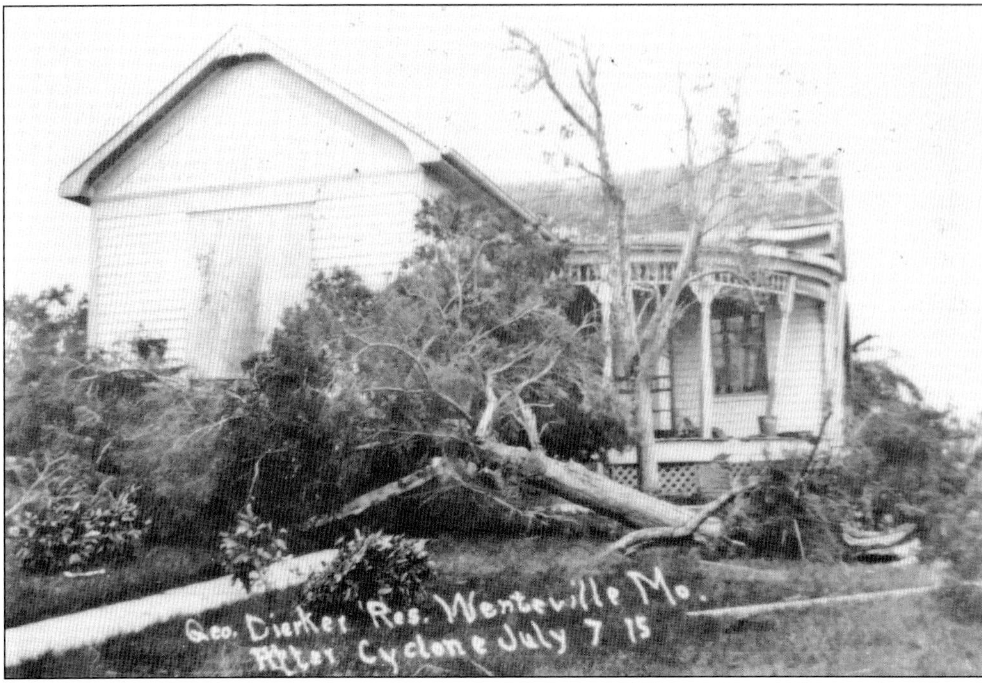

The classic porch of the George Dierker home was damaged in the 1915 tornado. Compared with the other 15 damaged homes in Wentzville, the damage here was less severe, although Dierker might have disagreed.

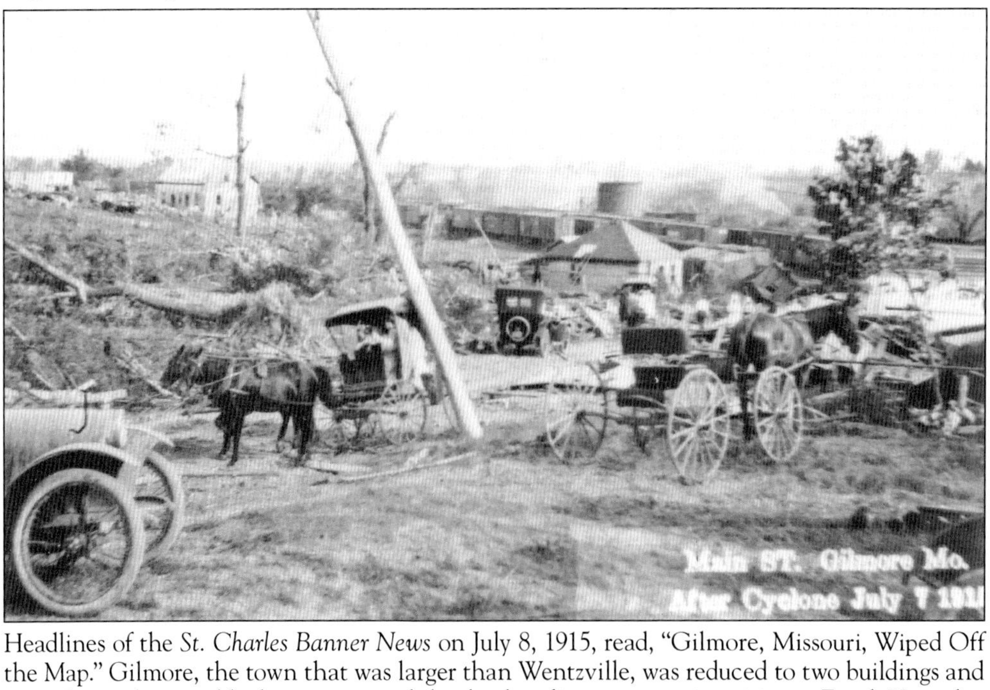

Headlines of the *St. Charles Banner News* on July 8, 1915, read, "Gilmore, Missouri, Wiped Off the Map." Gilmore, the town that was larger than Wentzville, was reduced to two buildings and was subjected to terrible destruction and the deaths of its unsuspecting citizens. Frank Hunsel, a station agent, was decapitated while attempting to prevent the train station door from blowing away in the storm.

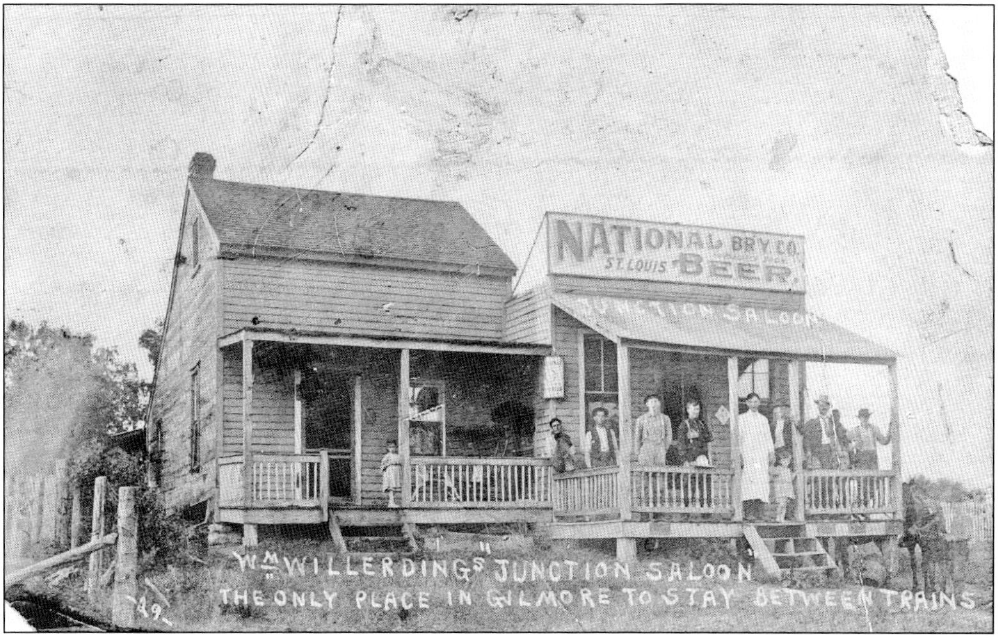

Only two Gilmore buildings survived the 1915 tornado: the Gilmore Hotel, which still stands today, and the saloon. William Willerding's Junction Saloon was touted as "The only place in Gilmore to stay between trains." Owners and customers are shown here in happier times, around 1890, before the tornado destroyed the rest of the town.

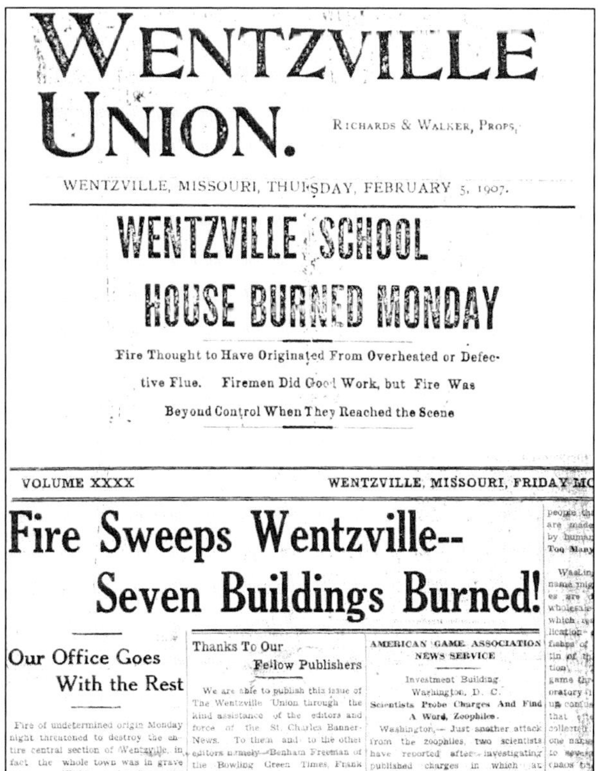

WENTZVILLE UNION. RICHARDS & WALKER, PROPS.

WENTZVILLE, MISSOURI, THURSDAY, FEBRUARY 5, 1907.

WENTZVILLE SCHOOL HOUSE BURNED MONDAY

Fire Thought to Have Originated From Overheated or Defective Flue. Firemen Did Good Work, but Fire Was Beyond Control When They Reached the Scene

VOLUME XXXX — WENTZVILLE, MISSOURI, FRIDAY

Fire Sweeps Wentzville-- Seven Buildings Burned!

Our Office Goes With the Rest

Fire of undetermined origin Monday night threatened to destroy the entire central section of Wentzville, in fact the whole town was in grave danger. Within a few hours the

Thanks To Our Fellow Publishers

We are able to publish this issue of The Wentzville Union through the kind assistance of the editors and force of the St. Charles Banner-News. To them and to the other editors namely—Benham Freeman of the Bowling Green Times, Frank Hollman, Warrenton Banner; F. J.

AMERICAN GAME ASSOCIATION NEWS SERVICE

Investment Building Washington, D. C.

Scientists Probe Charges And Find A Word, Zoophiles.

Washington,— Just another attack from the zoophiles, two scientists have reported after investigating published charges in which an "emergency conservation committee"

Large fires ravaged Wentzville from the 1850s until 1935, when the waterworks system was completed. Schools, churches, entire blocks of businesses, and many homes were destroyed. Sadly, along with the structures went much of Wentzville's history, including photographs and papers that went up in flames. City documents from 1872 to 1890 were all lost to fire, leaving a gap of 18 years.

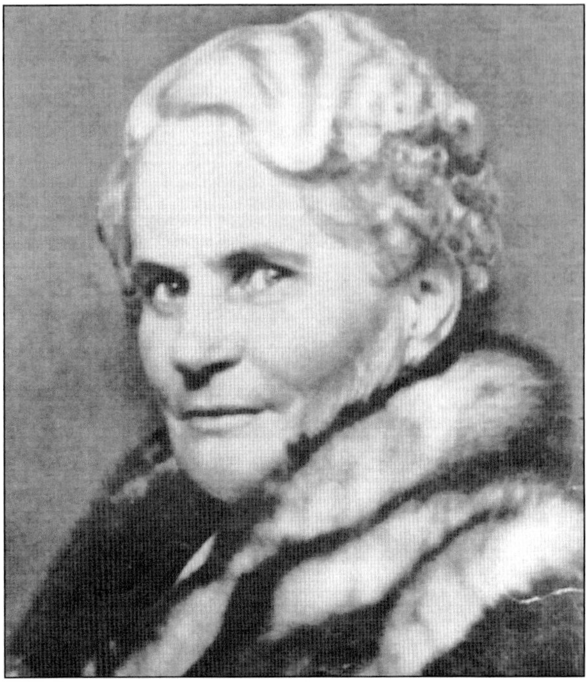

In June 1940, Wentzvillians were saddened to hear that one of their longtime fellow citizens had died, but they were soon horrified to learn that his new wife had murdered him. Emma Heppermann, they learned, had killed five husbands: one was burned to death and four were poisoned with arsenic in their potato soup. A sixth husband had disappeared. Heppermann became known as the "Death Angel" and made national news.

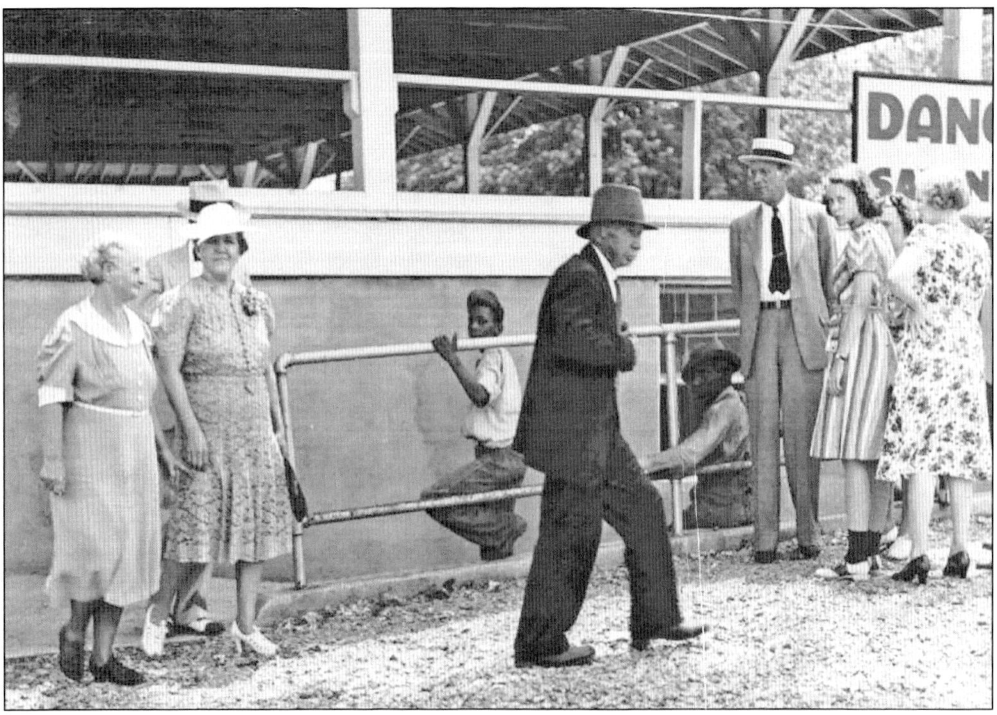

Emma Heppermann is escorted from her hearing in the Community Club pavilion by a county matron and sheriff. Before 400 citizens, Justice Gus Temme held her for murder without bail. The trial moved to Franklin County, where she was sentenced to life without parole. From her cell, when told her poisoned husband had died, she replied, "If that's all you have to say, I'd like to go back to bed." (St. Charles County Historical Society.)

Seven

Good Times

From the earliest records of Wentzville, reports abound of fun gatherings, from lawn fetes to tent shows and town barbecues. Stable owner and dairy farmer Charles E. Musick had a mansion and large tract of land on the west end of Main Street. He allowed his hilly, park-like farm, called Musick's Grove, to be the picnic grounds for city celebrations, such as the extravagant Fourth of July festivities.

An octagonal firehouse with a bandstand above it was used frequently by Wentzville's Craven's Band from 1905 until about 1912. Craven's Band played at most city celebrations, both large and small. The permanent bandstand atop the firehouse was located at the city's center at Linn Avenue and North Main Street (now Allen Street), next to the railroad tracks and directly in front of the Wentzville House Hotel. The band played to listeners who gathered in the streets and on the second-floor balcony of the hotel. Wentzville also had a baseball team; fans came from all over to watch their favorites play.

From 1935 to the 1970s, the Wentzville Community Club hosted an annual carnival and parade on Labor Day weekend. It was called Homecoming Jubilee, and people from all over the county attended. The original purpose was to raise funds for a waterworks. These huge celebrations included a carnival, a queen coronation, a motor parade, and a kiddie parade with bicycles and doll carriages. The Community Club raised thousands of dollars that paid for all the hookups for the waterworks to homes and businesses.

In 1963, a million-dollar racing facility was built in Wentzville called Mid America Raceway (MAR). It consisted of a drag strip and a five-kilometer racing course. The facility, whose motto was "MAR: where the big ones are," drew some of the most famous drivers and teams in the world, including Don Garlits, Tommy Ivo, A.J. Foyt, Mario Andretti, and Paul Newman. MAR brought millions of dollars into the Wentzville economy until it was torn down in 2005.

Whether listening to a band concert, watching a ball game, or attending annual festivities, small-town citizens have always enjoyed getting together for family fun.

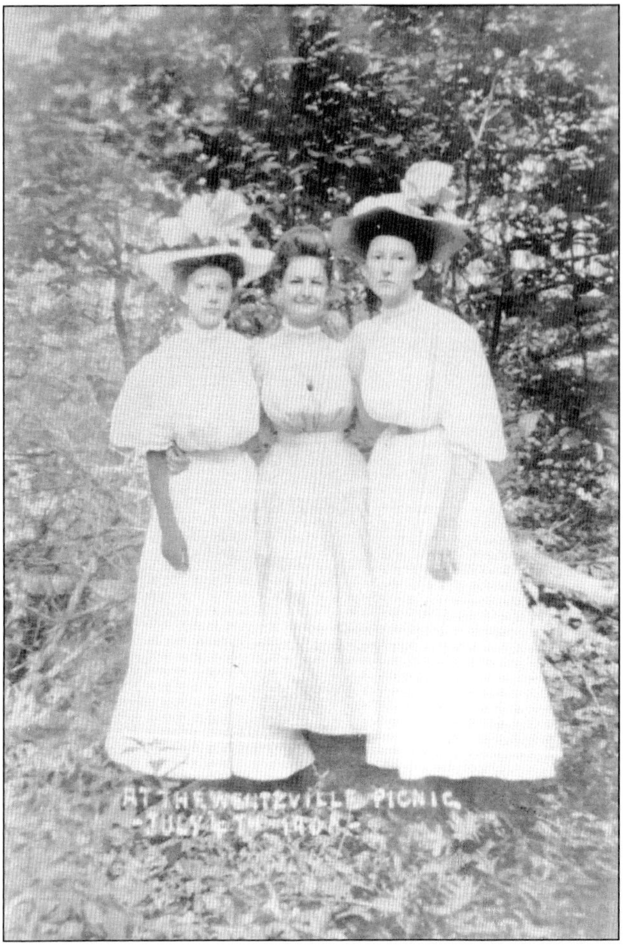

These lovely young ladies (from left to right), Olga Schramm, Carrie Hunsel, and Clara Koester, are attending the Fourth of July picnic in 1908, probably held in Musick Grove (currently the location of the Wentzville Community Club). Clara Koester is 16 years old in this photograph. (Clara Koester Schmucker.)

The year is 1942; the scene is the front of Smythe's Drug Store. Ruthie Parr (left) and Thelma Sinock (later Chilton) are being closely watched by a couple of hopeful admirers. They are probably getting ready to get a chocolate coke or root beer float at the drugstore's soda fountain. (Thelma Sinock Chilton.)

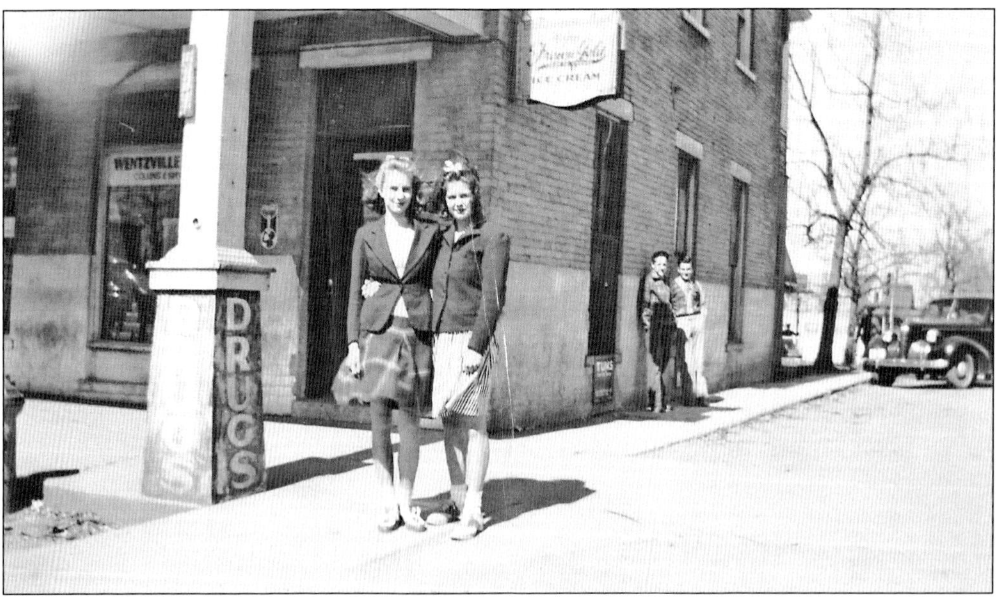

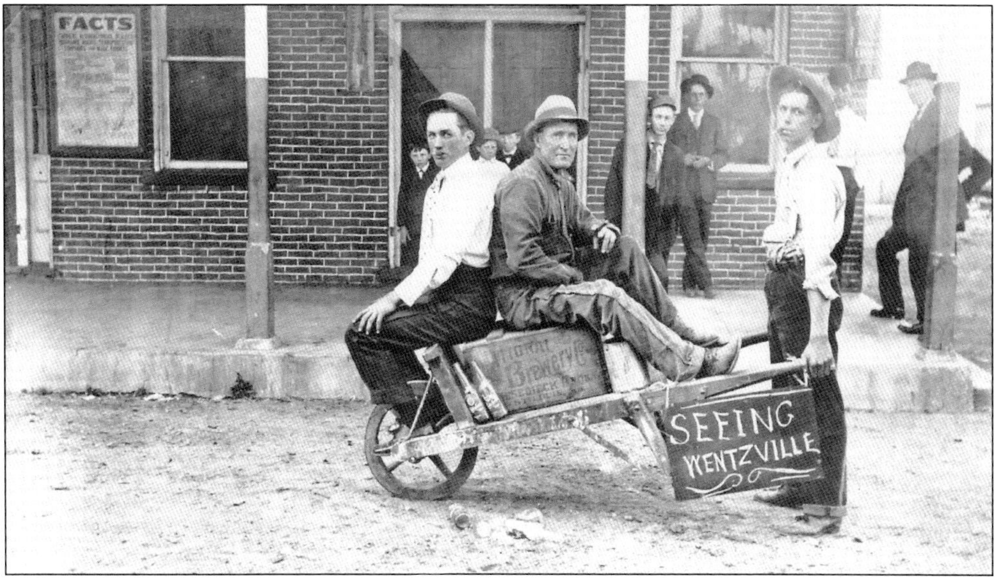

In small-town America, people go out of their way to have fun. Here, in front of the old Heady Hotel, from left to right, "Buck" Thomas, George Freese, and Tom Martin clown around with an apparent tour guide business, complete with bottles of beer on the side of the wheelbarrow. George Freese brought Wentzville its first automobile dealership.

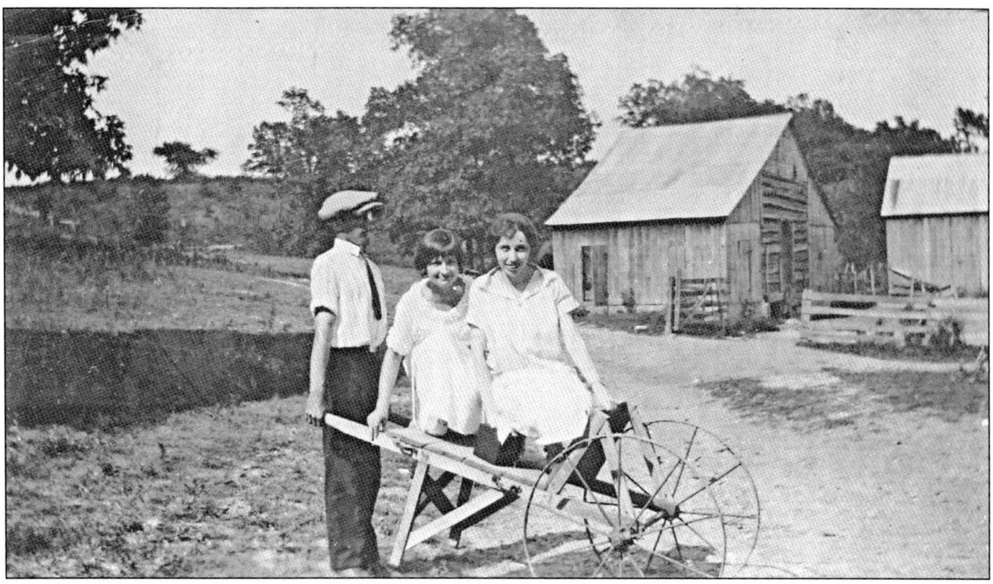

Wheelbarrows must have been the preferred mode of transportation in Wentzville during the 1930s. These young people are having fun on their farm, in spite of their dressy clothes. (Mary Moritz.)

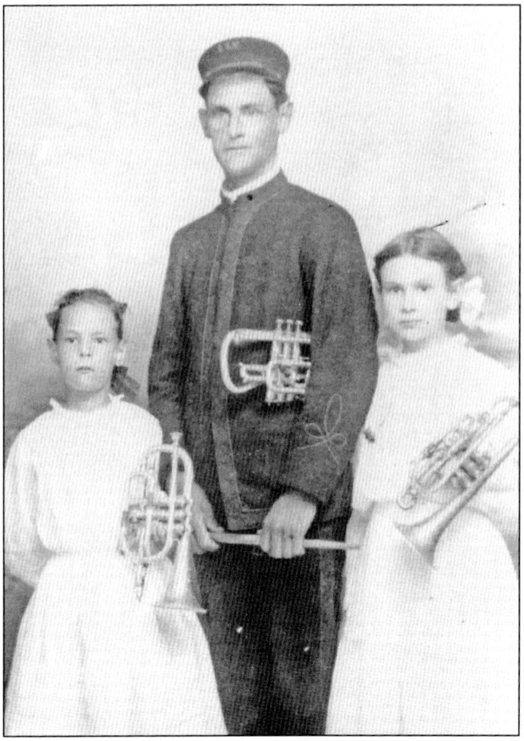

George Craven, who was a school teacher, formed and led Wentzville's Craven's Band. He is posed here with his daughters Erma (left) and Irene and their instruments. Many towns had their own Sousa-like band to play at picnics and other celebrations. Craven's Band entertained Wentzville and the surrounding area from around 1900 to about 1912.

Craven's Band is shown here around 1906. The band members are leader George Craven (center), Nat Cochran, Charles Richards, Fred Schultz, Ed Schierbaum, Fred Justice, Cleve Sidebottoms, Ed Williams, Theodore Schierbaum, Lloyd Allen, Edwin Talley, Horace Talley, Lou Willerding, and Al Vonderman.

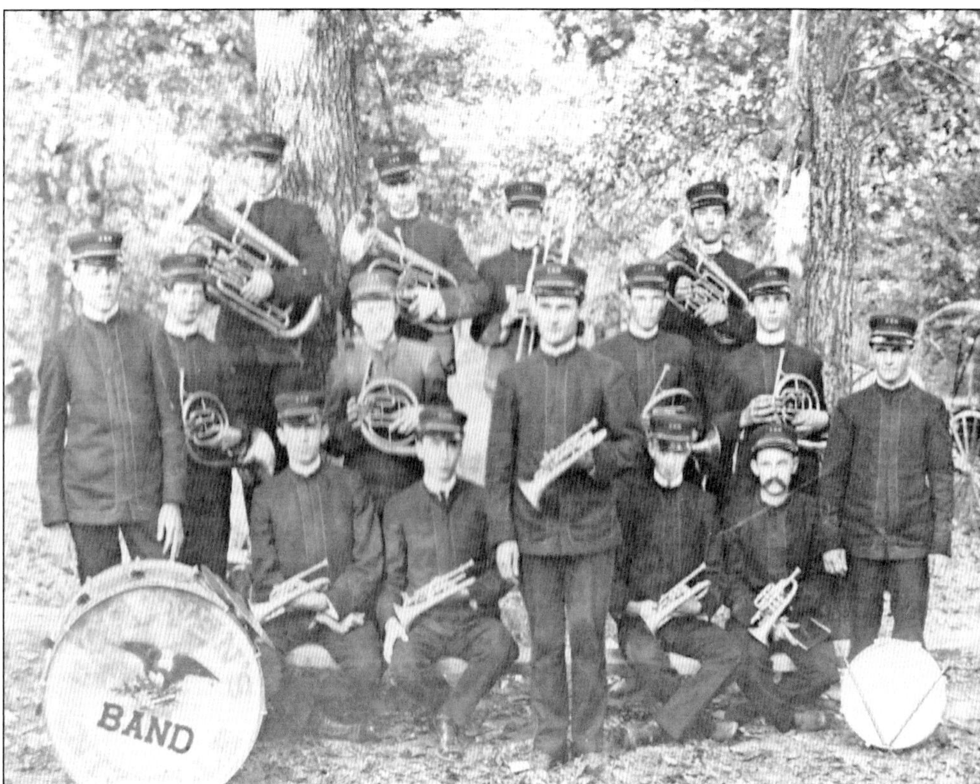

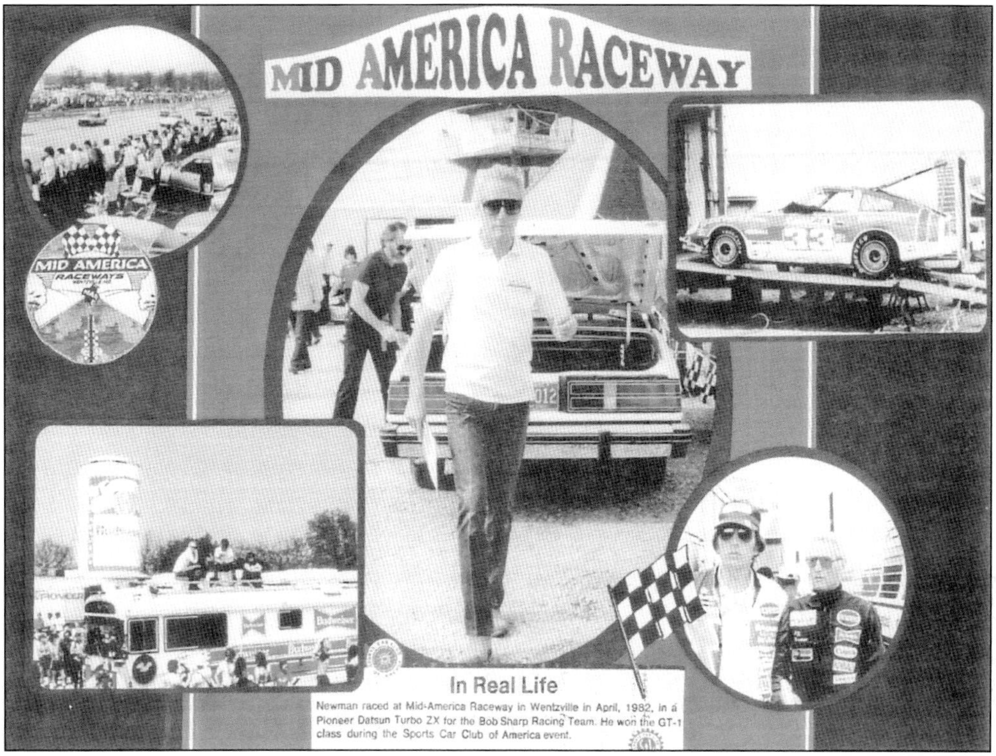

Mid America Raceway, built in 1963, brought millions of dollars to Wentzville's economy and brought big names in racing to town. The poster shown above was created to advertise Paul Newman, who raced at MAR in April 1982. He won the GT-1 class during the Sports Car Club of America event on the five-kilometer course. Most of America's top racing personalities raced at the Mid America Raceway's drag strip. The below photograph shows one of the best of all time—Don Garlits, with his open-wheel Dodge dragster and team. In 1971, the fans flocked around to get a good look at the man and his machine.

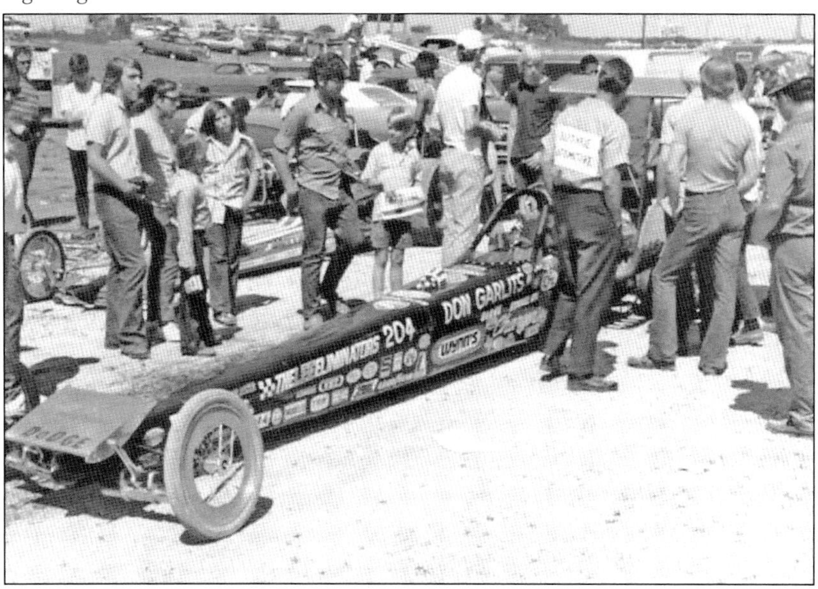

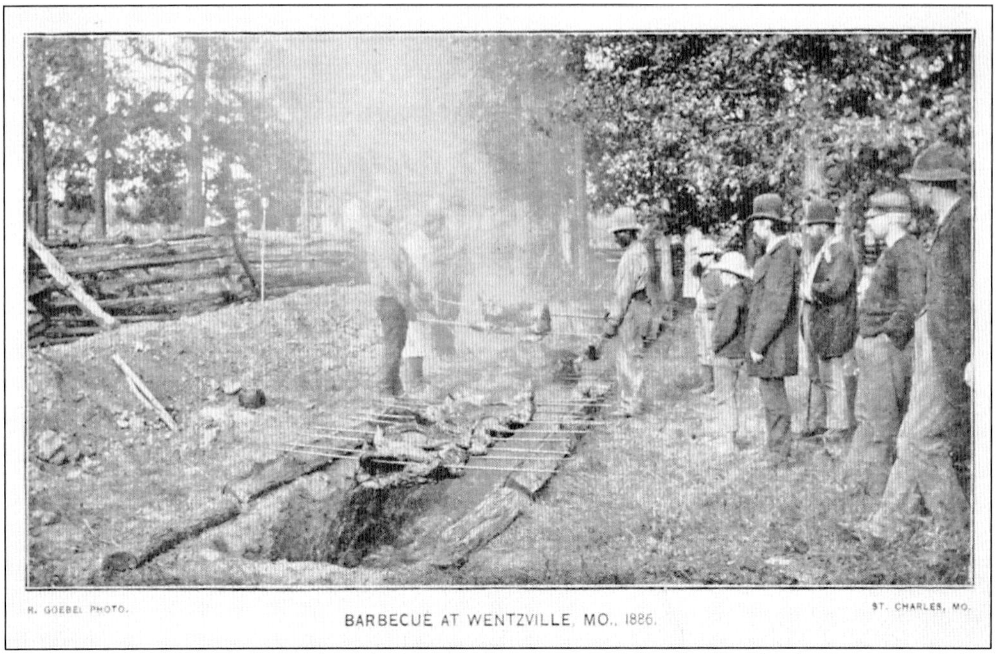

This Wentzville barbecue, which took place in 1886, was caught on camera by the famous Rudolph Goebel. From 1856 to 1916, he made his living as a professional photographer. Not satisfied with simply taking portraits and selling postcards, he created a visual history of St. Charles and other towns in St. Charles County.

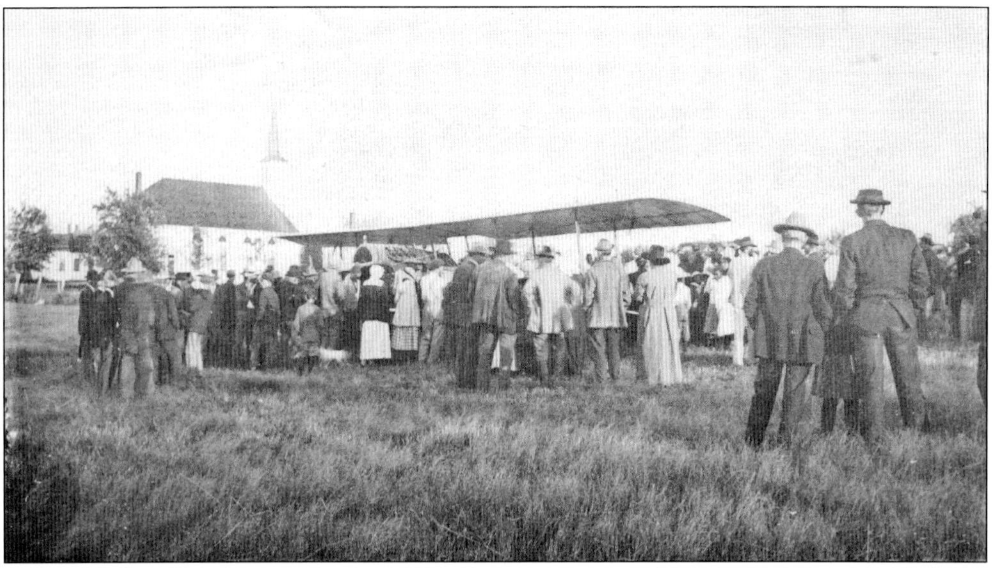

On September 20, 1918, a Curtiss Jenny airplane, originating from Scott Airbase, landed in a field west of Immanuel Lutheran Church. Lieutenants Marsh and Rudd stopped to refuel on their way to Columbia. Several planes landed in Wentzville during the war years, and they always attracted townspeople, who brought picnics for themselves and the pilots. A newspaper account said, "These visits are a good exhibition of what our war saving stamps can do."

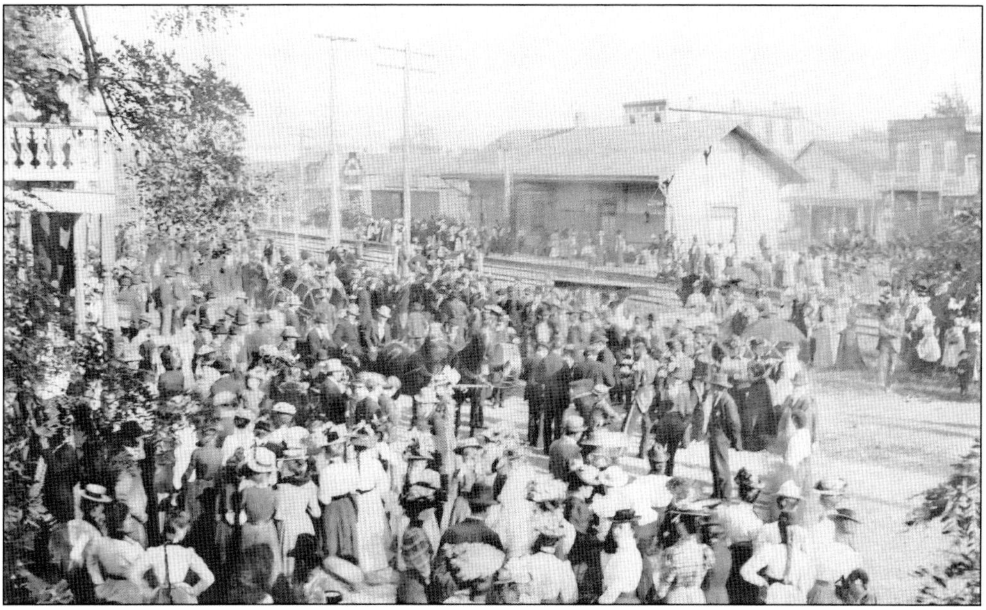

Citizens of the entire county gathered at the railroad station in Wentzville in 1892. Grover Cleveland was running for a second term and made Wentzville a destination on his whistle-stop campaign. Everyone dressed in their finest clothes and came from miles around to get a glimpse of the president. (Octavia Evans Sigman.)

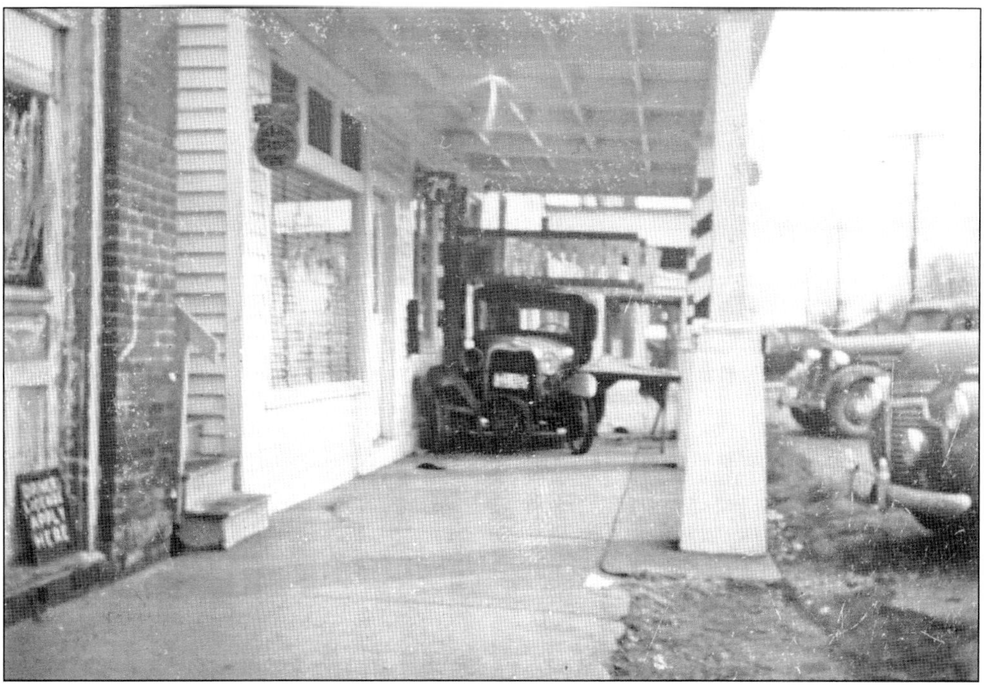

Halloween is a fun holiday for children all over the country, but it is also a great night for pranksters. On this particular Halloween in the 1940s, an ambitious group of young people decided to move an automobile onto the sidewalk in front of the barbershop on West Allen Street. (Nancy Frei.)

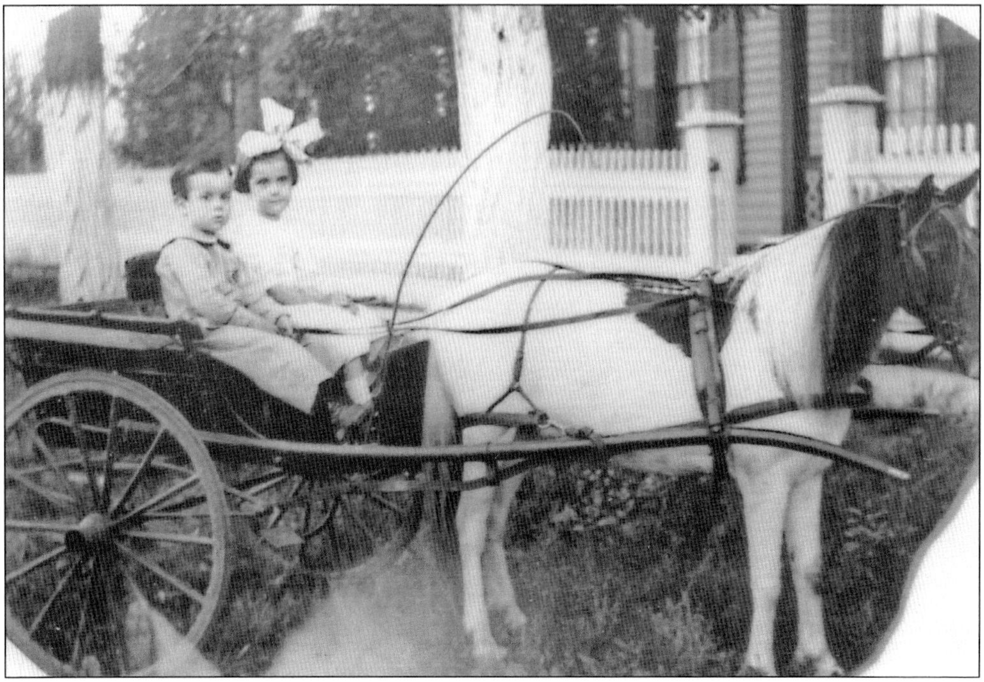

What could be more fun than getting all dressed up in Sunday finery (including an oversized hair bow), hitching one's pony cart, and going for a ride? Here Helen B. Foristell and her little brother John Emmett Foristell are ready to take off from their Wentzville home, led by their pony, Beauty. (Helen Foristell Southard.)

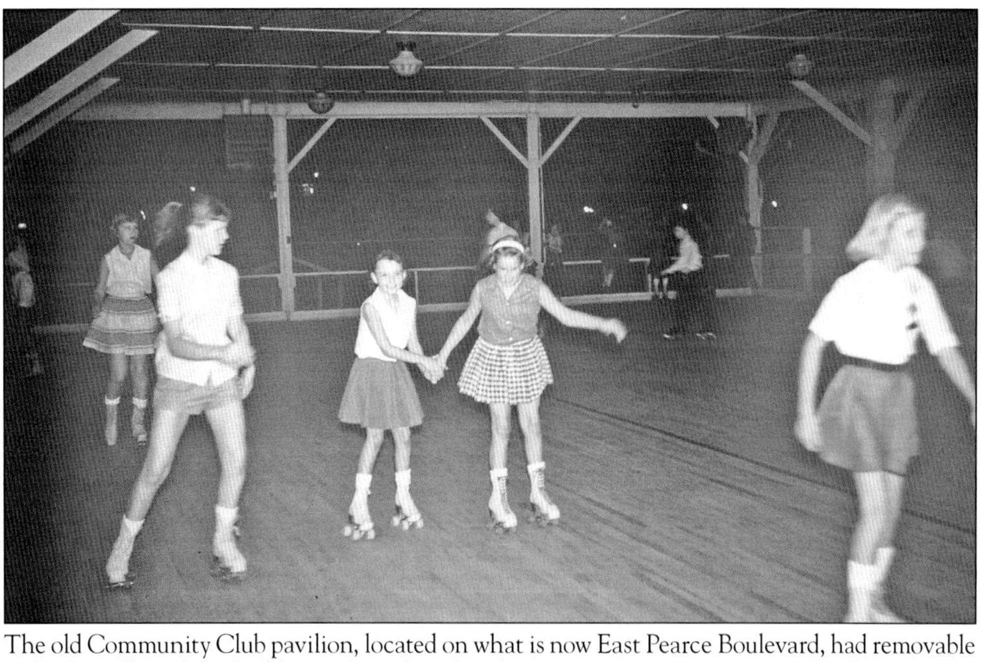

The old Community Club pavilion, located on what is now East Pearce Boulevard, had removable walls that allowed the building to be either closed or open air. Dances, concerts, and many other activities were held here. The pavilion was often used as a roller rink (weather permitting), as seen in this 1958 photograph.

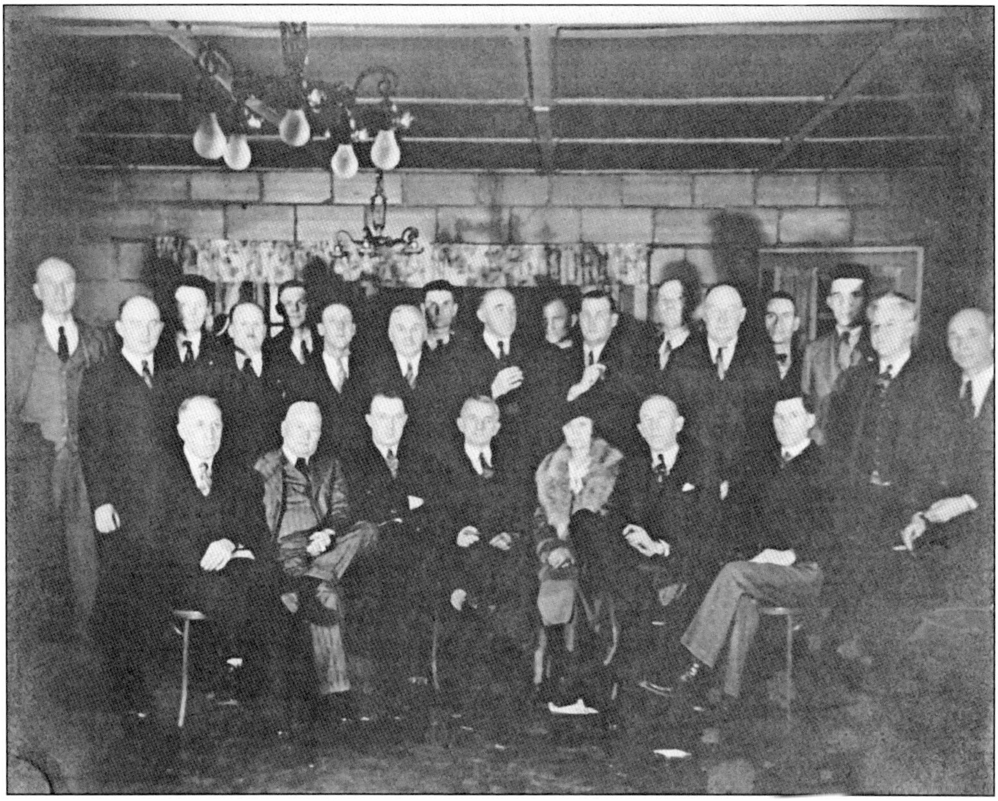

The Wentzville Community Club was founded at an enthusiastic meeting on December 26, 1933. Members of the Lions Club and representative business and professional people of Wentzville united to stimulate business in the town as well as to work for the general welfare of the community. Their first goal was to combat the effects of the Great Depression and bring an end to the town-threatening fires by building a waterworks. They met and exceeded their goals; they even paid the salaries of the mayor and aldermen through the hard times. The founders are seen above. At right is the group's first president, Charles Richards, with his wife, Alma Lee Musick, in 1908. The Community Club continues its good work today.

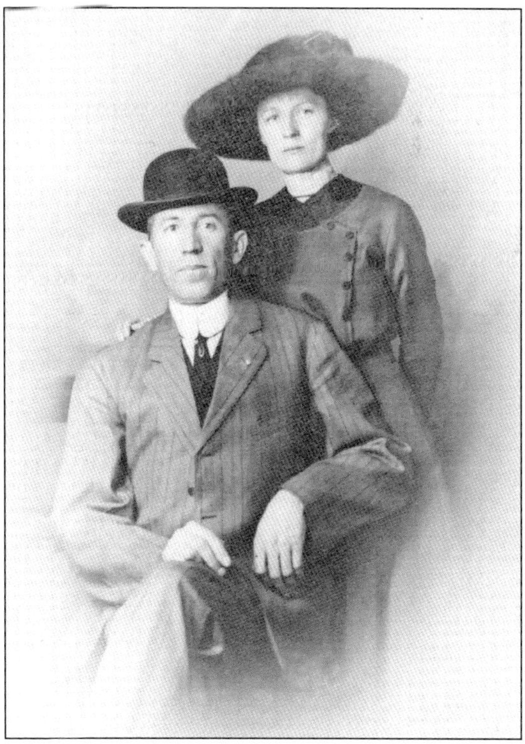

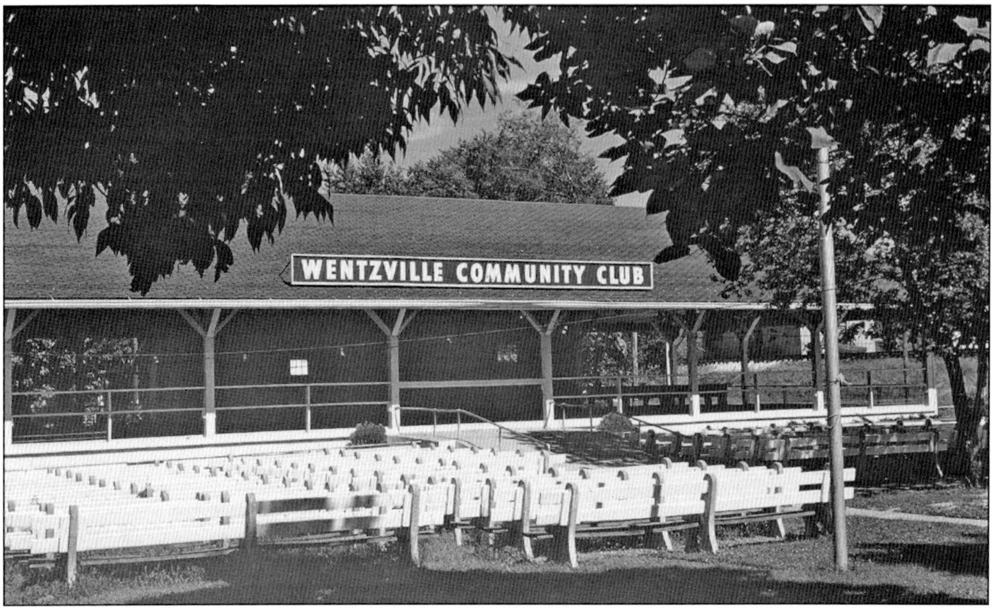

Completed in 1937, the Community Club pavilion, roller rink, and town meeting hall served Wentzville for almost 30 years. Every weekend, children and teens were entertained by dances and roller skating. The city government held meetings, and the municipal judge served in chambers in the basement. In the summer, the removable walls were taken down, and in winter, they were replaced. (Larry Wentz.)

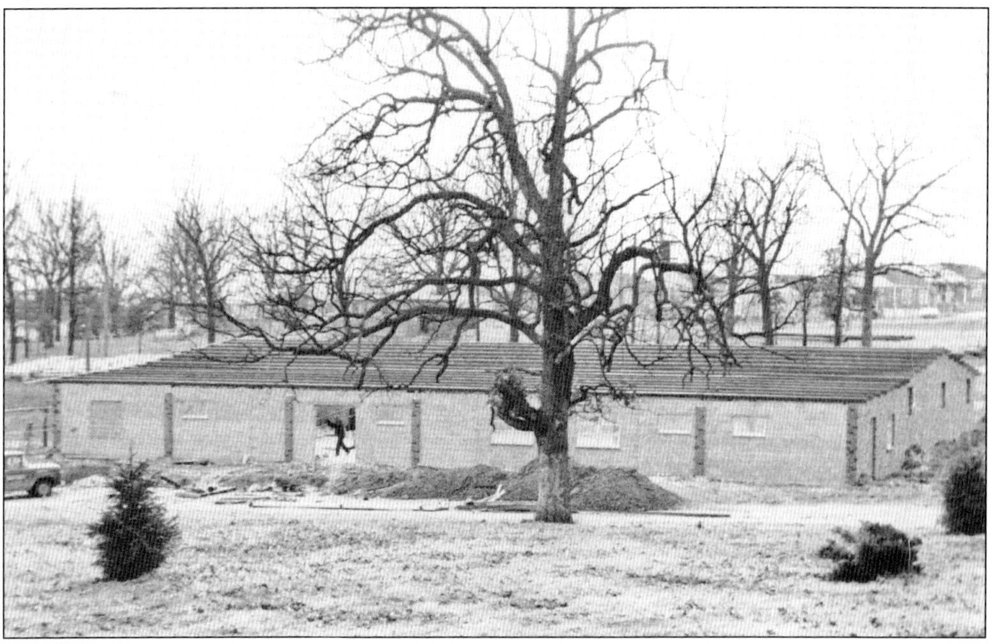

In 1962, the Wentzville Community Club began building a new roller rink, which developed into the current Community Club building on West Main Street. The club decided to sell its pavilion and property (which comprised a city block in the center of town) to a developer, who built a strip mall. Club leaders thought that the pavilion property could be better used to support businesses, create jobs, and generate tax revenue.

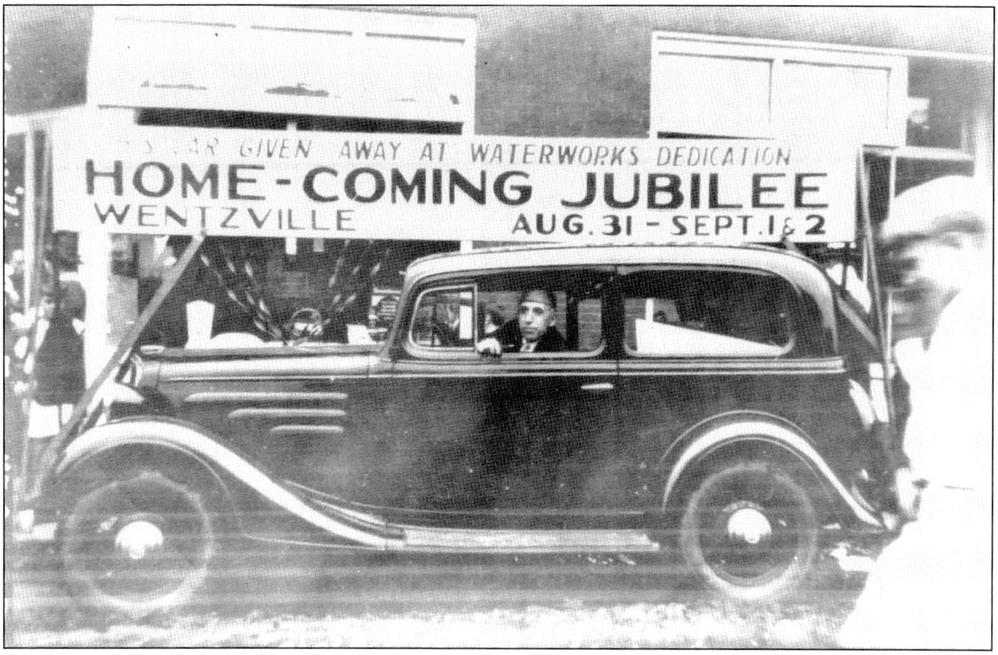

In 1935, after raising money for two years, the Wentzville Community Club had a townwide celebration to commemorate the new waterworks. The Homecoming Jubilee featured a carnival, stage shows, booths of every description, and much more. Each year the club raffled off a new car. Seen above in 1935, Emil Holt, a member of the Community Club and the school board, sits in the prize car. The celebration was so successful that it was held every Labor Day weekend for over 40 years. Below is a view of some of the booths and carnival rides in 1953. Ladies collected donations to fight polio, a dreaded disease of the time. The Homecoming Jubilee began to fade in the 1970s. People found other forms of entertainment, and the annual celebration was gone a decade later. (Below, Thelma Smock Chilton.)

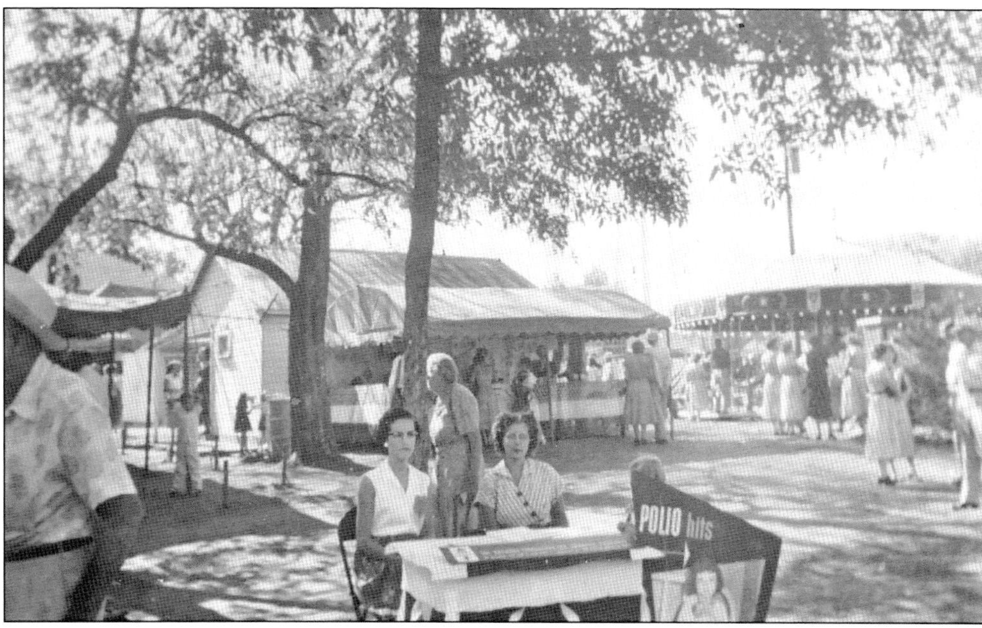

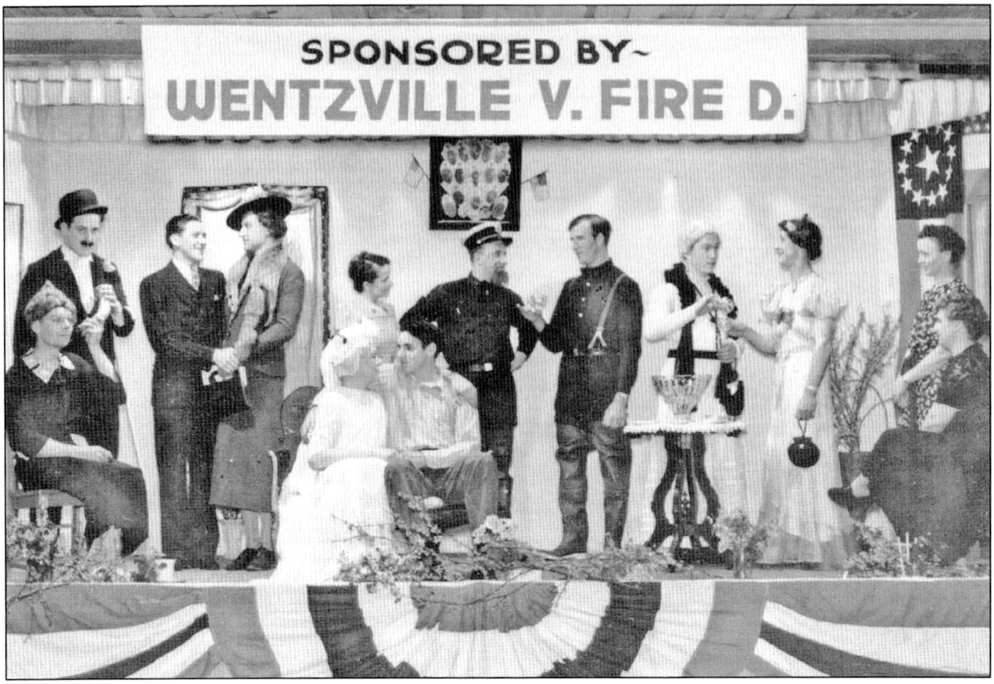

During the Homecoming Jubilee of 1935, the Wentzville Volunteer Fire Department put on a play in the St. Patrick's Church school hall. Money raised from the play and other activities was donated by the Community Club to the town or other worthy charities. (Adolph Buescher.)

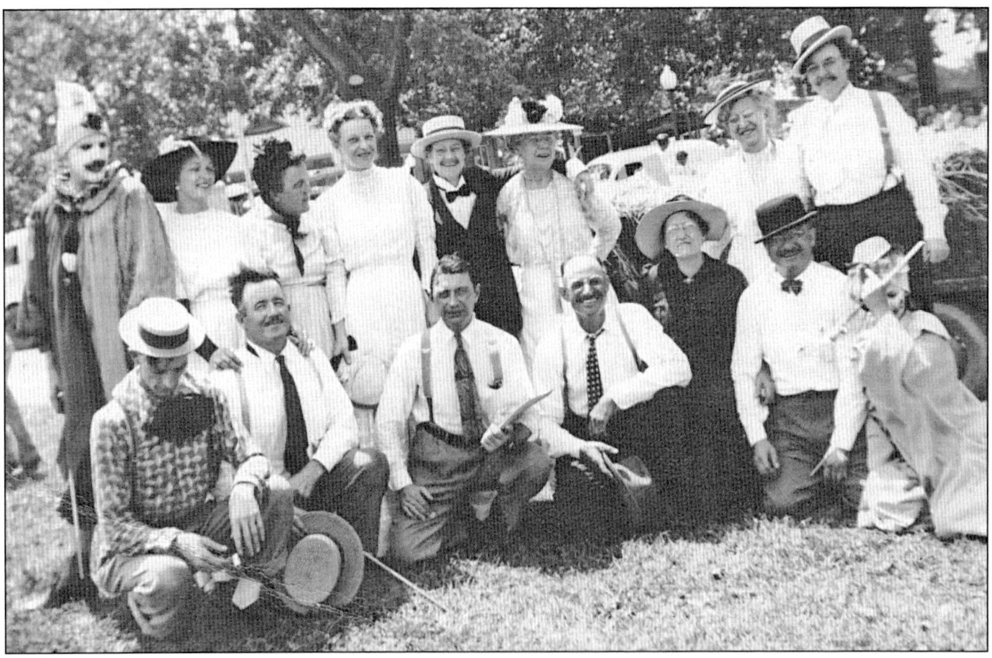

Homecoming was a busy time, especially for Community Club members, who volunteered their time the whole weekend. Club members are seen in 1955 ready to work. Many of the town's most prominent citizens and business owners are included. The clowns are John Eisenbath (standing on left) and Marie Dustman (kneeling on right).

"Aww Mom, can I please ride the Ferris wheel, please, please?" Taken at the 1937 Homecoming, this photograph shows the crowd enjoying the beautiful weather, taking time from their busy schedules, and watching the carnival. (Jim Roettger.)

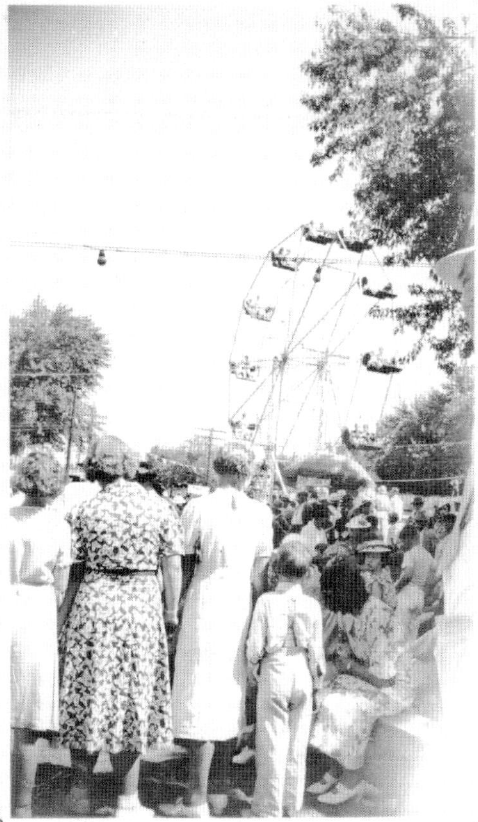

Games of chance were a big part of the Homecoming celebration every year. In 1937, the local Boy Scout troop sponsored and operated a ring toss booth. Even the children worked hard to raise money to help the Wentzville community. (Jim Roettger.)

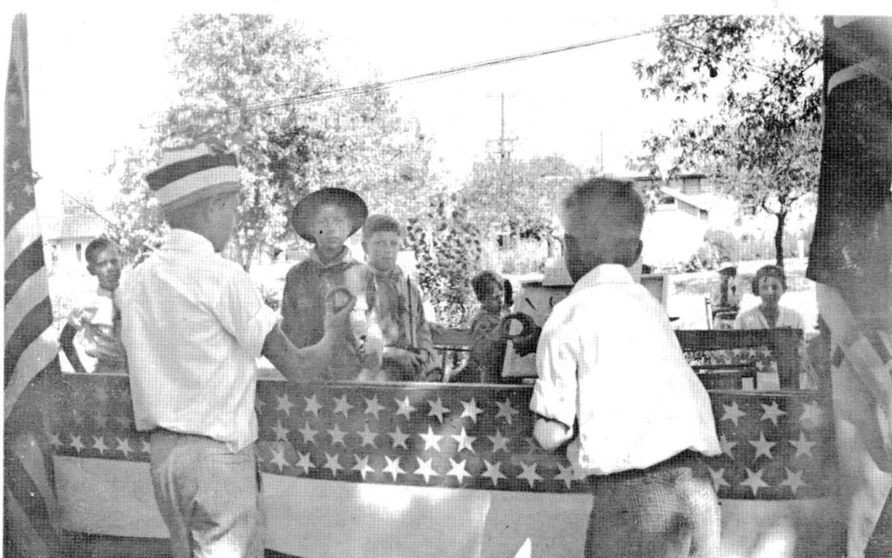

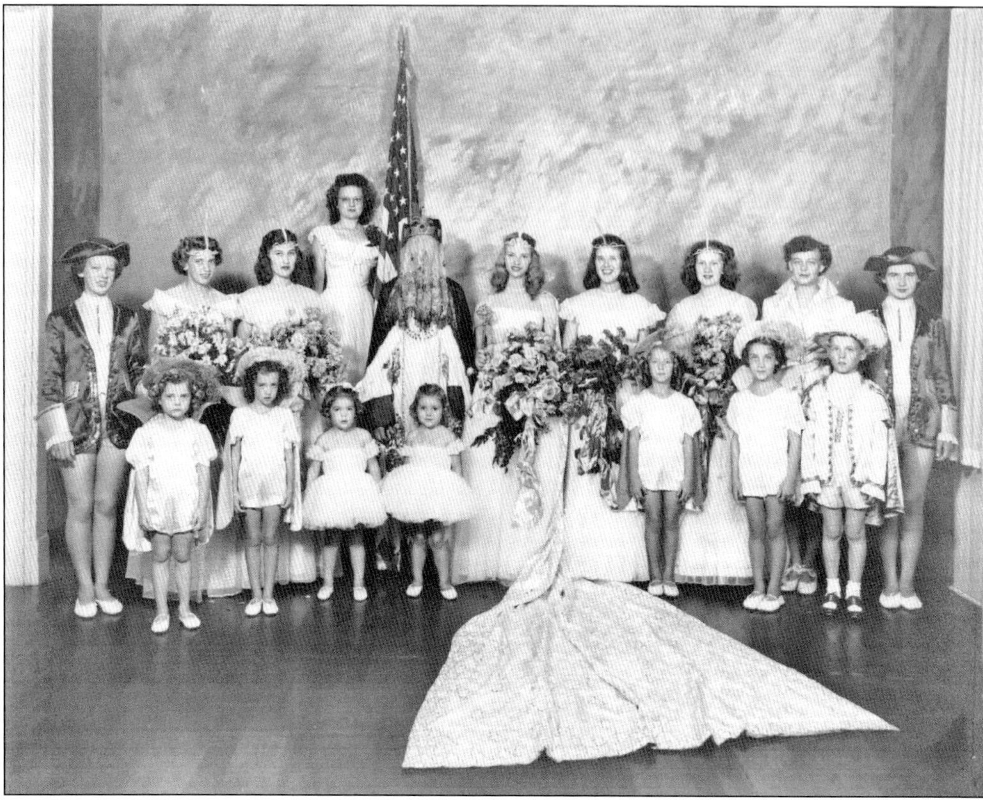

Homecoming queen Rosemary Diekroeger is shown with her court in 1948. Diekroeger is standing next to Community Club president Omar Neiderjohn. Neiderjohn is wearing the actual veil and robe worn by the Veiled Prophet, who presided over the Veiled Prophet Ball, held every year in St. Louis. The name of the Veiled Prophet Fair was changed to Fair St. Louis in 1992. (Rosemary Diekroeger Palmer.)

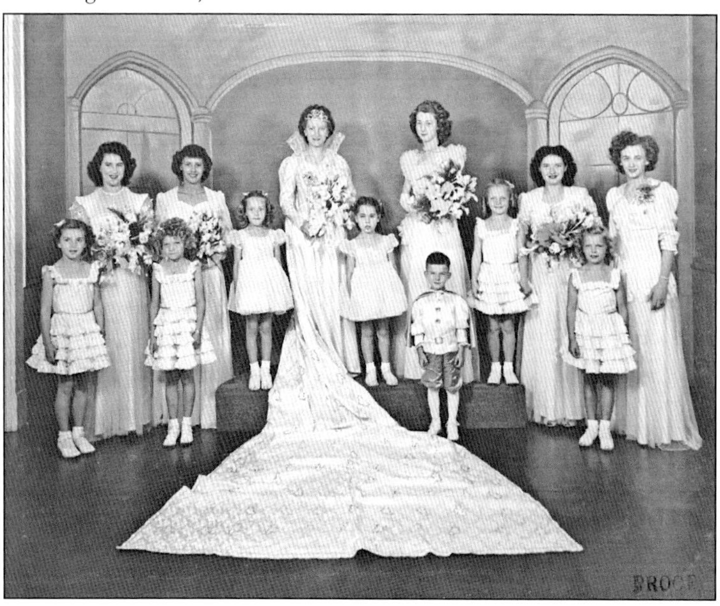

In 1945, Jeanette Rueter was named Wentzville Homecoming queen. She is shown here with her court of maids and pages. Queens for the Homecoming Jubilee were selected according to which young lady sold the most raffle tickets for the giveaway car or other large prize chosen for that year. (Jeanette Reese.)

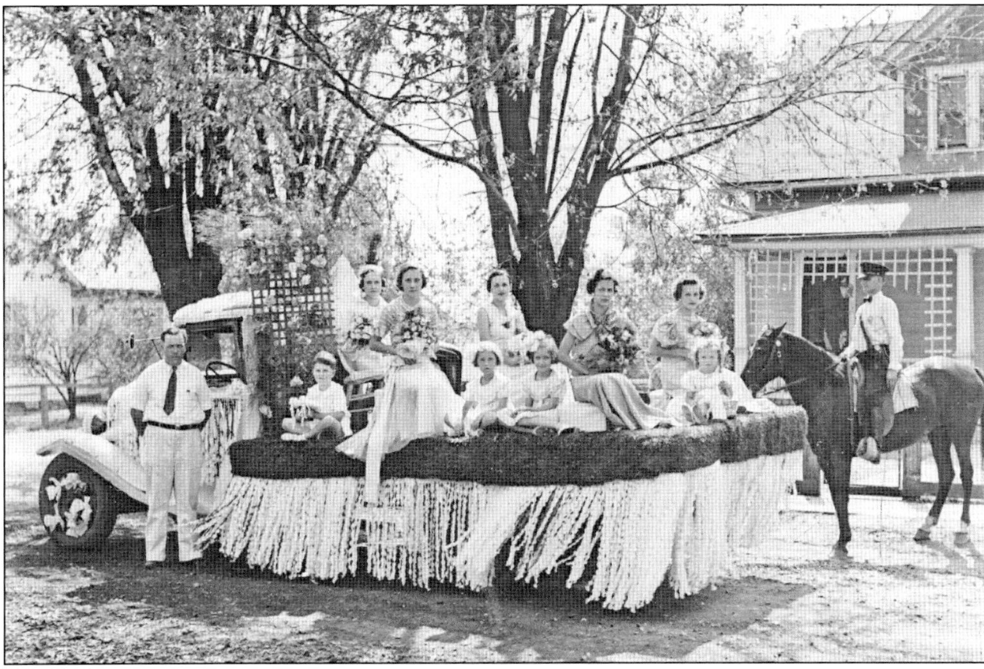

The Wentzville Community Club Homecoming parade was long and always had floats from businesses and organizations, along with a special float with the Homecoming queen and her court. These photographs were taken in the mid- to late 1930s. The queen float was often escorted by the city marshal. Above, Marshal G. Preston "Press" Heady accompanies the queen on horseback. The Heady family owned a longtime Wentzville landmark, the Heady Hotel.

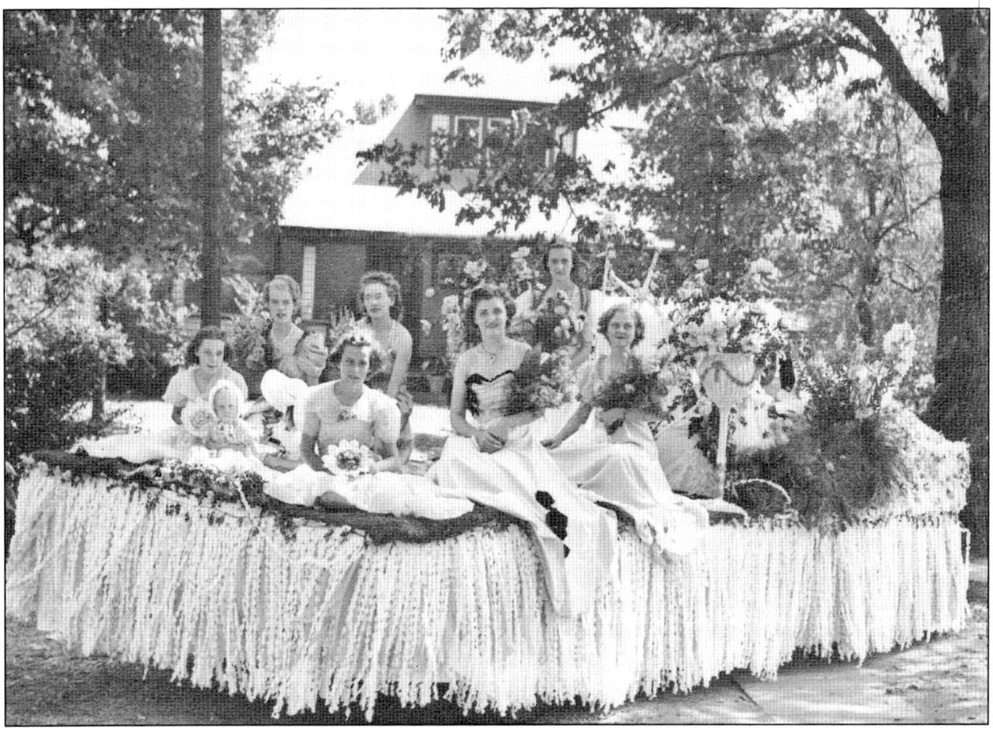

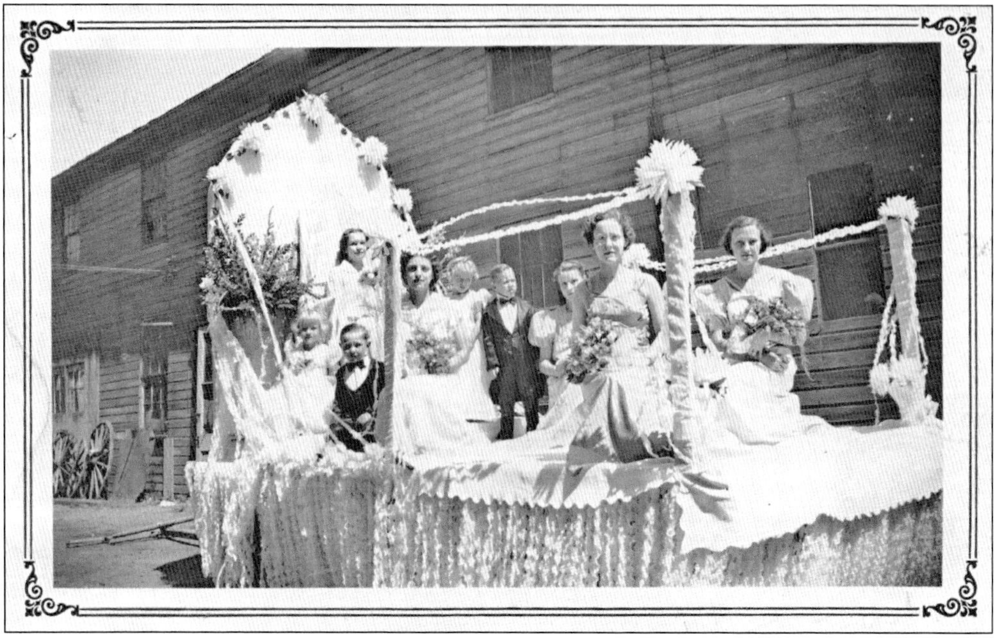

The 1937 Homecoming Jubilee queen float was driven by Louis J. Dubois using four white horses. The photograph below is another queen float from around 1940. In June 2008, the Community Club held a reunion of past queens. Sixteen attended: Elaine Rueter Swantner (1937), Arlene Jackson Kersting (1940), Jeanette Rueter Reese (1945), Melba Wilmer McCarver (1946), Rosemary Kiekroeger Palmer (1948), Darlene Sommers Pund (1949), Gwendolyn Schuchmann (1950), Geraldine Tochtrop Kerkemeyer (1951), Nancy Dickherber Frei (1953), Barbara Puff Wilmes (1955), MaryLou Brueggemann Kalleta (1958), Joyce Fearnley Dohack (1960), Pat Kammeier Dockler (1961), Maureen Miller (1962), Debra Miller Poeling (1964), and Marilyn Mispagel Birkenmeier (1965).

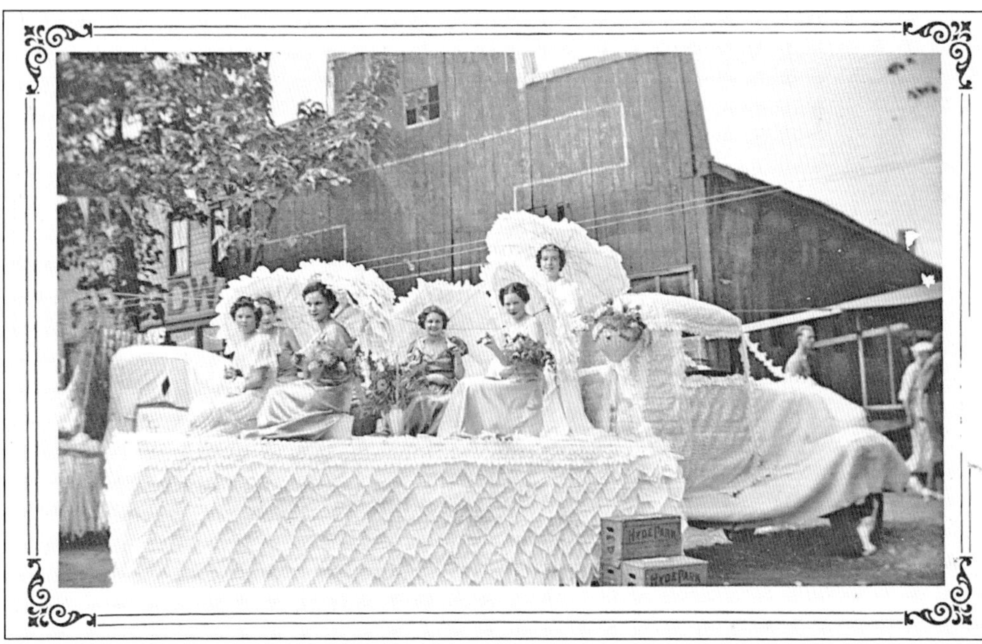

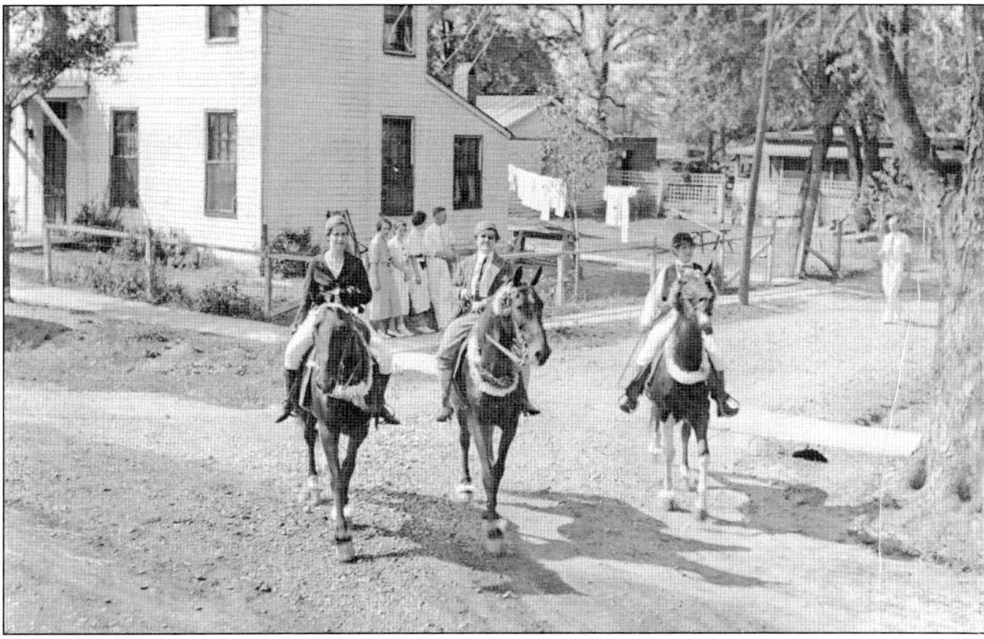

From left to right, Alma Heady, Meta Parr, and Dora Niederjohn were three of the volunteers who made the Homecoming Jubilee a success year after year. Alma was responsible for acquiring the Veiled Prophet costume, used for the queen's court. All three women were members of the Community Club and were leaders in the community.

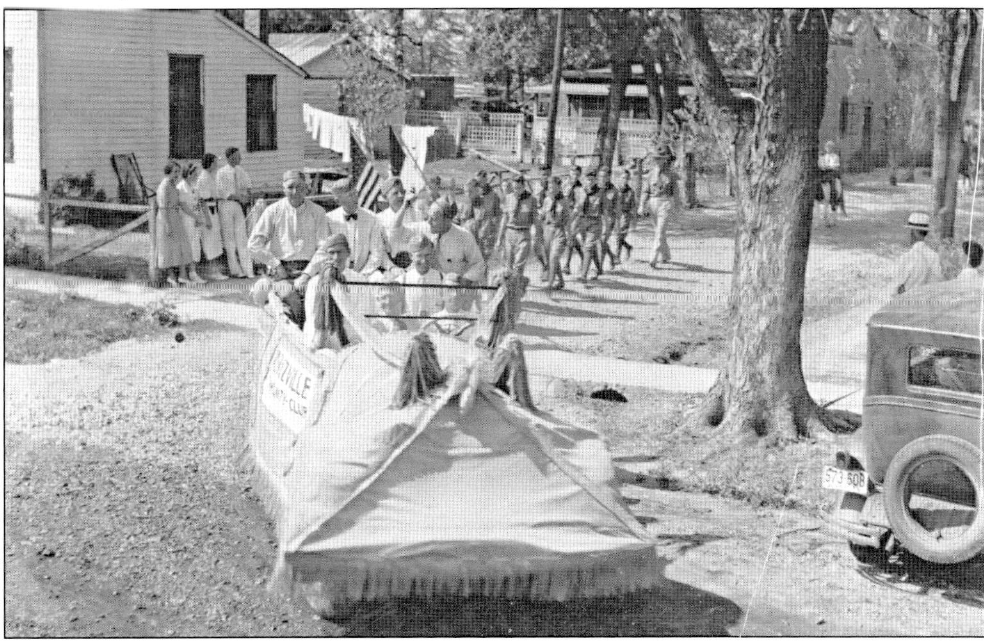

In 1935, for the first three-day Homecoming, the lead car consisted of Community Club board members and leaders of the community. From left to right are (front seat) Adolph Buescher and Clarence Schuemann; (back seat) Harvey Diekroeger and Elmer Minor; (sitting on top) Joe Kleeschulte, Charles Richards (Community Club president), Jerome Parr, and Mayor Jim Weir. The float was built on a 1930 touring car.

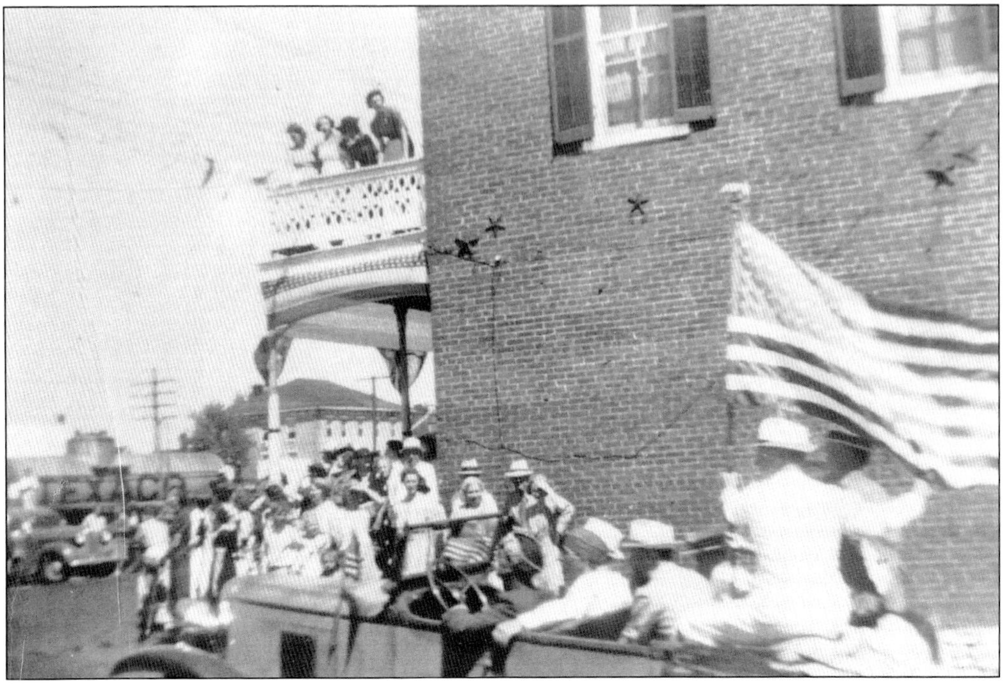

The Homecoming parade routes changed over the years. In 1937, as seen above, the lead car heads north on Church Street, getting ready to turn right onto West South Main Street in front of the railroad tracks. Onlookers on the second-floor balcony of the Wentzville Mercantile have a good view of most of the parade route. Across the railroad tracks, the old Wentzville House Hotel (also known as Heady Hotel) can be seen. Below, in 1935, Dr. W.C. Schroeder uses his personal car to advertise his office in the parade. "Doc" Schroeder, besides being Wentzville's chiropractor, also owned the phone company for many years. That building still stands at 205 East Allen Street.

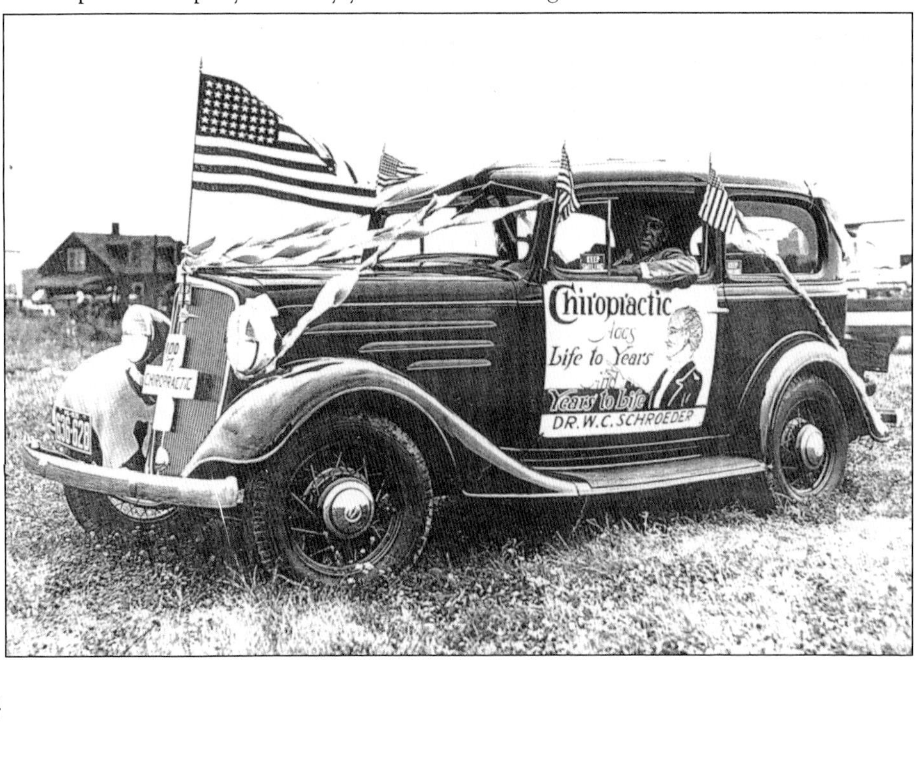

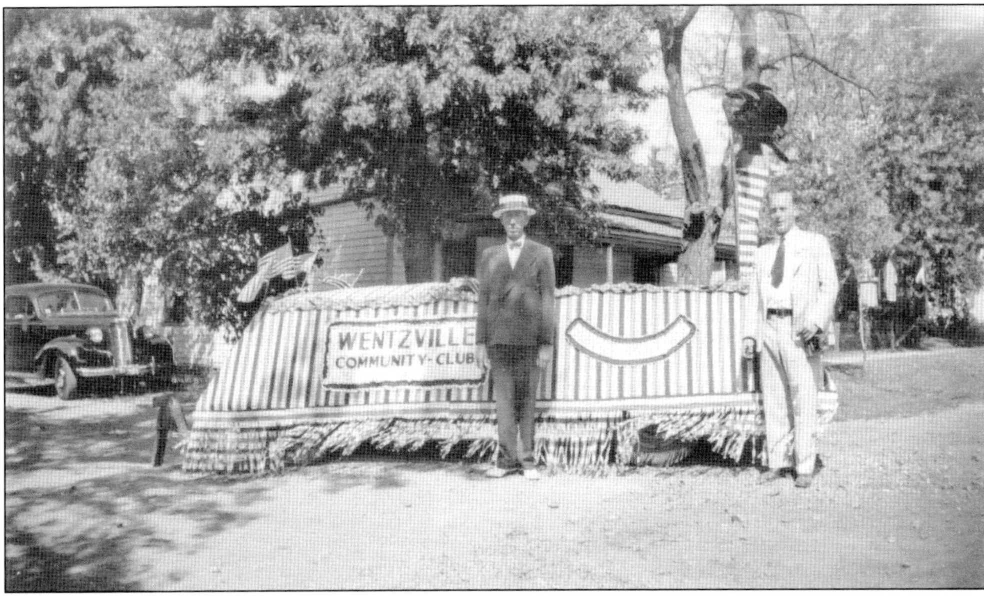

The slogan of the Wentzville Community Club, "Service above Self," appears on its float in the third Homecoming parade in 1937. Standing on the left is the first Community Club president, Charles Richards. On the right is club secretary Bob Brueggmann. Below, in 1958, four important Wentzville organizations work together to promote their causes with a float in the Fourth of July parade while celebrating Wentzville's slogan of "Crossroads of the Nation:" the Wentzville Chamber of Commerce, American Legion, Rotary Club, and Community Club. Thousands of red, white, and blue tissue paper flowers were made by hand to create this beautiful small-town float.

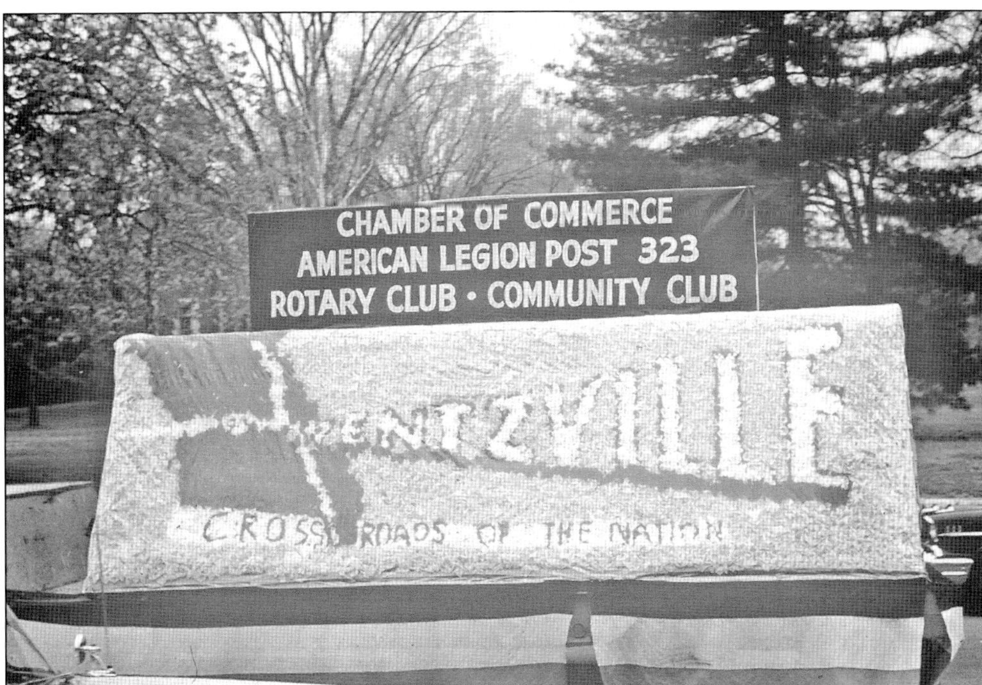

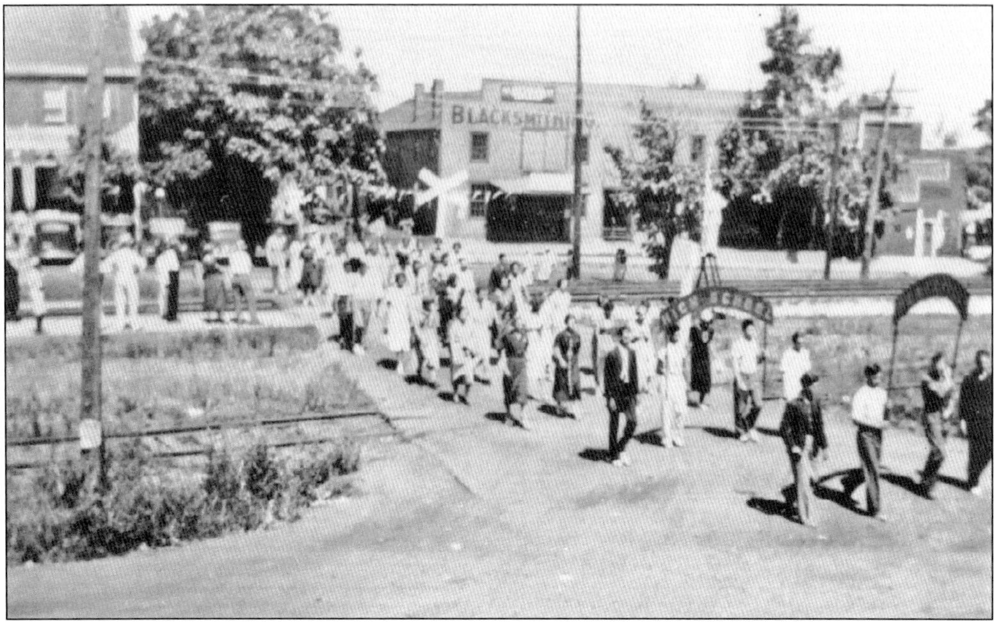

Photographs of Wentzville's Homecomings are useful for documenting the festivities but also for showing historians where long-gone buildings and landmarks once stood. In these photographs from 1935 (above) and 1937 (below), Rueters Blacksmith Shop can be seen, formerly the location of Schierbaum's Implement and Wagonmakers. This building was razed about 10 years later to make room for the American Theater. Most Wentzville citizens do not know there were once five railroad crossings between Allen Street (which was North Main Street) and South Main. North Linn Avenue is to the left of the Schierbaum home (far left in these photographs), but it did not connect to South Linn Avenue across the tracks until the 1940s. The man seen on the ladder was a railroad employee, alerting the parade participants of approaching trains. Many people were killed on these crossings over the years.

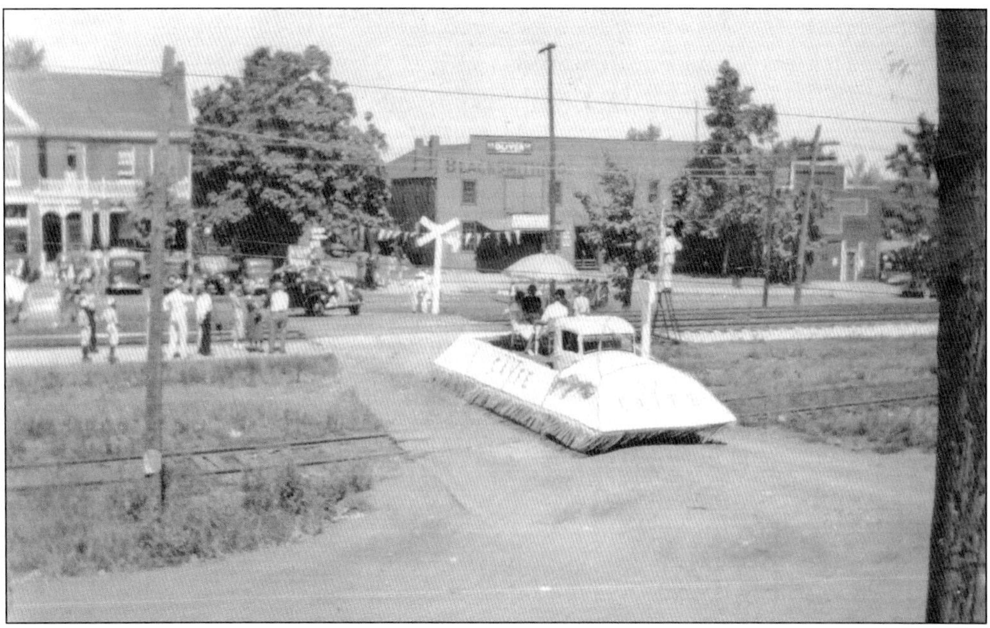

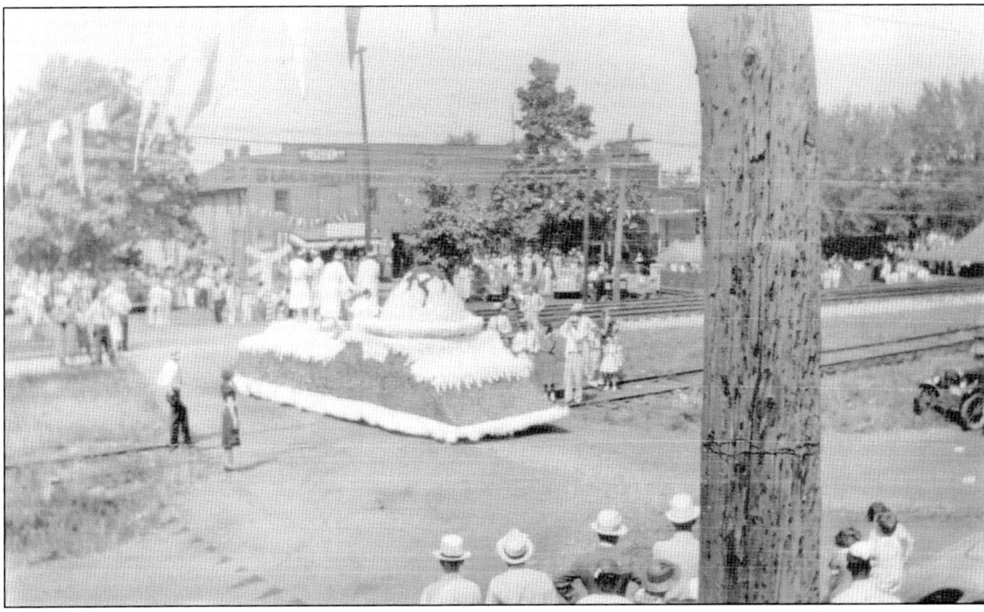

One of the many business floats in the 1937 Homecoming parade was from the Wentzville Creamery. Its claim to fame was the creation of Frozen Gold Ice Cream. The giant sundae on top of the float surely sent spectators in search of ice cream when the parade ended! (Roland Temme.)

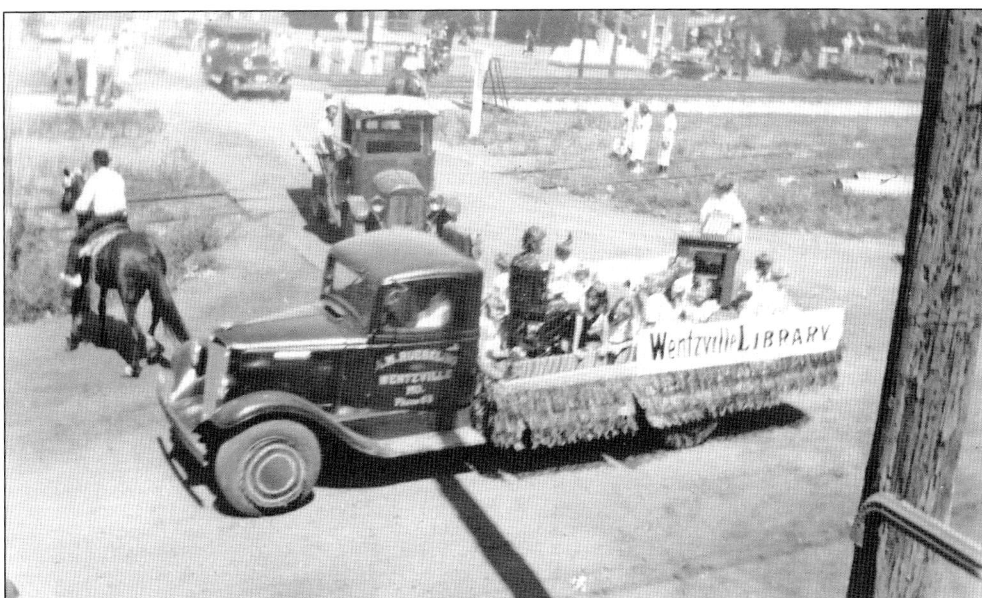

A.M. Ruebeling's flatbed truck serves as the platform for another 1937 float. The Wentzville Library has loaded its float with children listening attentively as the librarian leads story time (though some seem more interested in looking at the crowd). Notice the phone number on the side of the truck. To reach A.M. Ruebeling, dial 63.

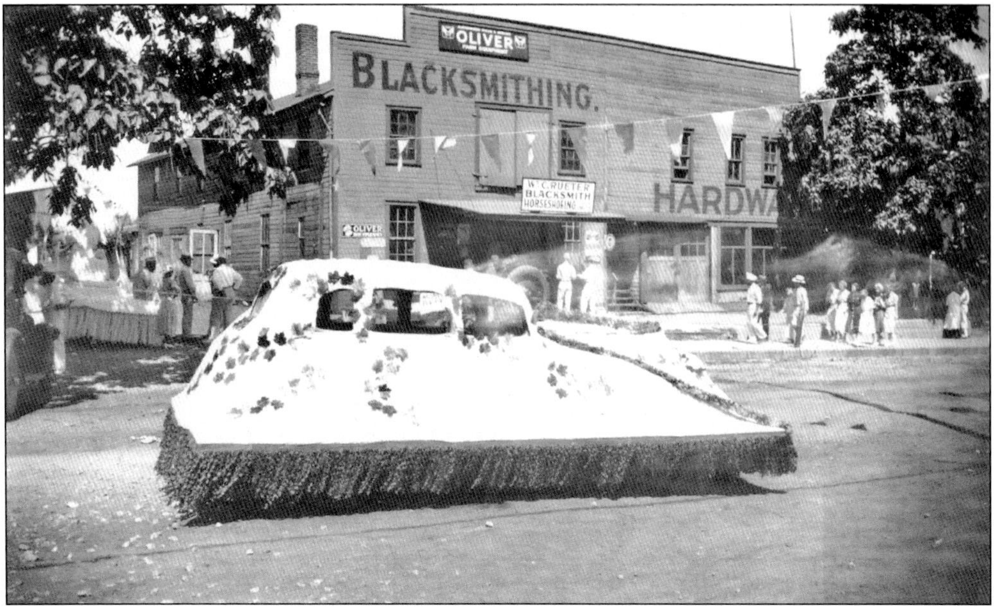

This 1937 Homecoming parade float was from the Karrenbrock Milling Company. It is about to make a careful turn to the right, over the railroad track, where it will pass the Reuters Blacksmith Shop, formerly the Schierbaum Implement and Wagonmakers building. (Jim Roettger.)

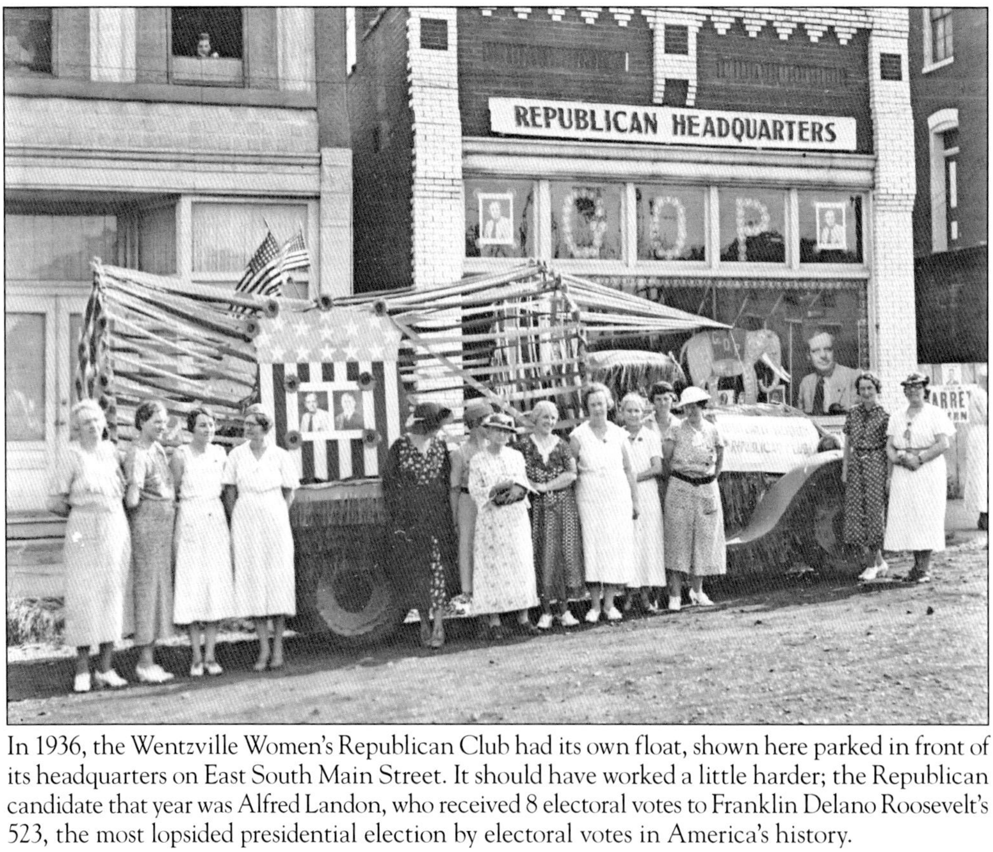

In 1936, the Wentzville Women's Republican Club had its own float, shown here parked in front of its headquarters on East South Main Street. It should have worked a little harder; the Republican candidate that year was Alfred Landon, who received 8 electoral votes to Franklin Delano Roosevelt's 523, the most lopsided presidential election by electoral votes in America's history.

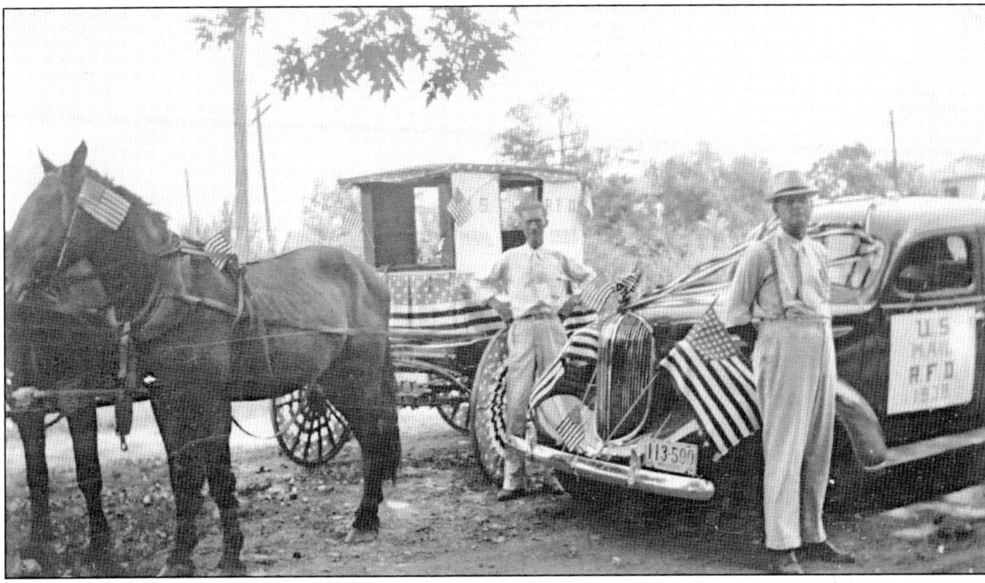

The old and the new clash in this photograph from the 1938 Homecoming parade. Frank Sommer is posing in front of Wentzville's horse-drawn mail wagon, used from 1908. Gus Ameling stands in front of his shiny new 1938 mail car. Thirty years of postal history were represented in the parade that day.

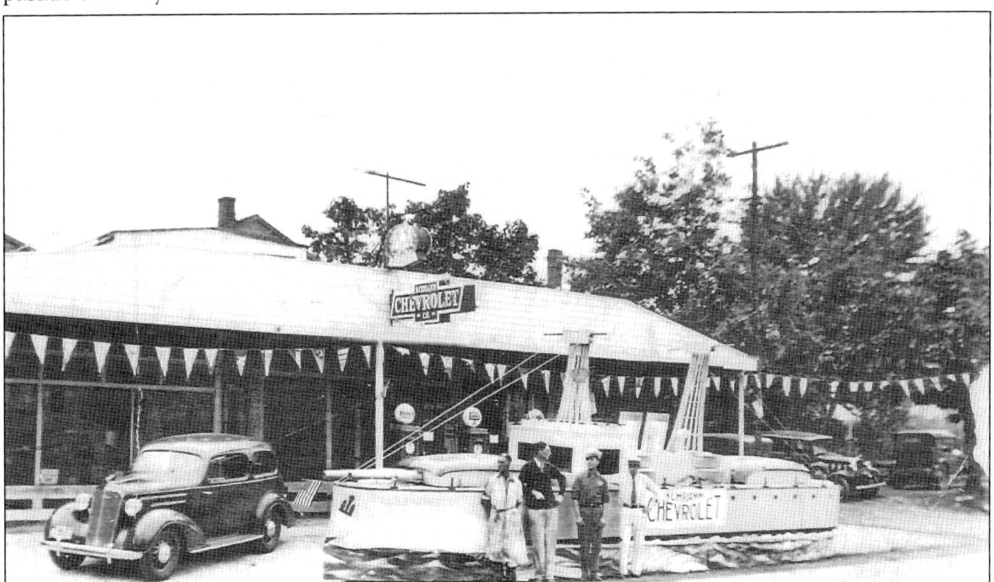

Not many people remember Schramm Chevrolet (currently Pogue Chevrolet) when it was located at the intersection of old Highway 40 (Pearce Boulevard) and North Linn Avenue. Owner "Dutch" Schramm stands with three of his employees in front of their 1935 battleship parade float.

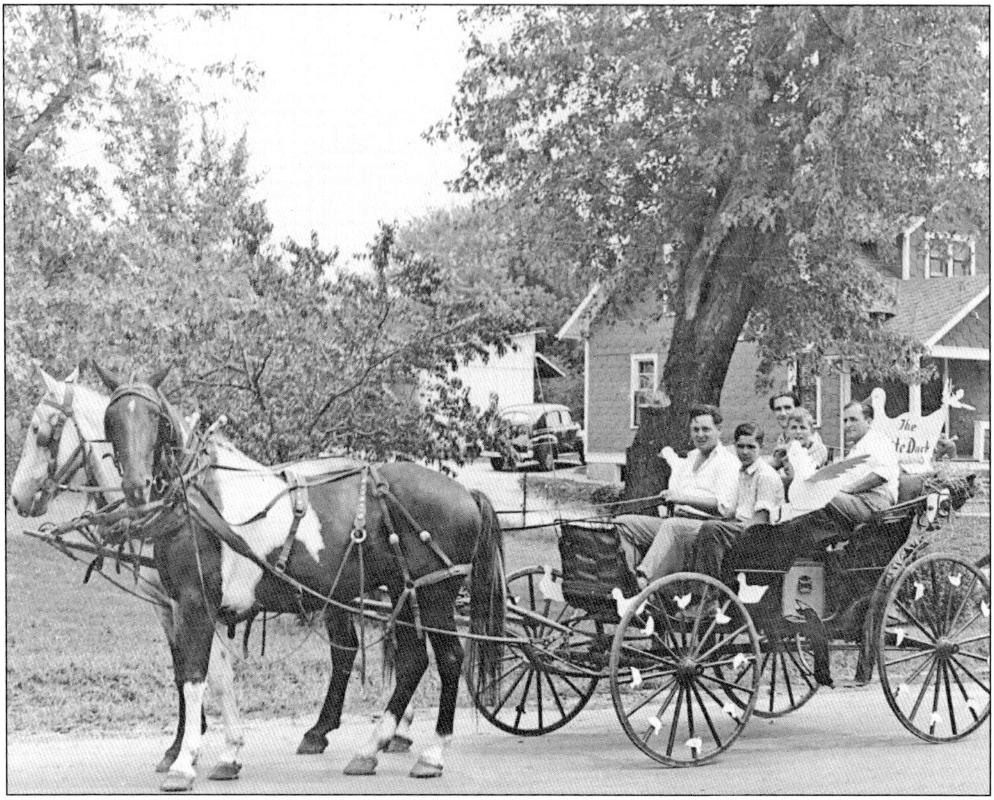

Charlie Willerding drives his White Duck restaurant team and wagon on Pearce Boulevard in the 1938 Homecoming parade. Notice the white duck cutouts on the back of the wagon and in the wheel spokes. The White Duck was one of the most popular restaurants in town. (Nancy Frei.)

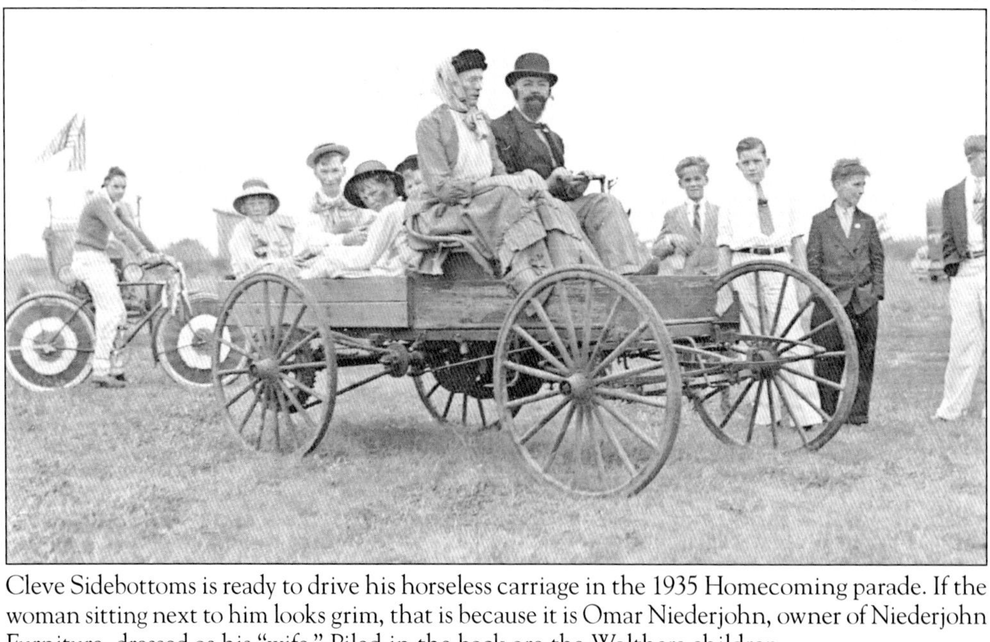

Cleve Sidebottoms is ready to drive his horseless carriage in the 1935 Homecoming parade. If the woman sitting next to him looks grim, that is because it is Omar Niederjohn, owner of Niederjohn Furniture, dressed as his "wife." Piled in the back are the Walthers children.

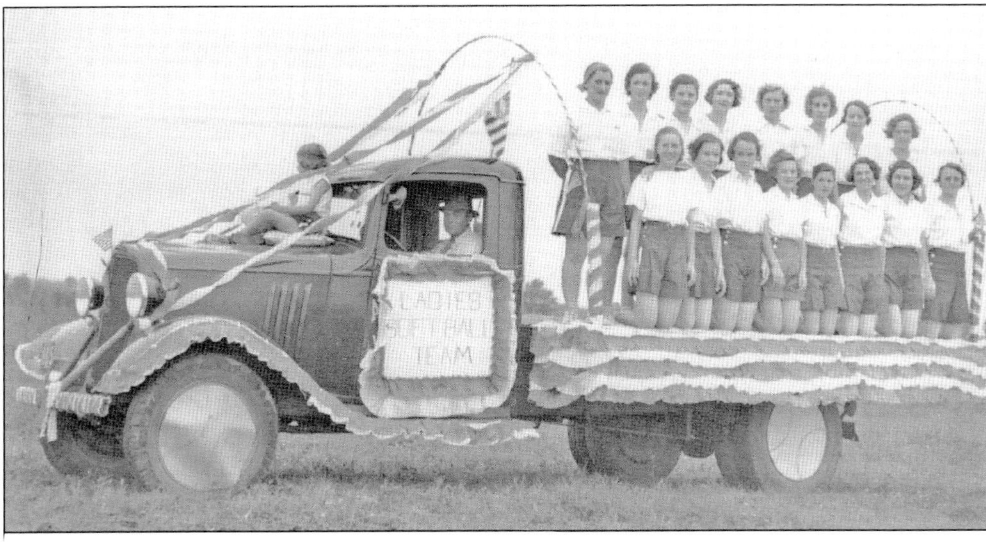

Another familiar entry in the annual Homecoming parade was the Wentzville ladies' softball team. Third from the right in the back row is longtime community-minded volunteer and Community Club member Viola Mispagel (later Boland). Below is the float for Niederjohn Furniture Company, owned by Omar Niederjohn. It produced beautifully handcrafted and carved solid walnut furniture. Samples of its work line the length of the float. (Above, Adolph Buescher.)

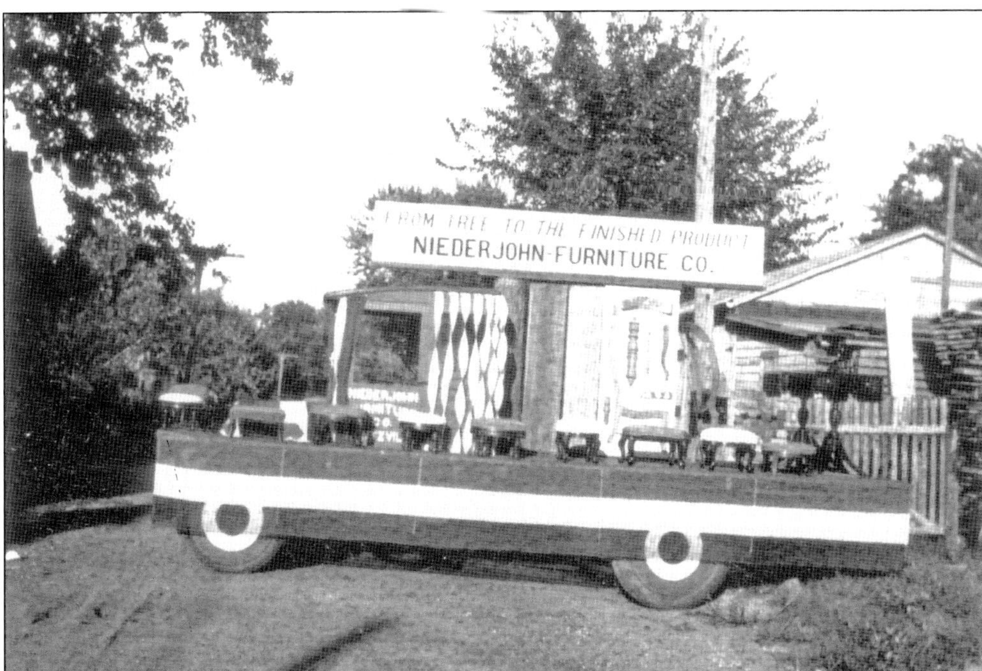

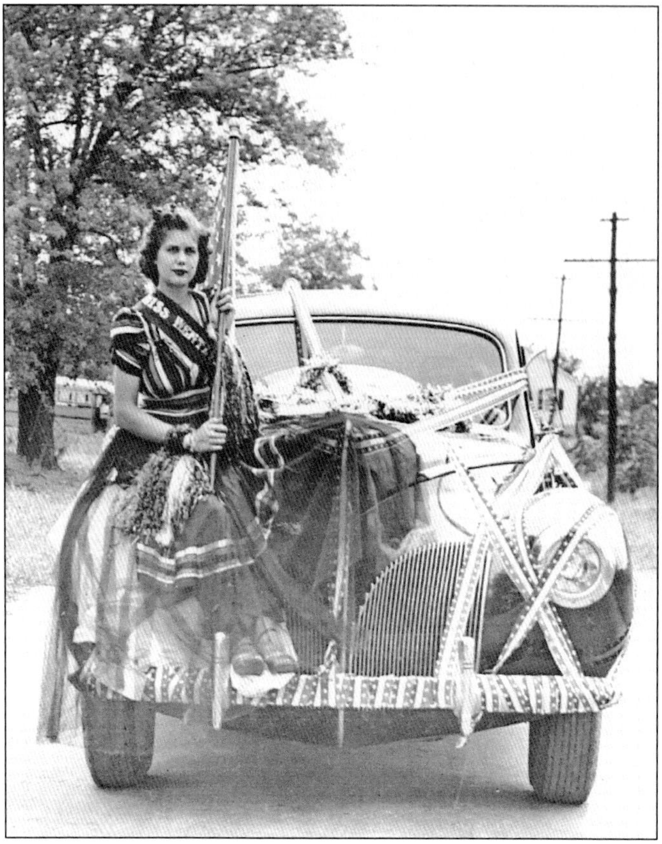

Community Club members were never afraid to be inventive; some years during Homecoming, a Miss Wentzville was chosen in addition to the queen. For Homecoming 1941, Thelma Chilton was named Miss Wentzville and participated in the parade by carrying the US flag while riding on the fender of a car. In 1942, a Miss Victory was also crowned. Below, in 1936, Santa Claus was a popular parade entry riding on the back of the Wentzville fire truck. The truck is parked in front of Jerome Parr's garage on Linn Avenue. Santa is posing with Charles Richards (left), president of the Wentzville Community Club, and G. Preston Heady, city marshal and Community Club sergeant of arms.

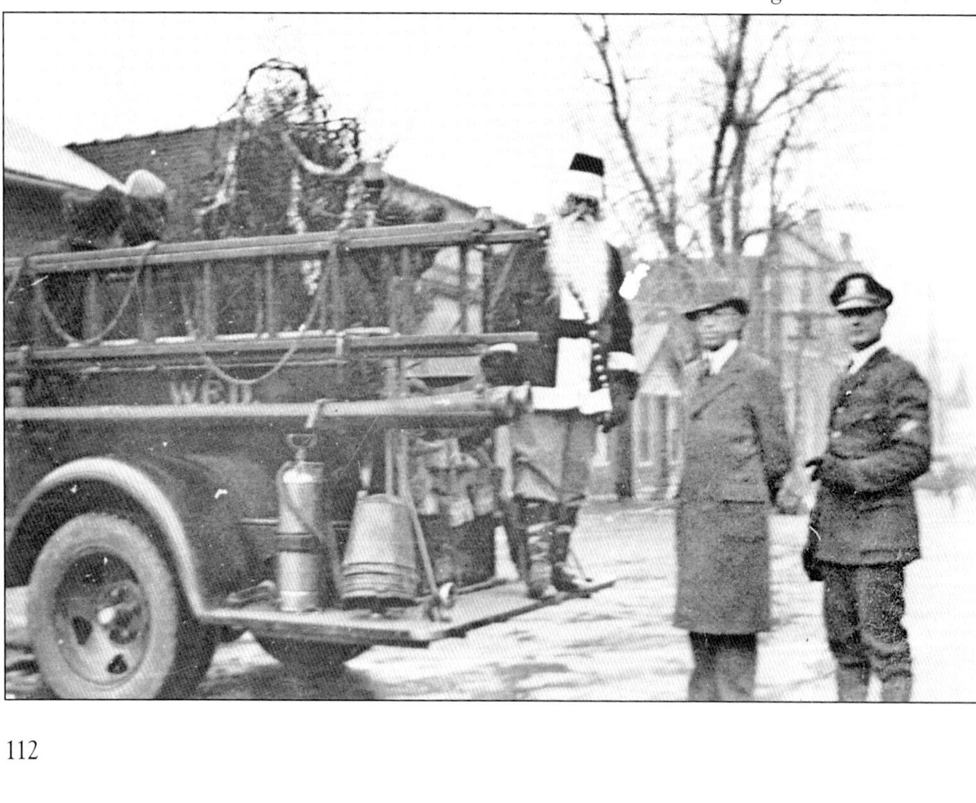

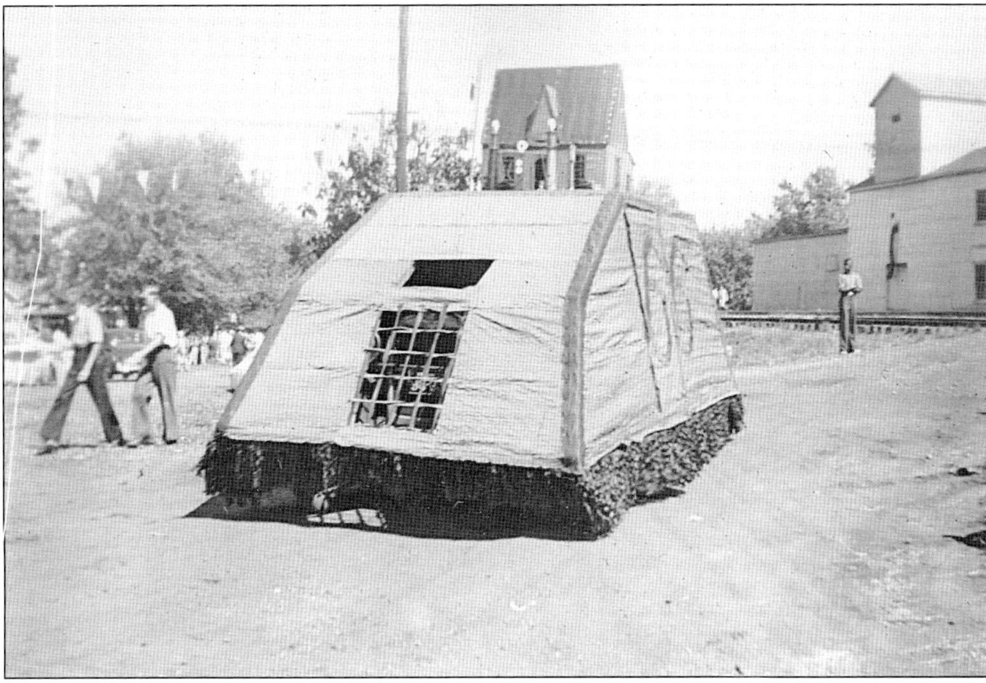

The Phillips 66 service station float has crossed the tracks and is making a left onto West North Main Street (now West Allen Street). Look closely at the top of the float to see a miniature replica of the station, exactly as it looked on the corner of Old Highway 40 (now Pearce Boulevard) and Linn Avenue (see page 56). (Mary Moritz.)

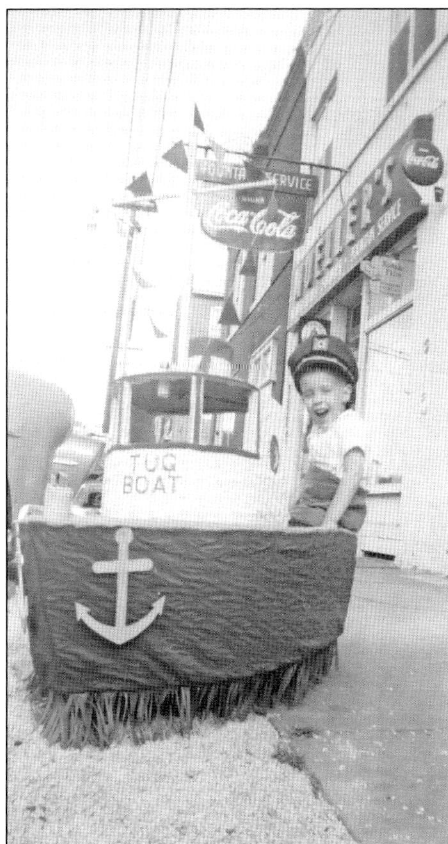

One of the most popular features of the annual Homecoming was the kiddie parade. Wayne Temme is ready for the 1957 festivities in his tugboat float, waiting in front of Mueller's Drugstore. Both adults and children went to great lengths to make Homecoming and the accompanying parades a huge success by creating ornate floats and volunteering where needed. (Roland Temme.)

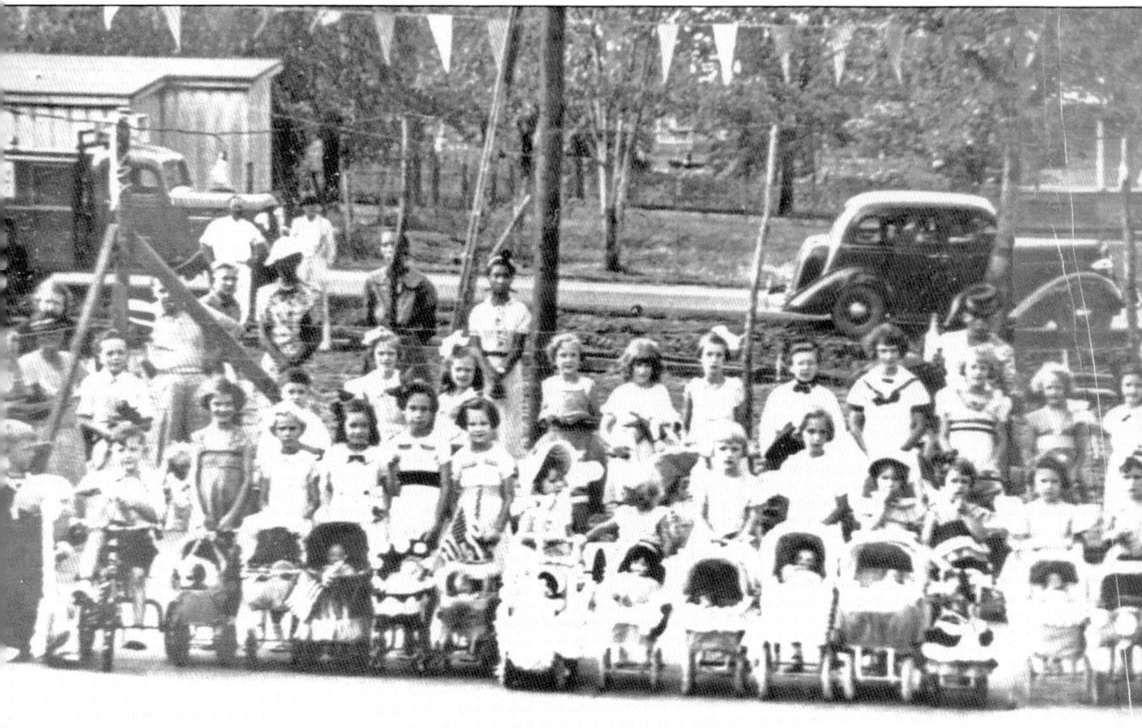

This rare panoramic photograph, taken in 1935, shows the kiddie parade entries. The population of Wentzville was around 1,200 at that time, so nearly every kid in town must have participated. The girls decorated their doll carriages, and the boys decked out their tricycles and bicycles.

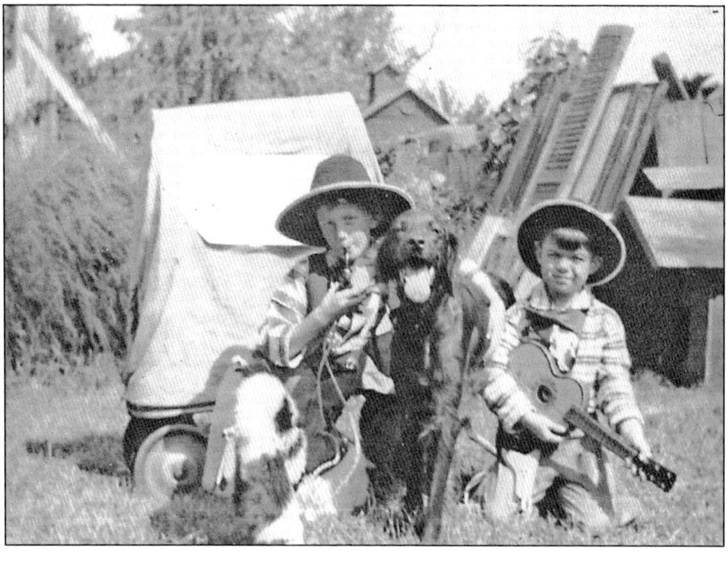

Hurley Carter Jr. (left), Jimmy Kelley, and an Irish setter named Old Red pose in front of their entry for the 1938 Homecoming kiddie parade. Dressed as cowboys, they set up their pup tent on an American flyer wagon, which was pulled by the dog. Their covered wagon and costumes won them first place. Even Old Red looks happy with the win. (Arlene Jackson Kersting.)

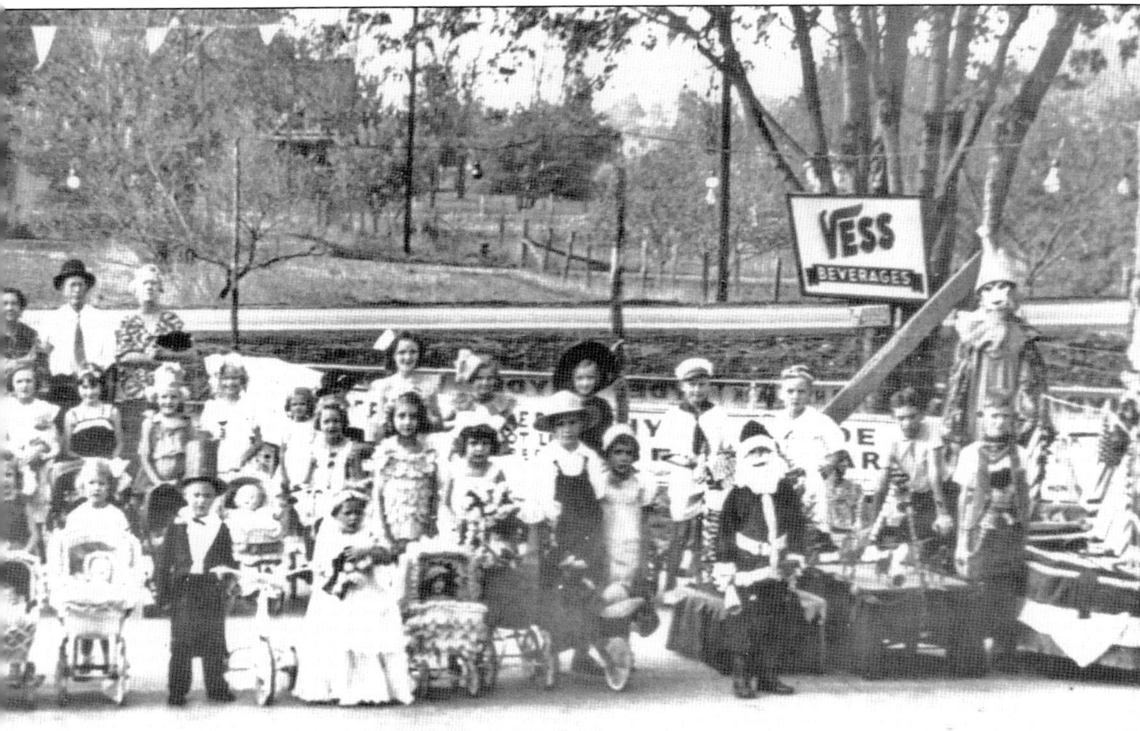

Their parade took place on a parking lot, where the boys and girls were judged on their creations and costumes.

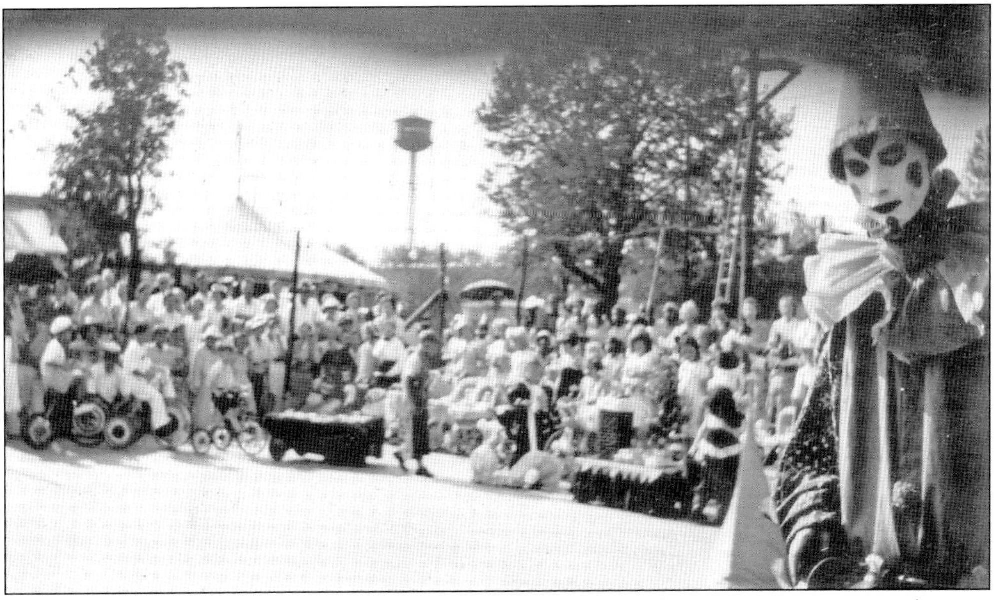

An eerie clown lurks over the kiddie parade judging in 1935. The new water tower can be seen in the background. The money raised in the early years of the Community Club's Homecoming Jubilees was spent on bringing a waterworks system to Wentzville. The kids are seen riding, pulling, or pushing their kiddie parade entries.

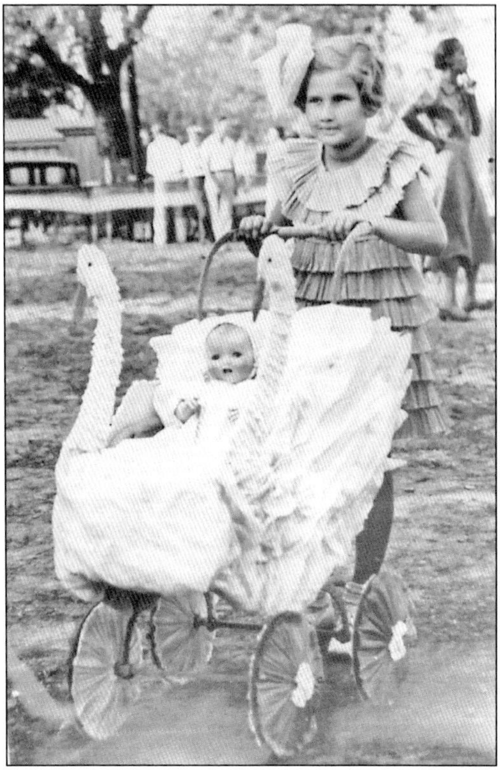

A young Glenda Temme was proud when she and her doll won first place in the 1935 Homecoming kiddie parade doll buggy contest. This photograph of her swan doll carriage (and her oversized hair bow) made it into the *St. Louis Post Dispatch* newspaper.

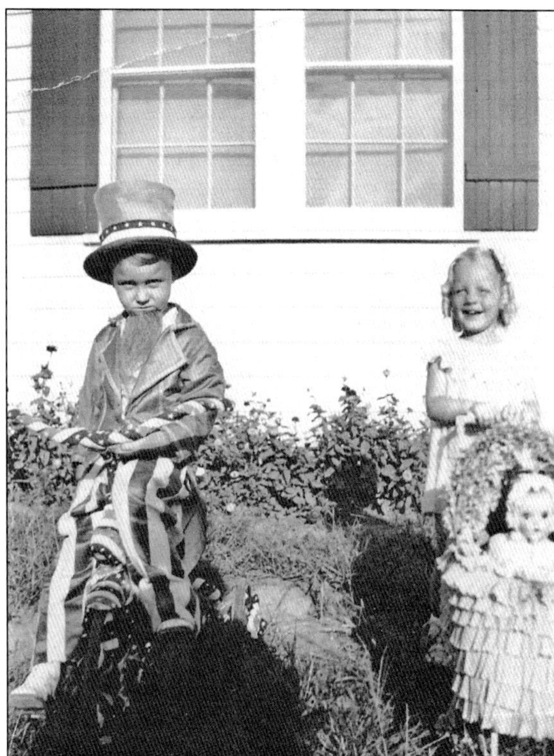

Donnie and Carol Shramm show off their entries to the kiddie parade in 1938. Carol decorated her doll buggy with ruffles, and her brother Donnie opted to go as Uncle Sam, complete with a beard and a bicycle festooned with stars and stripes.

Eight

Country Life

Immigrants began settling in western St. Charles County in the area that would become Wentzville in the 1820s. Well-known people like Daniel Boone and Lewis and Clark were here, but most of the immigrants were pioneers from Virginia and other eastern states, as well as from Europe, especially Germany. These men and women subscribed to the words of Horace Greely, "Go west, young man," and decided to lay down roots in Missouri.

Gradually, farmers and businessmen settled on the prairie, and villages began popping up along the Missouri River. Tobacco farms and plantations dominated the area until the latter part of the 1800s; the tobacco industry declined in the decades after the Civil War.

One of the largest tobacco plantations was owned by Missouri state senator William M. Allen, considered the founder of Wentzville. Allen was a member of the Whig party and was a strong supporter of the Confederacy. Unfortunately, most of the owners of Wentzville's larger farms kept some slaves.

The Civil War changed the way Wentzville did business. After the Battle of Wentzville, Allen and others were arrested and taken to prison in St. Charles. His plantation was seized by the US Army, and his property and home were sold on the courthouse steps.

The village continued to grow slowly in the years after the war, and the people of Wentzville began to heal from the wounds. Wentzville citizens in town and surrounding rural areas took a big step forward in 1872 when they voted to incorporate. As time went on, people got down to the business of living their lives and working their farms and businesses. Their creativity and entrepreneurial spirit helped them to move on and left some great images of their everyday lives, as seen in this chapter.

The strong work ethic and love of friends and family catapulted Wentzville citizens into the 20th century and helped the town survive the aftermath of the war. This spirit lives on today and has made Wentzville one of the fastest-growing cities in the country, but its people remain connected to the town's history.

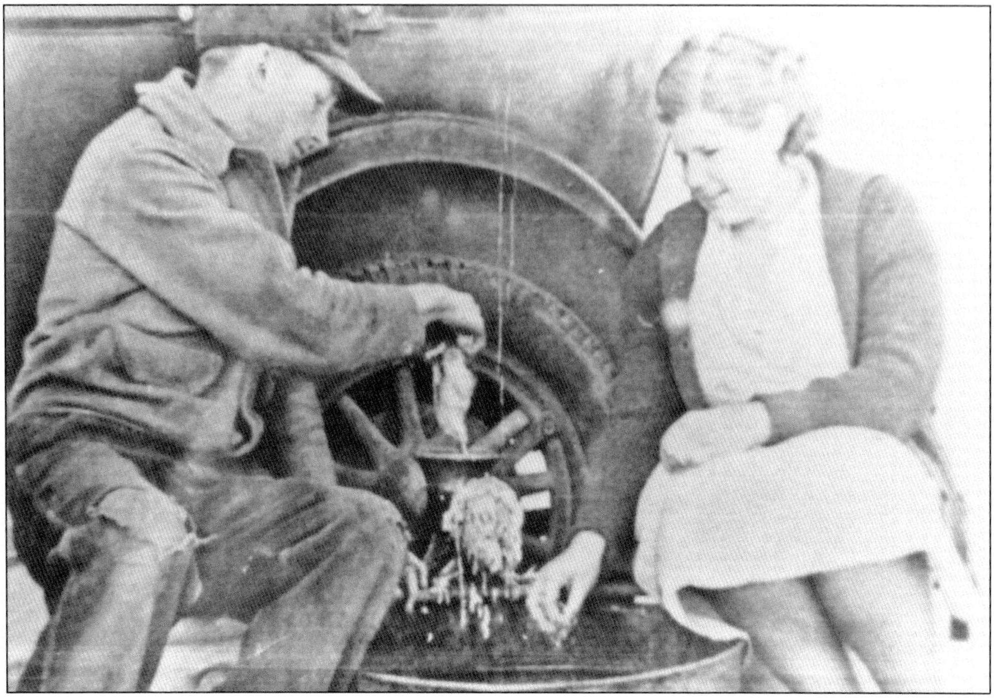

Life was hard in the early 20th century; most chores were labor intensive, unless citizens were inventive. This Wentzville couple used their Ford Model T to streamline their lifestyle by turning the rear wheel into an auto-powered meat grinder. Below, some resourceful family figured out how to jack up their Ford and use an old thrasher belt to power the wringer on their washing machine. Tricks like these gave people a little extra time and energy to enjoy Wentzville and its amenities, like the picnics and festivals or the movies that used to be shown behind Freese's barn on Saturday nights before the American Theater came to town.

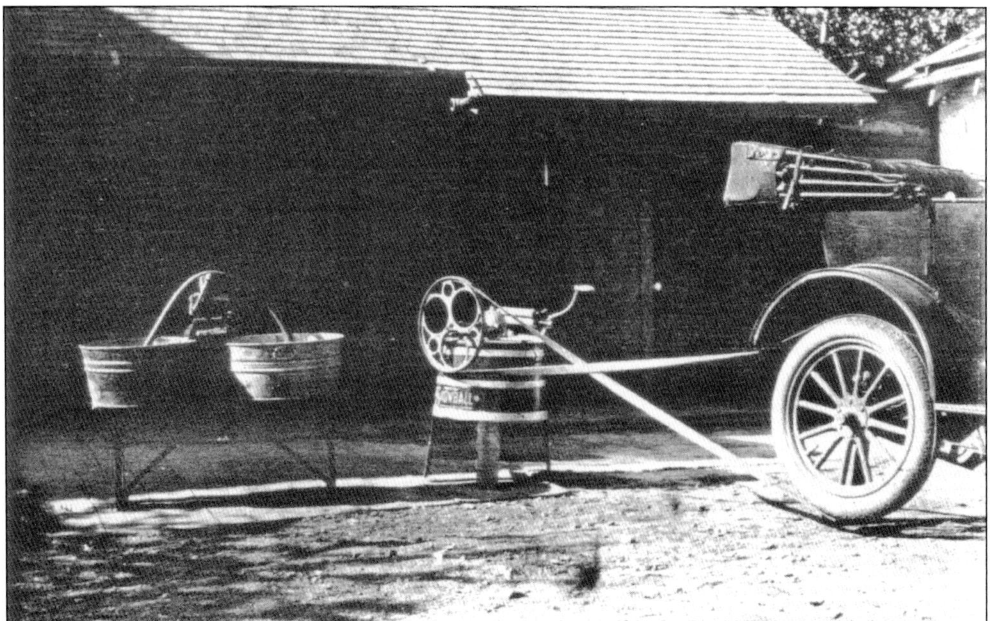

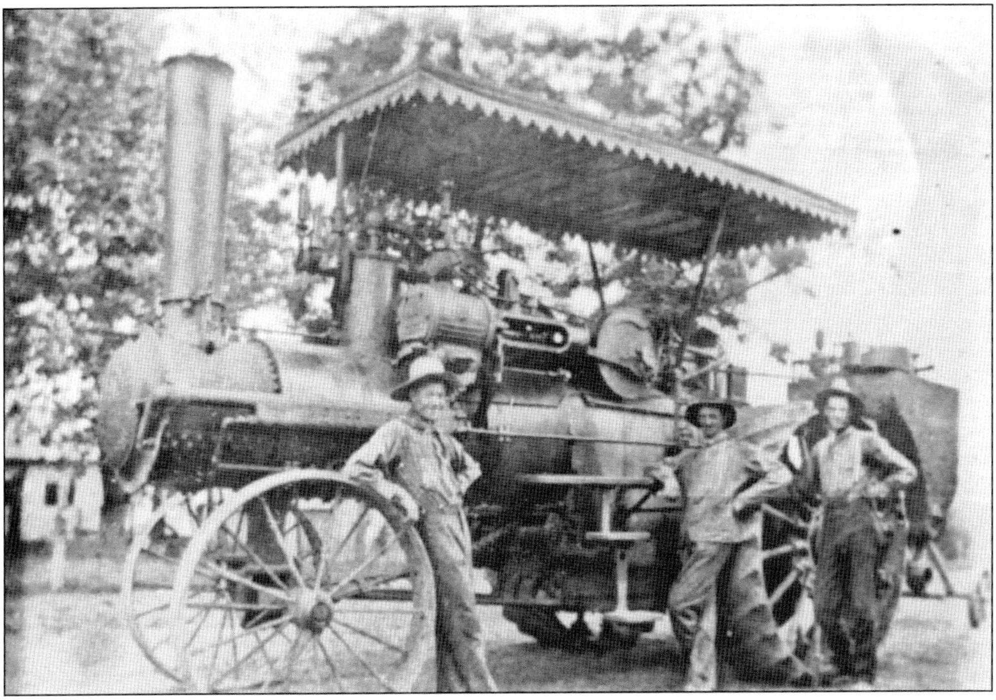

This farmer is grinning from ear to ear as he poses with his farmhands in front of his new steam tractor. No more hitching up a team to get the work done; he only had to saw down a tree and split wood to fuel it while his work horses lazed away their days munching on clover in the back 40. The picture below, taken around 1905, shows a thrashing party. People in those days pitched in to help each other, whether they were thrashing, digging a well, or raising a barn. They could always count on their neighbors to help with whatever needed to be done.

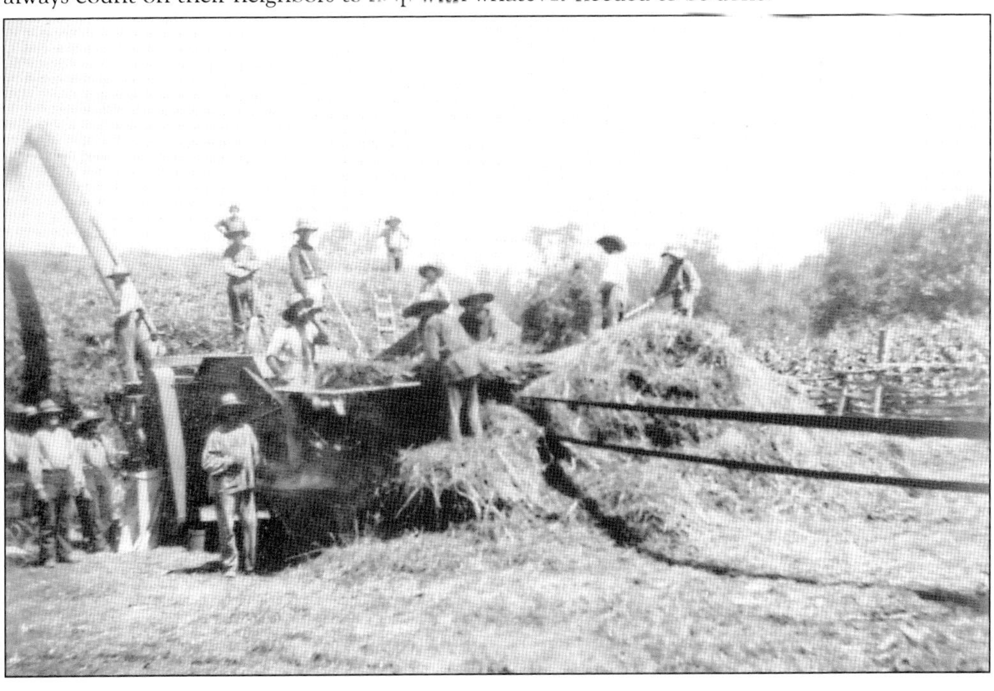

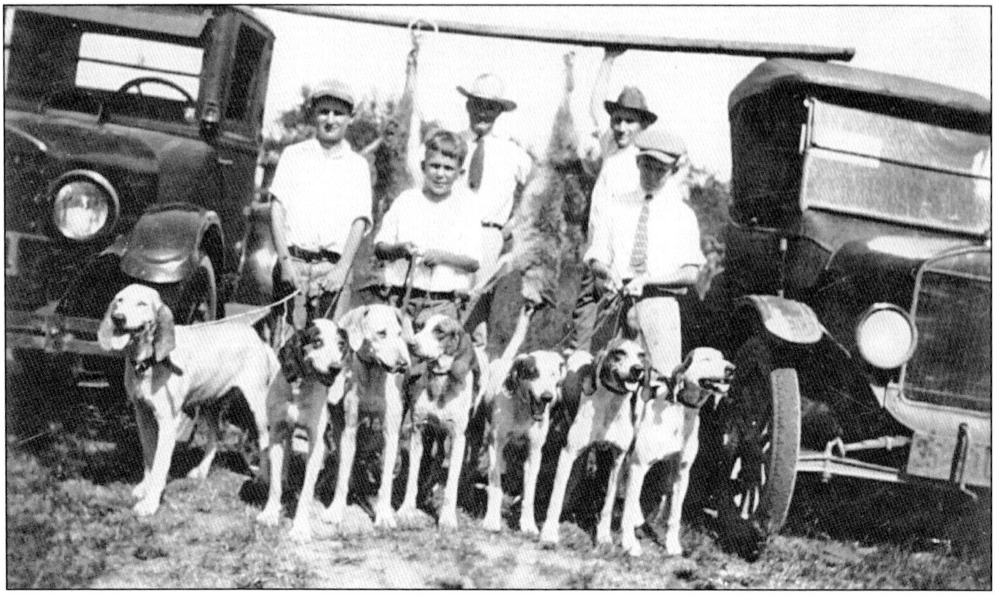

When the weekend came, Sam Anselm (second from right) and his good friend city marshal G.P. Heady headed for the woods with their dogs in search of fox, coyote, quail, rabbit, or squirrel. They are shown here after a successful fox hunt in the early 1930s. (Rick and Maxine Anselm.)

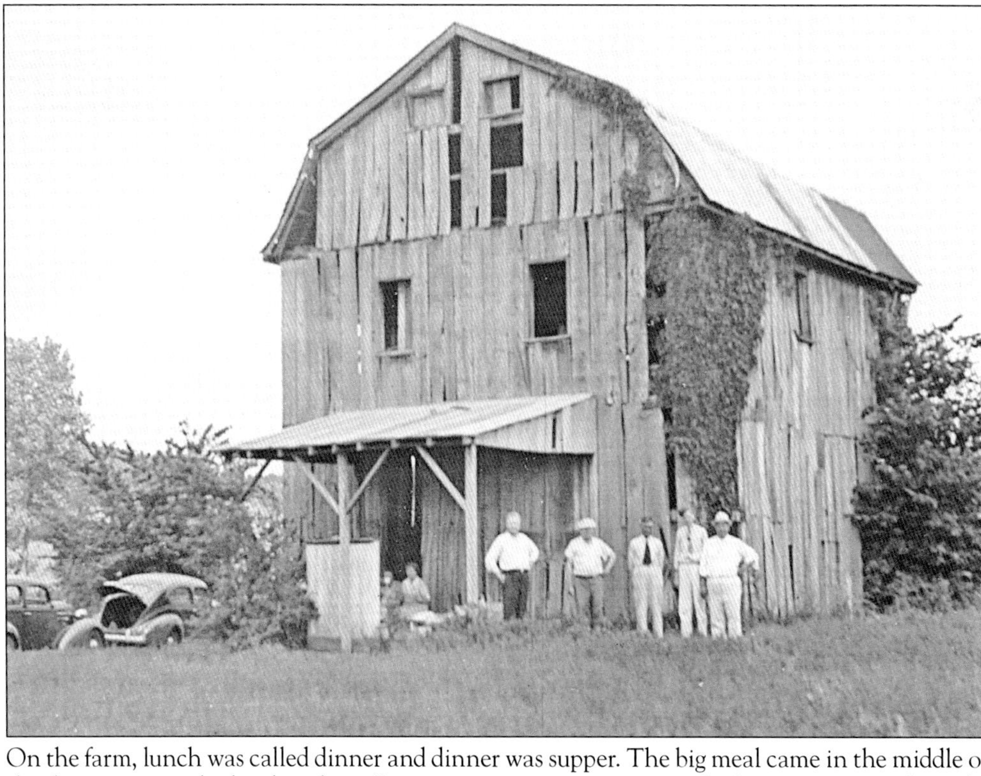

On the farm, lunch was called dinner and dinner was supper. The big meal came in the middle of the day to sustain the hard workers. Sometimes, to save time or just for fun, a picnic was brought out to the field or to the barn, usually with fried chicken and iced tea. Here, a family dines under the awning of the old barn. (Maxine Anselm Haynes.)

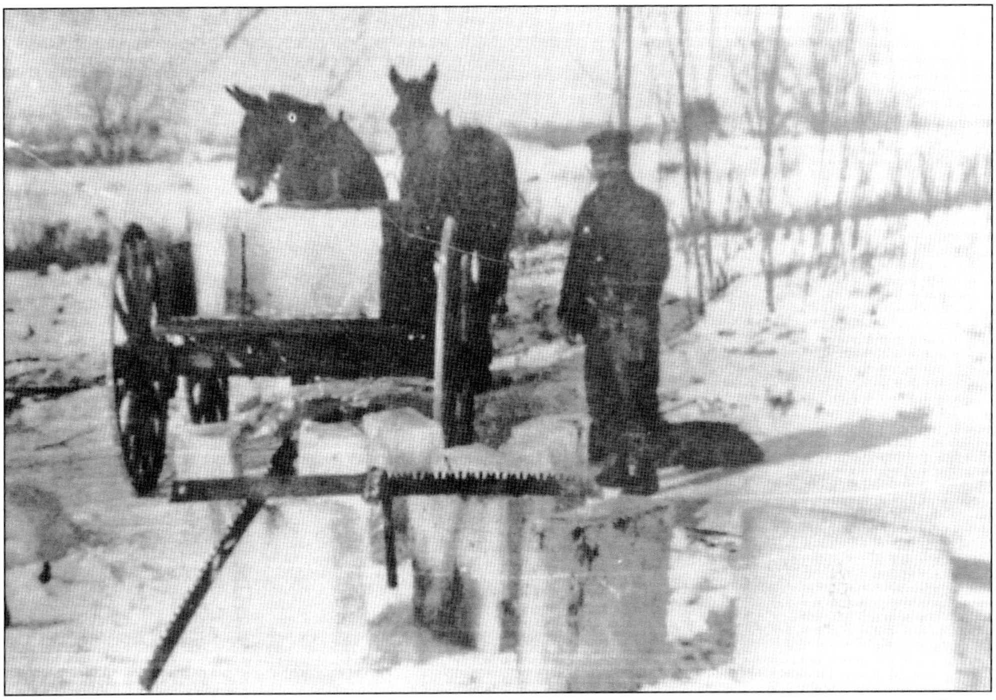

Wentzville got its first ice house in 1915. Before that, to get ice for the summer, Wentzvillians planned ahead. In winter, when the ice was over a foot thick, workers hitched a team of mules and trekked to the Missouri River, where they cut blocks of ice, hauled them back to the barn, stacked them, and covered them with sawdust so they stayed frozen well into summer.

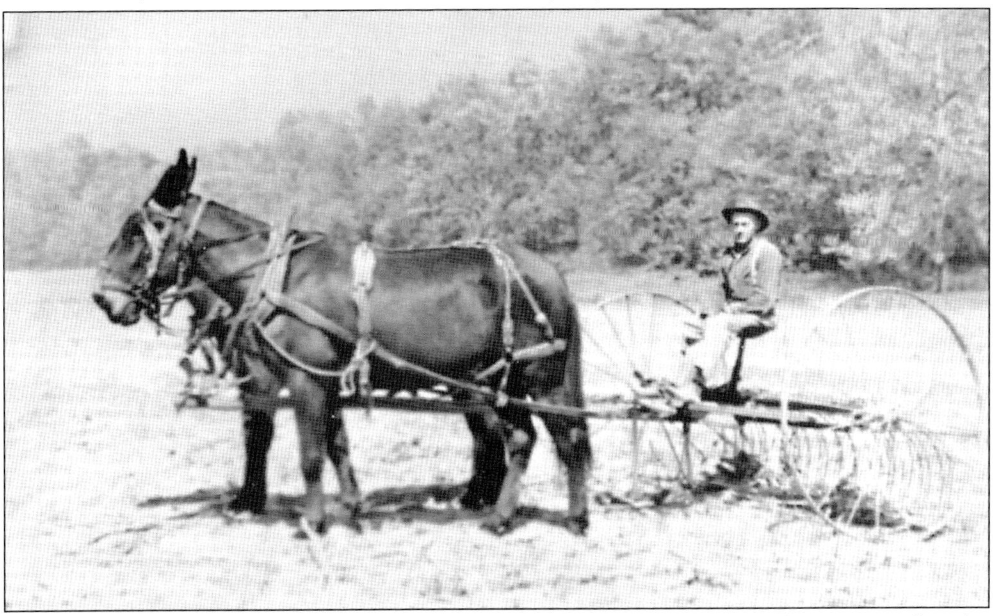

Farm work is never easy, nor does the weather always cooperate. In 1890, Alex Hemmer has the luxury of sitting on his rake behind his mules. What looks like a cushy job was actually miserable in late summer, when the temperature was 95, dust and seeds filled the air, and bits of straw worked their way down the back of the farmer's shirt and stuck to his arms and face.

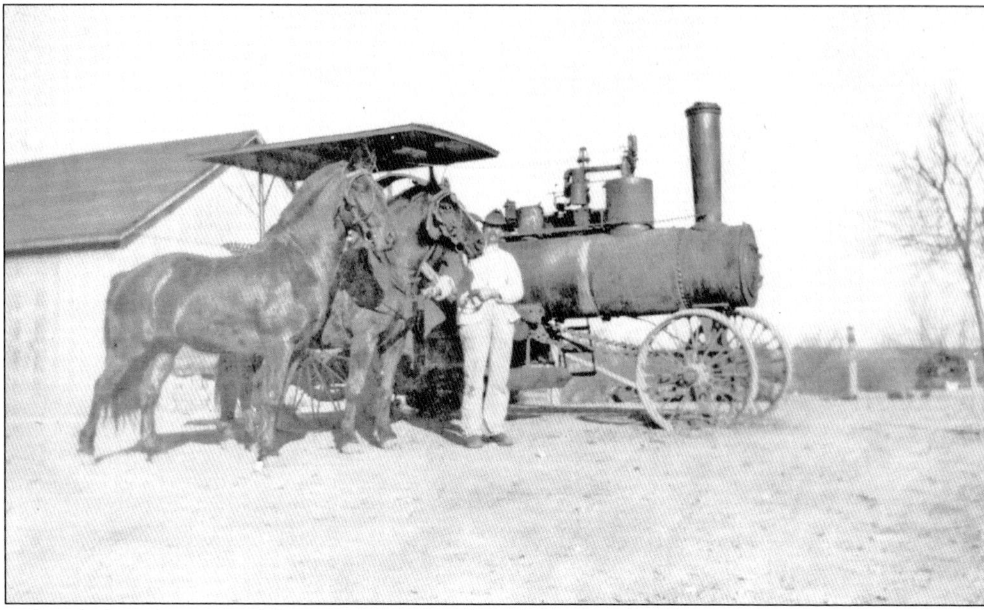

Taken before the turn of the 20th century, this photograph shows the old and the new side by side. The farmer stands with his two beautiful workhorses, who are being retired from field work in the name of progress. The new steam tractor stands by, ready to take over the work.

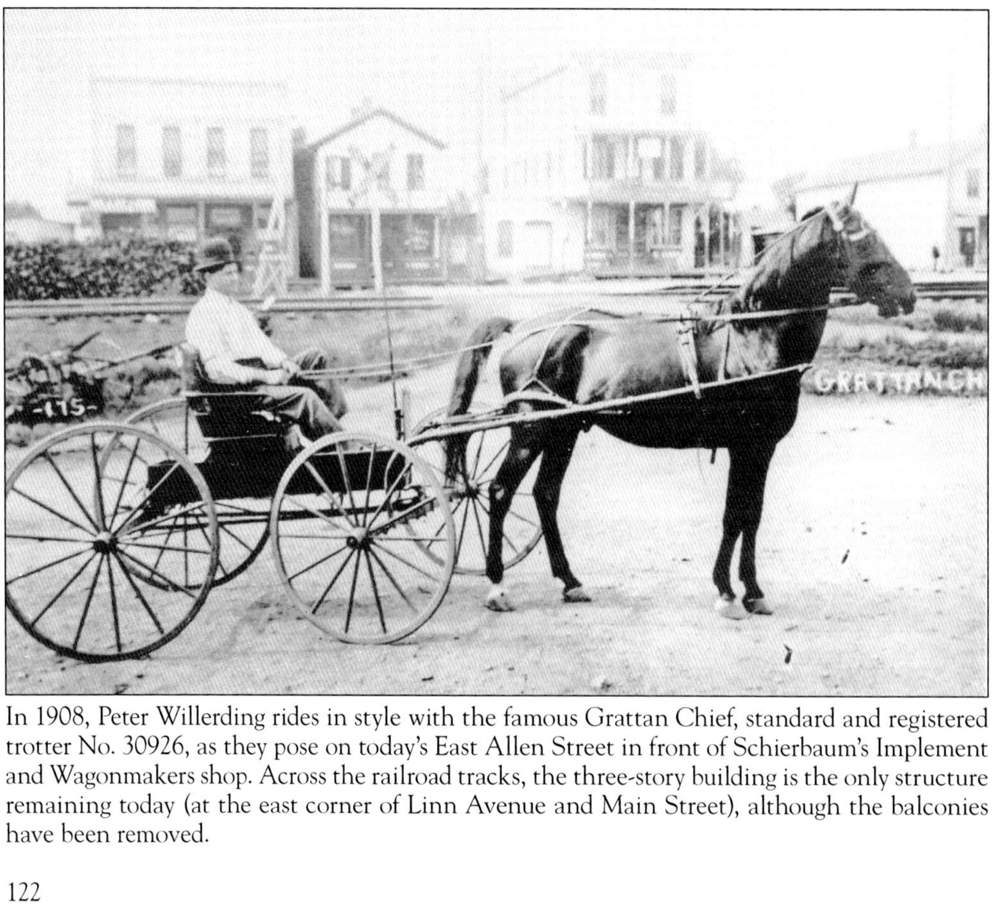

In 1908, Peter Willerding rides in style with the famous Grattan Chief, standard and registered trotter No. 30926, as they pose on today's East Allen Street in front of Schierbaum's Implement and Wagonmakers shop. Across the railroad tracks, the three-story building is the only structure remaining today (at the east corner of Linn Avenue and Main Street), although the balconies have been removed.

Nine

In Memoriam

Nearly every cemetery and burial ground in Wentzville contains the brave men and women who served their country. Before the founding of Wentzville in 1855, area landowners served in the Revolutionary War, Mexican War, and the War of 1812. After the establishment of the town, citizens served in the Civil War, World Wars I and II, the Korean War, Vietnam, and all of the wars in the Middle East. Wentzville has placed monuments and memorials for most of these devastating events and has plans for more in the future.

War has always been a primary danger, but other events caused grief to Wentzville residents. On July 15, 1920, Mayor J.C. Brown issued an order to citizens of Wentzville to keep their pets confined or the animals would risk being shot. The reason was a citywide outbreak of rabies. Children and adults were being bitten at an alarming rate, and then had to undergo the Pasteur treatment. Citizens panicked. Many took to their roofs, shooting anything on four legs. People were afraid to go outside for fear of being bitten—or shot.

In the 1930s, John Dillinger raced through Wentzville, confronting state patrol officer Fred Hagen, who tried to stop him from getting to St. Louis. Shots were fired, including some that lodged in the side of the Y Café. Emma Heppermann murdered husbands. Fires destroyed much of the town. Tornados flattened homes. But Wentzville picked itself up and went on.

John F. Kennedy once said, "We celebrate the past to awaken the future." Wentzville has faced it all: fires, tornadoes, wars, rabies, gangsters, and more. Yet the citizens have remained strong and continue to celebrate the past with an eye toward the future. They still respect and honor all those who sacrificed for their country and their city. That small-town feeling is alive and well in Wentzville.

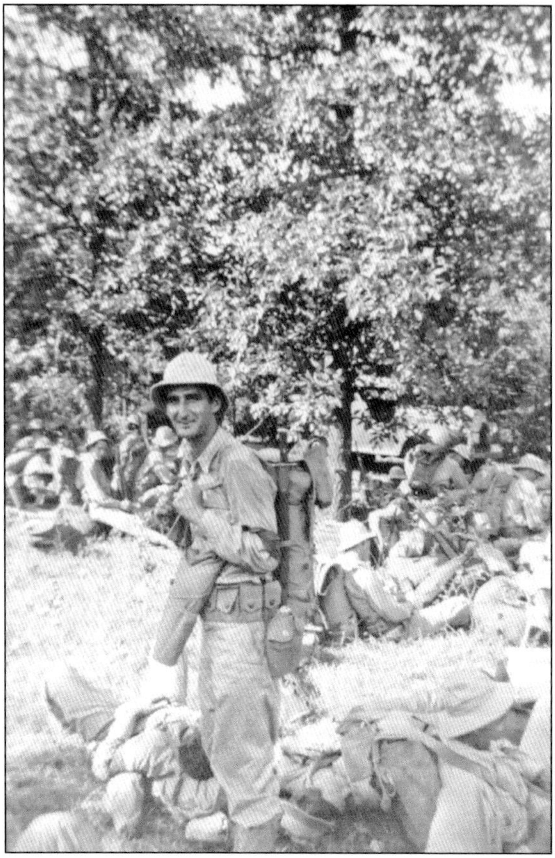

Sam Anselm, who later became the longest-serving city marshal in Wentzville history, is seen during a moment of relaxation with other US Army infantrymen somewhere in the South Pacific during World War II. Wentzville was well represented during the war. (Rick and Maxine Anselm.)

The man shown here in uniform in the 1940s is Charles Willerding, proudly standing in front of his restaurant, the White Duck, home of 5¢ hamburgers. Charles left his Wentzville restaurant in others' hands so he could serve his country. No wonder these people were known as "the greatest generation." (Nancy Frei.)

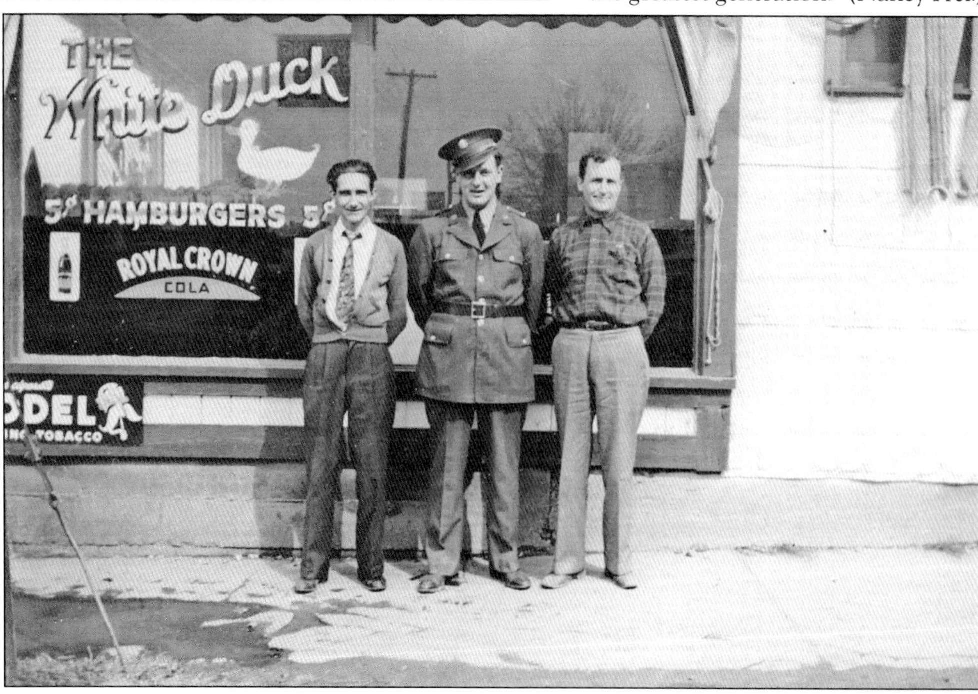

Wentzville's Vietnam Memorial has been a stopping place through the years for hundreds of Vietnam veterans on their annual "Ride for the Wall." Originally made of wood, the memorial was replaced by this granite monolith in later years. Recently, Wentzville has beautified the grounds, creating a stunning place to remember those who served in Vietnam. First erected in December 1967, it was the first Vietnam memorial in the United States.

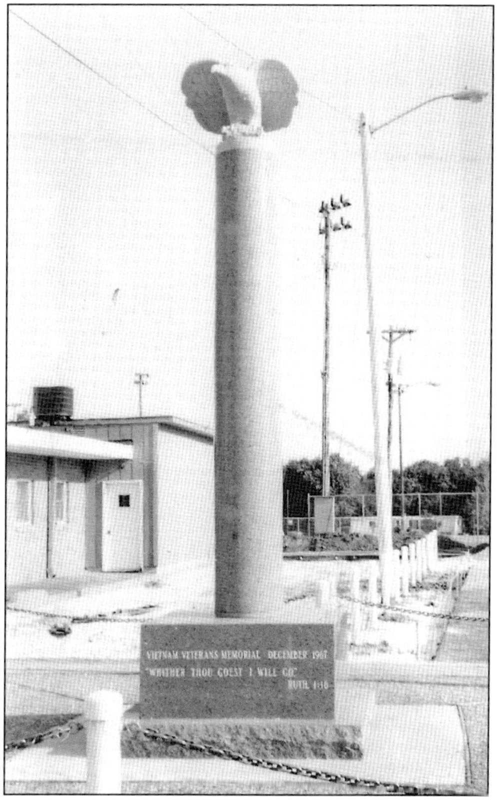

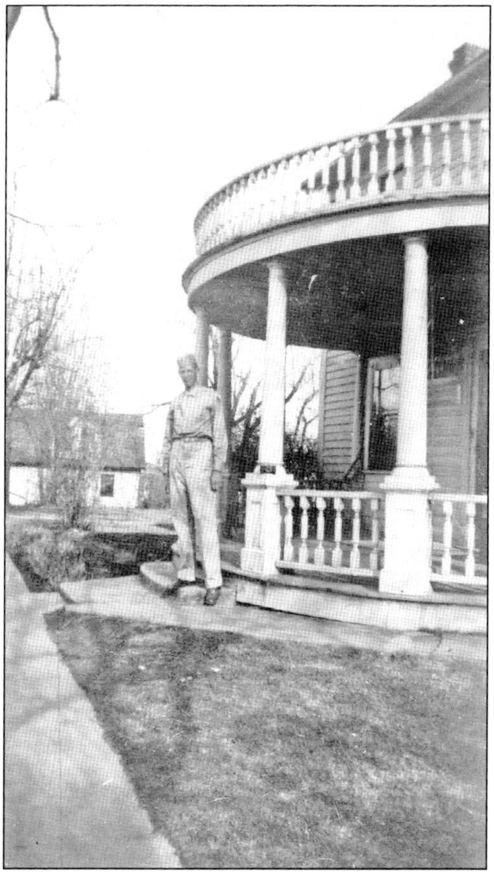

Arnold Hoeckelman poses in his uniform in front of his Wentzville home in 1945. This house is the only building on Main Street still standing from the original town of 1855; it was once owned by Robert B. Dula of Dula and Carr Tobacco Company. The Wentzville Main Street Association currently owns the house and is working to restore this piece of history. (Les Hoeckelman.)

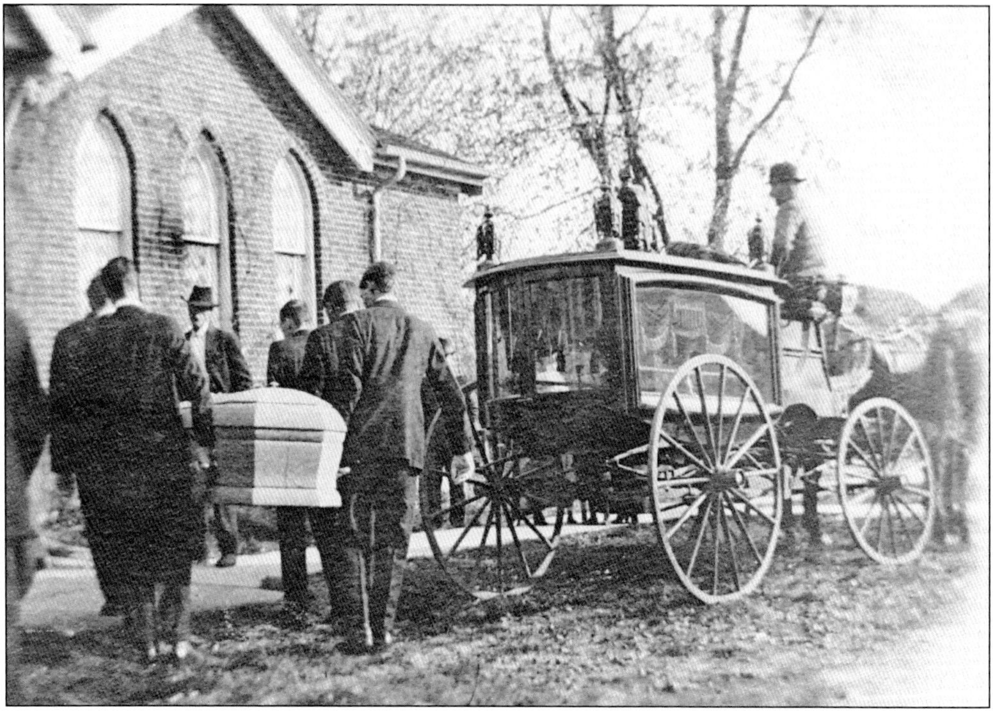

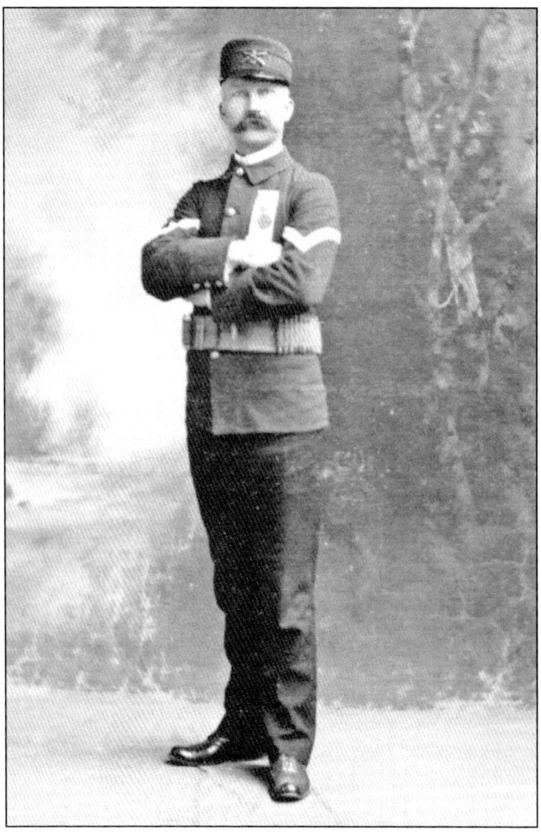

The Pitman Funeral Home has been in continuous operation since 1922. The founder, Tarlton E. Pitman, sits atop one of his horse-drawn hearses, waiting for a service to be completed so he can carry the deceased to their final resting place. The coffin is being taken into what is believed to be the Methodist church. This hearse was frequently used in parades.

Julius H. Kessler is shown here in his Spanish-American War uniform. According to draft cards, Kessler also served in World War I. He lived and is buried in New Melle, just south of Wentzville.

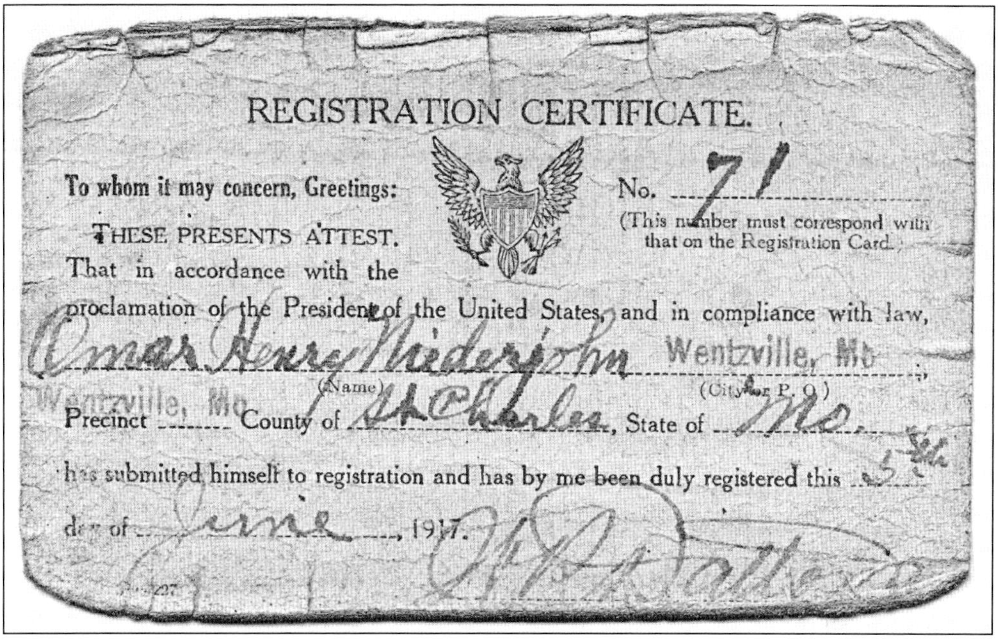
REGISTRATION CERTIFICATE.

To whom it may concern, Greetings:

No. 71

(This number must correspond with that on the Registration Card.)

THESE PRESENTS ATTEST.

That in accordance with the proclamation of the President of the United States, and in compliance with law, Omar Henry Niederjohn (Name) Wentzville, Mo (City or P. O.)

Precinct Wentzville, Mo County of St Charles, State of Mo.

has submitted himself to registration and has by me been duly registered this 5th

day of June, 1917.

This draft registration card was carried by Omar Henry Niederjohn, who served in World War I. He owned Niederjohn Furniture and was famous for his hand-carved walnut pieces. Niederjohn was very civic-minded and was a charter member of the Wentzville Community Club. He could be found giving his time as a volunteer at any event.

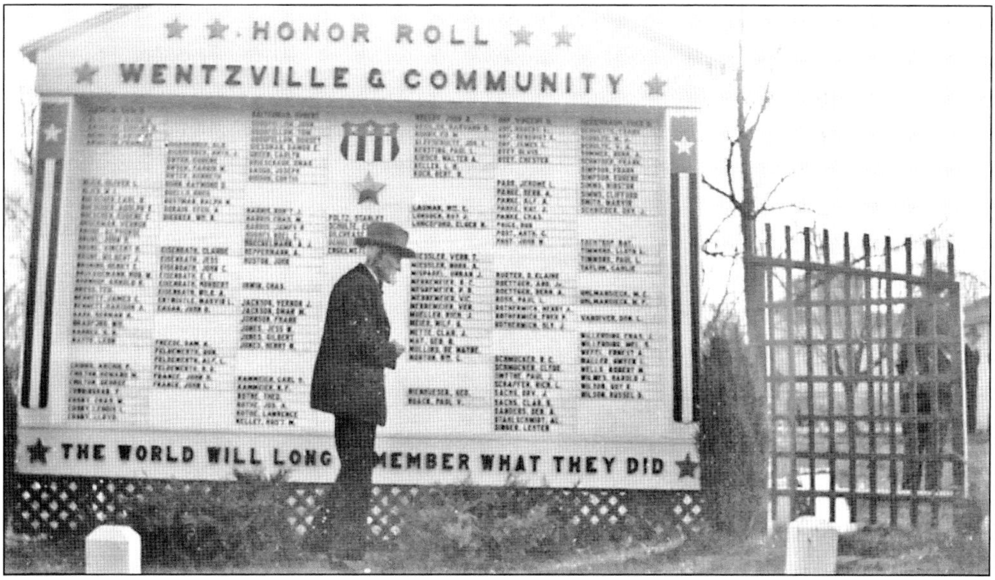

The World War II Honor Roll memorial was built and dedicated in 1944 on Pearce Boulevard at the Community Club pavilion. In 1963, when the property was sold, the monument was disassembled and, unfortunately, stored outdoors. It was never reassembled, and the structure deteriorated over the years. Now, in collaboration with the city, the historical society is re-creating this monument, along with World War I and other war memorials.